BURLINGAME PUBLIC
LIBRARY
480 PRIMROSE ROAD
BURLINGAME, CA 94010

WITHDRAWN

P9-DOH-030

Midnight
on the Line

Midnight on the Line

THE SECRET LIFE OF THE U.S. MEXICO BORDER

TIM GAYNOR

Thomas Dunne Books
St. Martin's Press
New York

364.137
G-256m

THOMAS DUNNE BOOKS.
An imprint of St. Martin's Press.

MIDNIGHT ON THE LINE. Copyright © 2009 by Tim Gaynor. All rights reserved. Printed in the United States of America. For information, address St. Martin's Press, 175 Fifth Avenue, New York, N.Y. 10010.

www.thomasdunnebooks.com
www.stmartins.com

Book design by Susan Walsh

Library of Congress Cataloging-in-Publication Data

Gaynor, Tim.
   Midnight on the line : the secret life of the U.S.-Mexico border / Tim Gaynor.—1st ed.
      p. cm.
   Includes bibliographical references and index.
   ISBN-13: 978-0-312-36671-1
   ISBN-10: 0-312-36671-X
   1. Illegal aliens—United States.   2. Border security—United States.   3. Mexican-American Border Region.   4. Mexico—Emigration and immigration.   1. Title.
F787 .G39 2009
364.1'3709721—dc22   2008035681

First Edition: March 2009

10 9 8 7 6 5 4 3 2 1

For Renata González

Contents

Acknowledgments

While working on this book, I got a helping hand from many different people. My heartfelt thanks go to all the U.S. federal, state, and local police officers, Minutemen volunteers, illegal immigrants, and smugglers that I named in its pages, albeit occasionally using pseudonyms. I also owe my thanks to the following people, who helped behind the scenes in one way or another during the research, writing, or editing process.

Lauren Mack, the public information officer with Immigration and Customs Enforcement, or ICE, in San Diego, put me in touch with special agents who had expertise in human and cash smuggling, and also arranged interviews with others who worked in the hunt for drug tunnels and corrupt border guards. Among those whose insights helped shape this book are John Mulvey, Johnny Martin, Dan Burke, and Mike Sauerborn. My thanks are also due to one special agent who worked south of the border in Tijuana, whom unfortunately I cannot name here for security reasons.

Misha Piastro, at one time the PIO for the Drug Enforcement Administration in San Diego, put me in touch with special agents who helped find a huge tunnel stretching half a mile from a shed close by the airport in Tijuana to a warehouse in Otay Mesa, California. While I cannot name them here, their insights into how that secret passageway was built and operated proved invaluable.

I spoke to dozens of Border Patrol agents, all of whom lent something to this book. I owe special thanks to Border Patrol supervisory agent Jesús Rodriguez, who placed me out on the line with two units in the Tucson sector that I had previously been told were off-limits. One was the Border Patrol's SWAT team, Bortac; the other was the horse patrol unit. Pat O'Donnell, the mounted unit's coordinator in Tucson, also helped to make that possible, as did all at the stables in Arivaca. Thanks also to James Jacques in San Diego.

The U.S. Customs and Border Protection public information officer in San Diego, Vince Bond, arranged several trips for me to the San Ysidro port of entry. The directors and inspectors he introduced me to at the border crossing gave me an invaluable sense of some of the systems, techniques, and technologies, from radiation sensors to sniffer dogs, used to screen out the smugglers from the legitimate travelers crossing up from Mexico, both there and at other ports on the line.

Brian Levin and Roger Maier, the PIOs with CBP in Nogales and El Paso, respectively, fielded numerous requests for information during my research. Together with Vince, they also helped to give me a sense of the rich strangeness of the border by peppering me with news releases detailing the bizarre things that inspectors encounter, such as smugglers carrying cheeses and sometimes even parrots.

Juan Muñoz Torres, the PIO for the agency's Air and Marine wing, arranged for me to visit the CBP's flight operations in Tucson, which are home to the most innovative air interdiction programs on the border. Flight crews there took me up in a Black Hawk helicopter and gave me excellent access to the Predator B drone program. Crucially, they explained how the helicopters and drones interact, a detail that has not been widely reported.

Cases involving corrupt border guards are on the rise. FBI special agents Andrea Simmons, Darrell Foxworth, and Rene Salinas fielded my inquiries about graft investigations and put me in touch with a number of special agents who led cases that I wanted to follow up on. Those agents, whom I cannot name here, set me straight on several details and helped me to establish a clear timeline in those investigations.

Bureau of Alcohol, Tobacco, Firearms and Explosives senior special agents William Newell and Tom Mangan took me inside the ATF's battle to curb the flow of arms to Mexico. In Detroit, the ATF's Philip Awe and George Krappmann also gave me a valuable primer on cigarette smuggling scams, and the alarming role they have played in raising funds stateside for Hizballah in Lebanon.

When I set out to write this book, I knew I needed to speak to the poachers as well as the gamekeepers. My special thanks go to Lizbeth Díaz, a prizewinning print and radio journalist from Tijuana who introduced me to human and drug smugglers in the city. Their perspectives helped give this book what I hope is its breadth and balance, as well as some of its most intriguing insights.

Victor Clark Alfaro, the director of the Binational Center for Human Rights in Tijuana, also shared his observations, as did the late Jesús Blancornelas, cofounder and editor of the investigative magazine *Zeta*. Don Jesús also gave me the useful observation that any traffic through a clandestine drug tunnel was likely to be two-way, not simply south to north.

I talked to scores of illegal immigrants about their journeys to the United States, some stateside, others in migrant shelters in Mexico. Aside from the many migrants themselves, I owe my thanks to Elizabeth García, the former coordinator of Grupo Beta in Nogales, and Father Luís Kendzierski, who runs a migrant shelter in Tijuana.

Many friends gave me help and support along the way. Susy Buchanan was until recently an investigative reporter with the Southern Poverty Law Center's Intelligence Report. She helped me to square away much of the history of the various Minutemen groups, and generously shared with me many of the documentary sources she used for her own reporting on the movement.

British academic Sophie Nield drove along the border with me from Texas to California. She also read the very first drafts of many of the chapters with great care and attention to detail. Her inspired advice helped me to find the narrative line and establish the sequence of chapters. It would be difficult to imagine having finished this book without her kind, patient, and diligent help.

Hugh Bronstein found me a literary agent. Then he lent me his home in Bogotá to write up a large chunk of this book, and while I was in Colombia, he shared his circle of friends there with me. A more generous friend it is difficult to imagine.

This is not a Reuters book, and all views expressed in it are my own. Nevertheless, my bosses Mary Milliken, Howard Goller, and Betty Wong supported me by giving me some time off to write. Bernd Debusmann also read part of the manuscript. Many colleagues in the United States, Mexico, and beyond also gave me encouragement.

Various media in the United States and Mexico report the border well and their coverage has often either led me to a story or broadened my understanding of it. I am grateful to Dennis Wagner of *The Arizona Republic* for his reporting on smuggling rings in Phoenix, which opened my eyes to the wiles of the traffickers in the city and spurred my interest in visiting a drop house. My thanks, too, to the Associated Press, *The San Diego Union-Tribune*, the *Arizona Daily Star*, the *El Paso Times*, and *The Brownsville Herald*, as well as *Frontera*, *El Mexicano*, *El Diario* (Juárez), and *El Mañana* (Nuevo Laredo), in Mexico.

My agent Paul Bresnick shaped this book from the outset and found it a home at Thomas Dunne Books. There, my editor Rob Kirkpatrick improved it considerably. My thanks also to Julie Gutin and Lorrie Grace McCann.

Finally, thanks go to my family scattered across the world, especially my father, John, my sister, Amanda, and her fine boys, Dan, Tom, and Pat.

Introduction:
An Offer I Couldn't Refuse

Mexico City (March 2004)

As corner offices go, Kieran Murray's was a great one. At his desk, the Reuters Mexico bureau chief was framed by a tall office building with a helicopter pad on the roof, buzzing with choppers hauling Mexico's movers and shakers. The vast city in the background was visible through a thick, yellow-gray caul of photochemical smog, with high-rises, volcanoes, and shantytowns playing peekaboo as the weather allowed.

He had invited me in to hear an offer. "Which do you want," he asked, "Guatemala, or the border?" Now, Guatemala is an amazing place—a country chockablock with colorful stories, and great to cut your teeth on as a foreign correspondent. But . . . the border!

I had stepped off a flight from London the day before and knew little more about the storied U.S.-Mexico border than any interested newspaper reader.

I knew it had rampaging drug gangs, and a million or more people each year tried to push across to the United States without visas or even passports. I also knew that it was getting to be a bigger story every day as concern grew stateside about safeguarding the homeland in a time of war and as illegal immigration crept up the domestic agenda.

Part of me was nervous. It would be totally consuming if I decided to take the challenge. But if, on the other hand, I walked away from it, I knew I would be dogged by regret for years to come.

"It's got to be the border," I said. Kieran nodded. He knew I couldn't turn it down. Who could?

The beat involved covering the whole border, from Tijuana on the Pacific Coast right through to Matamoros, where the Rio Grande spills into the Gulf of Mexico.

I would write about crime, security, illegal immigration, and pretty much anything else that caught my eye. I could work both sides of the line, tracking down the stories that would be of key interest to an international readership.

The decision to have an Englishman—I was born and brought up in the west of England—reporting the U.S. border, a place where men dress in plaid shirts and jeans with fancy tooled belts, was an interesting one.

It wasn't so much that as a European I would have, to borrow a gambling term, no "skin in the game," and be able to tell the story straight—any decent journalist could do that. I think it was more that everything would be utterly, completely, and bewilderingly new for me.

There were other factors, too. The fact that I speak good enough Spanish—I had lived in Spain and Central America for several years by the time I was hired—was an asset. Added to that, I happen to be physically resilient and can ride a horse—details that were to help considerably at one time or another.

The idea was that I should get out and talk to as many people involved in the story as possible, from U.S. federal police of every stripe to the Mexican "coyotes" and drug smugglers that they pursued, flushing out the best and most original stories: in short, to bring the border to life.

Dispatched to the industrial city of Monterrey, a powerhouse a few hours' drive south of Texas, I began a series of reporting trips that would take me to pretty much every city, town, and chicken-scratch village the length of the line, on both sides. Over the next few years I used just about every form of transport imaginable—cars, buses, trains, planes, choppers, and horses, as well as walking large tracts of the desert on foot—to try and get a unique perspective on what goes on down on the line.

This book threads together some of the insights from that trip. I wanted to show firsthand how the border is policed and the ways that it is beaten and subverted by smugglers working around the clock, along the length of the line.

I didn't want to write what everybody already knows—more or less what I knew when I set out—but what I found out firsthand, through five years of asking the right people questions on both sides of that line, working out what makes the border tick. I wanted to find its secrets, and tell them straight.

The story starts with the epic journey made by the millions of illegal immigrants who live and work in the shadows in the United States, busing restaurants and making beds.

It was the hottest month of the year, and I could hear the siren call of the desert. It was time to get my walking shoes out and head down to Altar, the place where it all begins.

ONE

The Gates of Hell

Amado Coello is sixty-two years old, a salt-and-pepper-haired retiree with a gentle, grandfatherly manner that gives him the air of a fairy-tale cobbler. He is in fact a retired paramedic, carrying out volunteer duty at a Mexican Red Cross station set up in a tractor trailer a few miles short of the Arizona border in Mexico.

The makeshift clinic is up a few wooden steps, and it's free. It's open twenty-four hours a day, year round, and attends to a constant river of people who draw up into the tawdry high desert town of Altar on buses in their tens of thousands each month.

The arrivals disgorged onto the sun-baked sidewalk amid a hiss of airbrakes are either prospective migrants seeking to trek across the vast desert to the United States illegally, or they are the failures—those broken by the desert's remorseless wheel and tossed back out by the U.S. Border Patrol.

Sitting at a desk in the cool interior of the truck, Coello is flanked by maps, one showing northwest Mexico in relief, the lay of the land—from the azure waters of the Sea of Cortez to the tall peaks of the Sierra Madre towering a thumb's width above them. The other is a simple outline of

Mexico, picking out more than two dozen states in a felt-tipped marker, noting the homes of the migrants who often come to the clinic hobbling on crutches after a bruising encounter with the blowtorch wastelands to the north.

"Welcome to the gates of hell. It's the gate to the next dimension." That's Coello, revealing a metaphysical bent as he talks about Altar in Spanish, the deeply expressive language of magical realism. "They don't know what awaits them out there! It could be that it goes well, that they get a good job, or that they stay out there . . . in the desert," he says, warming to his cataclysmic theme. "We get everyone. Entire families, pregnant women in the sixth or eighth month of their term, even older people in their sixties. The first thing we do is we try and convince them not to go, tell them that it is quite risky. We try and find ways to warn them that their families could be left to fend for themselves, but they justify the journey by saying they need an income, that they are going anyway."

The little clinic parked up on the broken asphalt is a triage station for one of the toughest foot journeys on earth. Coello has a small pharmacy with bottles of pills to treat high blood pressure for some of the older people intent on making the walk, together with electrolyte solutions to help border crossers offset dehydration. Then there are the treatments for those who have been sent back by the Border Patrol with injuries from their trek.

Casting an eye over the tight-stacked shelves, I see wound dressings, anti-inflammatory pills, painkillers, and even eyedrops. He has antiparasitic medication for people sick to the stomach after drinking at cattle troughs along the way, and antibiotics to treat cuts ripped by cactus spines and deep sores from rotten blisters.

"The worst are their feet, full of blisters. Their toes are beaten to a pulp with the nails hanging off them. They stumble against rocks in the dark, and that usually hurts the big toe," he says, blithely rattling off a litany of hurts in his lilting, singsong voice.

It is all of more than just academic interest for me. I am in his clinic with a Mexican colleague and friend of mine, Tomás Bravo, for a checkup. We are both reporters: I am part of a team that writes about immigration and the border, and he takes the pictures.

We are planning to follow in the footsteps of countless dirt-poor illegal immigrants from across Mexico and much of Latin America who make this clandestine journey north in search of a better life. It's a trip that I have imagined myself making countless times.

I want not only to see, at first hand, what it's like to break in to the United States, I also want to live that journey as much as I can, as the first part of this wide-ranging look at what smugglers do on the most contentious border on earth, and what the federal police agencies on the other side do to block them. I am doing it this way because I don't think what either does has been adequately reported firsthand, and certainly it hasn't ever been pulled together in a single book.

Altar struck me as a good place to start. It is a couple of hours' drive short of the Arizona border in Sonora. The sprawl of adobe stores, taco stands, and flophouse hotels lies on illegal immigration's superhighway. It is a kind of desert training post supplying and equipping tens of thousands of border crossers headed north each year, most with the aid of professional smugglers, in an illicit trade worth billions of dollars annually.

We are joining the band of hundreds of migrants who will be setting out tomorrow to walk the Sonora Desert to the United States. From Altar, we will take a van, or drive if we have to, over the desert to the frontier town of El Sásabe, from there walking forty-five miles up through the empty wilds of the Altar Valley to the hamlet of Three Points, Arizona, where many border crossers are picked up and driven on to Tucson and Phoenix.

It is late July, the most fatal month of the year. It is a time when searing temperatures reach up to 115 degrees Fahrenheit in the shade—only, of course, there is little real shade—and when torrential monsoon cloudbursts fill lonely desert washes with bucking torrents of water in moments. It is Armageddon scribbled across the calendar, the month when two years earlier, the Border Patrol pulled two corpses a day out of the deserts south of Tucson.

I swing my legs up onto the black vinyl gurney for my free checkup. Coello slips on the stethoscope, gazes absently into the middle distance, and listens to my heart. He checks my breathing and then finally wraps an inflatable belt around my arm to take my blood pressure. It is a little bit elevated, 130 over 98, perhaps driven up by my anxiety over the journey that lies ahead, or simply on account of his white coat. Doctors always make me nervous.

Next, Tomás lifts himself onto the gurney. From Mexico City, he is of middling height, with a head of corkscrew curls and a knockout smile, and he somehow quietly glows with well-being. The only concern Coello has is for his slightly accelerated heart rate. He puts it down to the heat, which is in the low hundreds, and cautions Tomás that he needs to start taking frequent sips of water as he is already getting dehydrated. Otherwise he is good to go.

Since Coello likely has more practical experience of what the trail can do to you than most in northern Mexico, I ask him if he has any more advice for us to keep us in one piece on the walk across the rough sun-blasted wilderness that could take us several days—if, that is, we succeed.

He thinks for a moment, then tells us to take several pairs of socks and change them whenever they get damp, as it is the rubbing of sweaty feet on damp socks that accelerates blisters. "The best thing would be to walk in open-toed sandals, but then there are the scorpions and snakes, and then, if you stub your toes . . . ," he says, trailing off, distracted by several new arrivals who have hobbled painfully up the steps into the clinic.

Elmer López is framed by the doorway. He wears a straw hat and a royal blue collared shirt that is encrusted with concentric rings of dried sweat radiating out from his armpits. A peasant farmer from a town on Mexico's border with Guatemala, he is accompanied by his wife and two weary young daughters in matching pink pants that look like pajamas.

The girls flank their mother, their arms draped around her waist, the eldest rubbing a puffy red eye, inflamed by grit from the trail. She is almost asleep on her feet.

Most families hire a guide, or coyote, to lead them over the desert, but the López family was too broke. Instead, the father explains, he led them alone through the desert at night until they were arrested by a Border Patrol agent and sent back over the border after agreeing to voluntary return to Mexico.

He shares some advice with me and Tomás as Coello rinses his daughter's eye and gently applies a white patch with tape, and it's not encouraging. "It's hard to cross right now, more so because of the rains. The washes are deep, and all the *bichos* are looking for high ground. The snakes will be where you are walking," he warns us. I hadn't figured on that.

Just as Coello is finishing up, another couple of young lads arrive at the clinic, one of them energetically levering himself up the steps on crutches, as if he were giving a particularly athletic performance as Shakespeare's Richard III.

José is a destitute teenage peasant from the southern state of Chiapas who is trying to make his way to a farm job in Florida. He has a large lymph-soaked bandage covering his left knee, which he wants Coello to take a look at. He chats freely as the paramedic unwinds the dressing.

Another self-guided border crosser, José was walking up a desert trail several nights earlier. In the inky darkness, he stepped out over the lip of a deep wash, and tumbled headlong into darkness, in a fall broken by knife-sharp rocks.

As Coello eases off the dressing, I see a deep, sickle-shaped wound carved beneath José's kneecap and reaching around the back of his leg. The sides of the gash are tagged together by a strip of stitches, some of which have tugged free, revealing an angry, suppurating gash.

"It looks bad, but it is healing," he tells me brightly. I look at him, look down at his cut. Trying not to wince, I ask him what his plans are. He shrugs. "I'll probably try again in a few days, once I've rested up."

Speaking of rest reminds me. Tomás and I need a bunk for the night. We say our farewells to Coello and head back out to the street, which by now is as hot as a baker's oven, and see a mirage dancing on the simmering asphalt.

The sign to the Casa de Huéspedes Martínez is propped up on a brick in the street. It has a black arrow pointing guests down a dusty back alley from the main strip in Altar to a single-story brick building.

It is a flophouse for illegal immigrants heading up to cross the deserts of the U.S. border, and it is exactly the sort of place we are looking for to bed down for the night. The clerk is sprawled on a couch in a windowless room, watching television. He looks up, somewhat put out by the intrusion, and tells us there are vacancies. It costs three dollars, but a blanket is included in the price, which I would have thought went without saying.

He jabs a hand toward a dark, airless room next door where rows of metal bunk beds stand three tall like storage racks. It gives the place the feel of an office storeroom, or perhaps a jail. I claim the top bunk against the back wall, under a hand-painted image of San Judas Tadeo, the patron saint of lost causes. The figure has a flaming sacred heart in his chest, and his hand is raised in benediction atop a staff. He looks like he is setting out on a trek.

As I stretch out on my back on a thin strip of gray office carpet—the only mattress on offer—I find his prayer is somehow appropriate.

Holy Apostle San Judas, friend and servant of Jesus! The Church honors and invokes you universally as the patron of difficult and desperate cases. Pray for me. I am without help and so very alone. . . . Make use, I implore you, of the special powers to swiftly and visibly help when almost all hope has been lost.

The sun has been beating down all day on the tin-roofed ceiling, backed with black plastic sheeting, about eighteen inches above my nose. I stare up at it, feeling more than a little daunted. The dorm is dispiriting enough. Then there's the journey itself that lies ahead of us.

Before we set off on the trek over the desert, we have to drive for a couple of hours over a potholed road to reach the border line at El Sás-abe, passing through an area along the way controlled by well-armed drug trafficking cells and the ruthless human smugglers called coyotes.

The little I know about these thugs makes me nervous. The drug smugglers are loyal to the Sinaloa cartel, and they haul tons of pot each week over the desert back trails to Tucson in specially adapted trucks and SUVs, on horseback, or on foot.

Once over the line, Tomás and I will be in perhaps the only place in the United States where you can still be held up at gunpoint by armed bandits, the so-called *bajadores* who specialize in stealing drug loads and robbing migrants of their every last peso.

They ambush the groups in the desert, offering them a stark choice: your money or your life. If a group is in a truck the bandits suspect is filled with dope, sometimes the first thing the passengers will know about it is the heavy assault rifle rounds raking up the hood and punching through the windshield.

And then there is the walk itself. It will take us between two mountain ranges that flank the searing Altar Valley, a broad highland plain of prairie grass spotted with cactus and mesquite trees that is baking during the day and extremely cold at night. It is also home to some of the most venomous animals on earth: the rattlesnakes, scorpions, and black widow and brown recluse spiders that can send you to the emergency room with a swift nip or glancing sting. The only thing is, there is no emergency room.

I am, selfishly, very glad that I am not doing this alone. Aside from being a witness to whatever happens out in the desert, Tomás is great company. He also has a straightforward, easygoing manner that is already proving to be a great help on this trip. He is very disarming and friendly, and just hanging out with him is making life a lot easier for me in the grimy bunkhouse, which is starting to fill up with people.

Our roommates are from a roll call of the poorest states in Mexico, crashing for the night on their way up to the border. Putting down their packs, water jugs, and meager rations of food, they glance up at me with clear suspicion.

I'm above six feet in height, weigh over two hundred pounds, and fill out the top shelf of the bunk. I have fair skin and a shaved head, and totting up the pointers, most people I meet in the borderlands tend to take me for a policeman rather than a reporter. They turn to Tomás for an explanation.

"So what's he doing here?" asks José, a tall youngster from Querétaro.

"We're both reporters. We are doing a story on the journey to the United States."

"Can't you afford to stay in a proper hotel?" he asks, clearly puzzled.

"Yes, but we want to do it like you guys. . . ." Tomás is off, animated, winning everyone over with his charm, easygoing manner, and conversation sprinkled with phrases that mark him out as a *paisano,* and as a friend. Within a minute or two we are all sitting on the bunkhouse floor, chatting.

José is a very good-looking kid. Dressed in a black T-shirt and with sharp razor-cut hair, he looks like he could be in a boy band. He is in fact an agricultural worker from central Mexico on his way to Kentucky to muck out horses at a stud farm. He tells me he was working there illegally a few months earlier but came home.

"Why?"

"*Por pendejo*—because I'm an idiot," he says with a shrug. He got homesick for his wife and young child, and came home to unemployment. Within a few weeks it was time to set off again, rattling north across Mexico in a bus to once again make the desert hike up through Altar.

Then there is Mario, another farmer with a gentle voice, this time from Oaxaca. He cradles a plump, sleeping baby gently in his arms, and has an awkward, rattled expression. The reason he is out of sorts is that the tiny bundle is the daughter of a woman he met moments earlier in the dorm room, who has now stepped out, leaving him quite literally holding the baby.

A short while later Leticia reappears. She is in her early twenties, wearing a white T-shirt, black shorts, and slip-on plastic sandals. Apart from the baby, she appears to have very few possessions. Speaking slowly and with a far-off look in her eye, she tells me that her child is just four months old. The baby's name is Crystal Esmeralda, the only hint of beauty in the guest house, with its stifling dormitory, sweaty blankets, and plastic bucket shower.

The father of her child is somewhere in southern Mexico, and it becomes clear over the next few hours that she has something of a complex life, with a series of entanglements with one or more of the men in our dorm room. Rather than passing through, she has been living in Altar for the past eighteen months. It isn't quite clear when she will be moving on, or how she supports herself.

I stretch out on the meager strip of carpet on my bunk. Exhausted, I pull my shirt up over my head to block out the buzzing strip light on the ceiling, and slip into a deep, dreamless sleep until dawn. It will be a puzzle to me on this trip, but I will have some of the best nights' sleep in years, snatched in a flophouse dorm, then slumped way out in the desert. Tomás is not so lucky.

He is kept up by five boisterous roommates drinking cheap rum and bothering Leticia, who sleeps in a tiny, windowless room behind our bunk. At about 3 A.M., a bare-chested guy in shorts bangs on the door of Leticia's room and barges his way in for sex, but not before turning on a noisy air-conditioning unit to drown out the sound of his activities.

It later occurs to me that Leticia may be a prostitute, a camp follower for this legion of migrants on the march, like the women who gathered up their skirts and followed Napoleon's armies across Europe two centuries earlier, and armies before that, reaching back in an infinite regress.

At first light, Tomás and I gather our few belongings and step out into the street. Only Leticia is awake, and she follows us out to the curb. She has a look of deep sadness on her face that makes me think of Peter Lorre in the film *Casablanca,* as he promises Rick his "letters of transit."

"Have a good trip, and take very good care of yourselves," she says distantly. I don't look back.

An awning stretches over the sidewalk, throwing the row of shops into deep, welcome shadow. We need to get equipped for the trip, and since all the thick-walled adobe stores sell the same things—backpacks, baseball caps, sunglasses, and headscarves—it hardly matters where Tomás and I stop.

We dive into the first, blinking in the darkness of the windowless interior. It feels more like a Bedouin tent than a shop. Stacked high on tables and in deep shelves ranged along the walls are black school backpacks priced from five to fifteen dollars, and all the clothes we might need for the trip.

The wares range from cheap hiking boots and knockoff athletic shoes to long-sleeved plaid shirts and heavy denim jeans offering protection against thorns. There are also racks filled with baseball caps and cotton headscarves to keep the sun from burning your skin and sucking the moisture clear out of it until it looks like a wizened old prune.

The proprietor of the store is called Lourdes. She sits in a plastic patio chair in the dark interior of the shop, which somehow has the feel of a traveling bazaar that could be packed up and sent on across the wastes on camelback.

Far from simply being a cut-price outfitter for migrants, this souk sells items that are also a rich repository of folklore, offering a dazzling array of consolations for the journey.

Lourdes, like all the other store owners, sells a selection of caps and headscarves decorated with images of the Virgin of Guadalupe, Mexico's most revered icon, depicted in a shawl fringed with rays of light, and with an adoring Juan Diego kneeling at her feet, interestingly, in a desert dotted with nopales.

San Judas also features prominently, offering forlorn hope to the dispossessed. One headscarf, though, is eye-catchingly different, capturing the hopes and dreams of material betterment that are implicit in the journey that hundreds of thousands of illegal immigrants make each year. The cotton rectangle is printed with a flurry of twenty-, fifty-, and hundred-dollar bills, set against a backdrop of green. Migrants who buy it are literally wearing the American Dream on their heads as they set out for the north. I finger its meager selvedge, lost for a moment in that enticing reverie of riches. I slip it over my head and anchor it in place with a cap. I decide to buy them.

In a bewildering irony of globalization, I notice that the scarf is made in China and the cap in Vietnam. I find the thought of factories in the Far East running off caps and scarves for a target market of penniless migrants from Mexico mind-boggling. First, how did they ever find out about their journey? Then, how do they turn a buck out of pitching to the borderline destitute?

Other popular items on sale are soccer shirts for teams in Mexico's Primera Division league. Lourdes has the blue and white stripe of Cruz Azul, a team from southwest Mexico City, and the red and white colors of Las Chivas from Guadalajara, famed as the one club in Mexican soccer that has only ever signed Mexican-born players.

"We sell a lot of them," Lourdes says as I hold one of the shirts in my hands. "They like to wear their colors. Their teams carry their hopes and their dreams."

Seeing the shirts reminds me uncomfortably of the story of a condemned man on death row in the Jim Crow South decades ago that had touched civil rights leader Martin Luther King, Jr. In some macabre twist, the prison authorities had decided to place a microphone in the gas chamber just before the man's execution, to capture his last words. As the pellet dropped to release lethal cyanide fumes, he was overheard making a desperate appeal to then world heavyweight champion Joe Louis. He expired whispering, "Save me, Joe Louis! Save me!"

Could it be, I wonder, that soccer-mad Mexican migrants in extremis in the desert call out through cracked lips to top goal scorers like the Chivas' Salvador Reyes for salvation? It's a strange and disquieting thought.

It's time to pay up and get our provisions. Earlier, I had picked up a guide at the Catholic church refuge, which contains a helpful shopping list. It advises migrants to stock up on canned food, candy, peanut butter, chocolate, and *suero* (electrolytic rehydration powders), and of course water. If the water runs out, the guide advises migrants to suck a pebble as they walk, to stop their mouths from drying out—an old Native American trick.

We head along the broken sidewalk to Pesqueira Hermanos, the largest supermarket in Altar, to fill our rucksacks with food and fluids for our trip. It's strange. As we head into the store with our church shopping list, there is something different, out of place. Then I realize what it is.

I lived in northern Mexico for a couple of years. In most supermarkets you tend to see middle-class housewives *haciendo super,* as the weekly shopping is known, often dressed and made up to equal the glamorous presenters on *Televisa*. Here, though, the aisles are packed with tight knots of men pushing carts conspiratorially, locked in animated discussion about the items they need for the grueling journey ahead. We follow them around with our shopping list, starting off with water.

You see the gallon water jugs strewn across the deserts in southern Arizona, an unwelcome addition to the landscape, by now as commonplace as the saguaros themselves. Here they are, stockpiled in huge quantities in the far corner beyond the produce department in a massive display.

The opaque plastic containers rest on pallets stacked ten tall against the wall. I see that border folklore is also to the fore here. The local brand, Agua Purificada Santo Niño de Atocha, is pure marketing genius, specially targeting superstitious migrants. The brand is named after the holy child who appeared to a group of miners trapped by a cave-in at a deep mine in the desperately poor central state of Zacatecas. In answer to their prayers, the tiny figure led them through the mazelike underground galleries to safety.

Perhaps not coincidentally, Zacatecas is one of the states with the highest rate of emigration to the United States. What better figure to accompany Zacatecans on a walk through the hazardous desert labyrinth, then, than the image of their very own holy child? Slapping the figure on a bottle is inspired.

Another brand of water that one Arizona rancher told me he had come across comes in a gallon jug stamped with a picture of Baboquivari Peak, a sugarloaf-shaped dome sacred to the Tohono O'odham tribe that towers over the route north through the Altar Valley.

For those making the trek on foot, the jug in their hand serves as a basic map, accompanied by text advising migrants to keep the peak on their left-hand side during their three- to six-day walk up through the valley to Three Points and other load-out points on Highway 86 as it sweeps in across the desert toward Tucson.

I look around for the brand in the store, but can't see it. I figure that perhaps it's like a Coke and Pepsi thing. In Altar you either stock Santo Niño or Baboquivari water or lose your refrigerator. We load six gallons into the shopping cart and trundle on down the aisles. We figure it may be just enough fluid if we walk in the cool of the night and sleep during the day.

Tomás and I agree on a dozen cans of tuna fish and four large cans of refried beans. We also load up on a packet of flour tortillas, broad discs bound with suet, which we agree will make good fat burritos out on the trail. Chocolate, except in fiddling packets of cookies, is nowhere to be found, so we settle on a cone of *piloncillo*—raw cane sugar.

It has the rough texture of a cattle salt lick, and we figure it will be good for a no-frills energy burst should we need it out on the trail. Now all we need is garlic. It's an odd one, but it comes on doctor's order: Coello himself told us to buy it.

The stinking rose is high on every migrant's shopping list, as it is held to be an effective repellent for the night-walkers: the poisonous spiders, scorpions, and reptiles that hunt out on the trails the migrants walk over. Groups of migrants are in particular danger of treading on them or even sitting down on them, as they travel at night without a flashlight so as not to draw unwelcome attention to themselves from border police.

The technique, according to Coello, is to slice a fat, fresh clove in two and rub your feet, socks, shoes, and pants with the gleaming juice. When this is done thoroughly with a fistful of cloves, the clothes are said to be pungent for life, although whether this is effective at warding off predators is difficult to either prove or disprove.

Garlic does, however, have one proven property that could provide an unsought benefit to migrants: It is a natural and effective antibiotic. The presence of the microbe-fighting juices may well help migrants who continue to walk on, day after day, with ripped blisters steeped in increasingly bacteria-rich socks. We toss four or five heads of garlic into the cart as it can't hurt. Next stop, the pharmacy.

The Border Patrol say that walking in temperatures above one hundred degrees, you can lose up to a gallon of water an hour. The life-giving moisture evaporates through the pores, leaving vital salts encrusted on clothing in stale rings like those on López's cotton shirt. The *suero* on sale includes a balance of all the essential metabolites, combined in a strict ratio with sugars to aid their speedy uptake by the body.

The supermarket pharmacist is dressed in a white lab coat, and stands before neat, well-stocked shelves eyeing me somewhat impatiently. She holds up two kinds of *suero* to a circular hole cut in a glass window that seems to seal off the unwashed shoppers from her sterile domain. The choice is plain or lemon flavor. The lemon costs three times as much, but somehow it looks more refreshing, so we buy several boxes of sachets to add to the distinctly holy-looking water.

I also wonder about pep pills for the journey, and I ask her straight out about the best of them: ephedra. The compound was sold over the counter stateside as a weight-loss product and energy booster for years, and it is rich in ephedrine and pseudoephedrine, the principal ingredients of methamphetamine that fire up the metabolism like a blazing gas poker stuffed into a reluctant coal fire.

Aside from its use as a slimming aid, it has been used for its supposedly performance-enhancing effects by troops on exhausting military exercises and by athletes in training. Border Patrol agents that I have spoken to say that it is also sometimes fed to migrants by coyotes seeking to get groups of people to cross open ground faster.

Ephedra, though, was banned for a reason. The preparation has a range of dangerous side effects, including heart attacks, strokes, and overheating, and has been implicated in the deaths of soldiers and athletes including Orioles pitcher Steve Bechler, who died during spring training in 2003 after taking the drug.

The pharmacist looks at me blankly. I dictate the letters *E-P-H-E-D-R-A* for her to note down. She looks the name up in a guide, but finds she doesn't have it. What she does have is a codeine pill, laced with caffeine, which she says will also do the trick. I can't make up my mind about it. I don't like popping pills unless I really have to, and decide to pass.

It's time to get a little last-minute professional advice before we hit the border.

Tomás and I head out to the square and loiter in the shade of some eucalyptus trees on the corner opposite the Banorte office. It's a spot where Altar's coyotes congregate, doing business beside a line of white Ford minivans that run migrants up to the border line.

You have to be careful talking to smugglers, as our TV cameraman Manuel Carrillo found out last time he was in the town. Then, as he was standing in the plaza filming, a man on a bicycle rolled up to him, flashed a long, sharp knife, and warned him and the reporter he was with to skip town.

We are rather furtively on the lookout for Carlos, a smuggler with whom Tomás, ever friendly and disarming, was talking the day before. We catch sight of him leaning heavily on a pay phone, barking into the receiver. Muscular and short, he wears a pair of reflective sunglasses. He has close-cropped hair and rolls of skin that gather up on his neck like the thick roiling furrows on a shar-pei pup. He is dressed in a pressed white T-shirt, notable for having been ironed, and some khaki shorts and smart sneakers. It is a purposeful, distinctively cared-for look that makes him stand out amid the crowd of broke and shabbily dressed migrants. To me, he looks like a well-turned-out fighting dog.

Originally from Guatemala, he has been running migrants over the border from Altar to Phoenix for the past five years. Tomás greets him with a smile and handshake, and explains that we are going to cross the border that day. Would he, perhaps, have a little breakfast with us? He nods.

Strolling along the main strip, Carlos eyes the stream of well-equipped buses from the south unloading their cargo of farmers and the urban poor from across Mexico, heading on up to the United States for work. He looks at them, looks at me, then whips out his wallet and opens it to flash a thick wad of banknotes. "They think they have to cross to the other side to make money, but they don't. There's plenty to be made here in Altar if you know what you're doing," he brags.

It was no coincidence that we found Carlos using one of several Telmex phone cards to work the shiny bank of telephones in the street. He has one family in Guatemala and also a wife with children in Maryland he hasn't seen in three years. Aside from keeping in touch with them, his chosen profession is one that requires a large network of co-workers carrying out a variety of tasks that require close coordination on both sides of the border.

There are the *ganchos,* or "hooks" in English, who recruit the migrants in their hometowns across Mexico and beyond, some working right down in the highland cities of Central America. Then there are the coyotes proper, the guides who lead them over the desert, usually on foot, although occasionally in trucks or even on bicycles.

Then there are the short-haul drivers who spirit them on from desert load-outs to Tucson, or more commonly Phoenix, where they are held prisoner in drop houses until their fees are paid by their sponsors, usually anxious relatives already living in the shadows stateside.

In a conversation with Tomás a day earlier, Carlos explained that he operates a two-tier charging system. For somewhere around $1,200 a head, a guide will walk migrants over the desert as part of a group, in a trek taking several days, before handing them off to drivers taking them on up to Phoenix.

If they are prepared to pony up a few hundred dollars more, there is

An agent for Mexico's Grupo Beta migrant welfare agency watches over a group of people who had spent the night attempting to crawl up and over the border to Arizona. They failed, but there's always tonight. (Courtesy of Reuters)

an express trip by truck that will take just a few hours. As we plan to go it alone—an increasingly long shot in a time of ramped-up border security—Carlos volunteered to show us the best places to cross, and, naturally, those to avoid.

The taco stall is open to the street. The lemon yellow walls of its sunlit interior are decorated with a picture of Jesús Malverde, the drug traffickers' saint, and a poster of Valentín Elizalde, the Stetson-wearing balladeer of the powerful Sinaloa cartel who was gunned down a few months earlier after recklessly playing a concert in rival Gulf cartel territory south of Texas.

The display is a subtle message that the owner of the stall is open to the boys from Culiacán, the violent capital of Sinaloa state, who have moved into Sonora and secured local trafficking routes at gunpoint for drug lord Joaquín "El Chapo" Guzmán, Mexico's most-wanted man.

Carlos hasn't removed his sunglasses. He reaches across the floral tablecloth for my notebook and pencil. Hunched over, he sketches out a map with an almost childlike concentration. It shows the road we will need to take to El Sásabe in meticulous detail, and marks out key trafficking back roads branching out like the limbs of a saguaro as they lead up to the international line.

On the far side of a penciled fence marking the international border, he blocks out the serried peaks of the Baboquivari and San Luis mountains that stand over either side of the Altar Valley like a fistful of smashed knuckles.

"If you cross through here, you are entering the lion's mouth," he says, tapping the pencil sententiously over the tiny border town. "There's a lot of *migra,* and nobody crosses through there anymore. They are there day and night with motorbikes, quad bikes, and in cars tracking you, and they also have a helicopter and dogs."

Three greasy meat tacos cool in front of him on the oilcloth as he sketches trails out to the west through the vast, empty deserts of the Tohono O'odham nation, west of the sugarloaf dome of Baboquivari Peak, and east toward Green Valley and the border city of Nogales. He suggests we take either one of them to avoid the ramped-up vigilance.

"They have left a little space on either side, and that's where people get through."

Carlos's advice to us is to hug the mountains flanking the valley, where access trails for the Border Patrol are further from the main highways, and more difficult to watch and to track.

He warns us that it could likely take up to six days to cross up to Highway 86, the main corridor taking migrants out of the desert and into Tucson. It will be tough, he says, but we just have to be determined like the highly motivated migrants who get through.

"They succeed because they have the same dream you have," he says, revving us up like an L.A. life coach. "The American Dream."

Back in the park, the rank of vans is doing brisk business running migrants up to the border. The trucks have sliding doors and bench seats, and some of them have thick pile carpet on the floor. They have remolded tires plastered with mud, and their battered chassis rest up on flattened leaf springs.

The vans are filling up with scores of men, women, and children, who look to have gone to the same outfitters that Tomás and I visited. For the first time I notice that the predominant color is black: They are clearly going to walk at night, and it is rudimentary camouflage.

After Manuel's rather chilling experience, I am clearly pushing my luck, but I lean into one van where a group of migrants sit clasping day sacks and water jugs, and ask the driver if he will take me up to the border. He looks at me askance, tells me it will cost a hundred pesos—about ten dollars—and I should come back in forty minutes. When I return he has changed his mind. Not even Tomás can persuade him.

There's nothing for it but to go with our backup crew of Manuel and Robin Emmott, who are colleagues from our Mexico bureau. Between us we have their rental car, a less robust-looking minivan, and my new four-wheel-drive Toyota pickup truck that I have driven down from Phoenix. We will just have to ride in our own convoy up to the border.

With our bags tossed in the back, we roll on out onto the highway in searingly bright sunshine, past the guest houses, outfitters, and grocery stores, and head up toward the Arizona border on this highway taken by tens of thousands of people seeking to cross illegally to the United States each month.

I am excited. It is one of the most emblematic journeys of our times, although to my knowledge it has never appeared in the travel section of any newspaper. Travel means moneyed leisure, and there is nothing either moneyed or leisurely about this ride we have embarked on.

We find the turnoff to El Sásabe just outside Altar, opposite the scruffy Pemex gas station, just as Carlos noted in his sketch. The asphalt surface smudges into ungraded dirt a few yards off the highway, and is cut off by a chain drawn across the road between a metal post and a small tollbooth.

An old man in a white straw hat takes the three-dollar fee charged by the communally held farm, called an *ejido,* lowers the chain, and we are on our way up the sandy track, flanked by broad reaches of mesquite and clumps of livid green ocotillo. The track looks abandoned although it is, in fact, busier than the blacktop we left behind.

There are dozens of minivans barreling down the track, interspersed with pickup trucks. Some are new Chevys and Fords with tinted windows, others decades-old rust buckets with lifted suspension and fat, underinflated tires for off-road roaming. They are more likely to belong to drug runners than ranchers. I try not to catch the eyes of their drivers, and wish for a moment that my gleaming new truck had an inch of mud and a few dents to blend in on this outlaw highway.

The drivers clearly believe the best way to take the rough trail is at full tilt, covering the long miles of bone-rattling track up to the border line in top gear. Van after van roars by us kicking up a cinnamon cloud of moon dust, although it's not clear that their suspension will bear it. One passing truck has splayed front wheels dangling from a suspension like a snapped wishbone. We pass several others stopped at the roadside, their drivers changing flat tires or peering blankly at radiators belching steam.

As I gawk, Manuel is at the wheel, driving cautiously, rolling gently up and down the frequent washes, and driving around the deepest potholes. I am glad he's there, and I feel in safe hands. After a few miles we hit our first serious patch of mud: a thick, heavily churned axle-deep stretch the length of an Olympic swimming pool, which has traffic backed up at either end. A couple of trucks lie marooned, like ships beached on a sandbar.

Manuel stops, backs up, slips into four-wheel drive, and churns through it up to the wheel arches in mud. I look back, and Robin has gamely followed on, but after a few yards he is stuck fast, the rear wheels of his people-carrier spinning uselessly and throwing up a thick chestnut plume of mud. His expression is wide-eyed dismay as his shiny hired van wallows ever deeper into the mire.

We don't have a tow rope, and I don't fancy wading back into the muck to pull him out. One of the stranded smugglers has a chain and gamely offers to trudge in to attach it to Robin's van. Robin, though, has not given up. He turns the engine over once more, guns it hard, and the van glides on spinning tires, striking a hard crust at the edge of the pool. It gains traction and we are on our way again! It's a brief lucky break.

Bouncing on down the road, our little convoy is now caked in a thick impasto of mud and dust. Then I hear it, the unmistakable flapping of a ripped tire. We shudder to a halt on a hard patch of the road, get out the jack, and start grinding the Tacoma up off the ground, and find that, even with the jack pushed up to its limit, we somehow can't get the new wheel on. I start thumping out a hole in the packed sand beneath the wheel, thinking all the while about the drug runners who haul dope up the same road we are on.

According to border police, pot smugglers heading out over the open desert often pack as many as two spare wheels in among the pungent *costales* of Mexican grass. The reason, as I am beginning to discover, is that the trails are covered in cactus spines, some as tough as sailmakers' needles, that slice through tire walls like a hot spoon through ice cream. One spare wheel may well not be enough, and I find myself wondering if we are going to make it.

On the road again, we see more evidence of the *narcos,* as drug smugglers are known in Mexico, and it is disquieting. At the side of the road there is a rusted, burned-out hulk of a minibus, flipped on its back like a roach. As we lurch on down the road we count eight or nine more people-carriers trashed and set ablaze in the same way on the desolate stretch of highway. It gives the trail the unsettling look of a war zone.

According to news reports, the vehicles are among a dozen or so that were destroyed by gunmen from the Sinaloa cartel on the same day. The rifle-toting enforcers stopped traffic, ordered the drivers and passengers out, doused the trucks with gasoline, and tossed in a match. None of the passengers were hurt in the coordinated attacks, which the drug lords used to claim the route and the *plaza* as their own. It did not mean an end to human trafficking along the route, it simply meant that now it was subordinate to the dopers.

According to chatter in Altar, the *narcos* now charged the human smugglers for protection, thereby claiming a hefty slice of the profits from the booming illegal immigration routes to Arizona. Not only that, we learned, they also now called the shots, telling the human smugglers when and where to cross, to provide cover for their own cross-border smuggling activities.

What better way could there be to ensure that a high-value load of grass will get through than by first tying up finite Border Patrol resources with one or more large groups of immigrants? The Border Patrol agents have to call in more cops to assist them, and then to drive the detainees off for processing. Most of the detainees will be posted back in a few hours anyway, after agreeing to voluntary return, free to try to cross again the next day, so it's no real loss to the coyotes.

After a couple of hours on the trail, we rattle into the outskirts of El Sásabe, once a dirt-poor brick-making and ranching town and now one of the most notorious smugglers' hubs on the border. As we bounce toward the low brick outskirts we see an eye-catching, though utterly incongruous, racetrack. With its smart starting stalls and post-and-rail track, it stands in stark contrast to the humble brick and adobe homes and dirt streets of the town, and speaks volumes about life in the borderlands.

Local drug lords and their lieutenants are flush with hot money in a part of Mexico where there is little to spend it on and where police are at their weakest and most intimidated. Discretion is thrown to the wind, and profits are splurged on whims that are often as bizarre as they are ostentatious. The racetrack reminds me of a drug lord's caprice in the plunging gorges of Mexico's Copper Canyon system in the highlands of Chihuahua. There a notorious marijuana grower had built a dry ski slope into the cliff edge, creating a bizarre private theme park that local residents called simply *narcolandia*.

I find myself imagining a day at the races in El Sásabe. Drug lords in Stetsons, plaid shirts, and ostrich-skin boots, rattling their *esclavas* (as their chunky gold bracelets are called), swilling back beer, and cheering for their riders. I doubt there will be Thoroughbreds or hundred-pound jockeys, just the tough quarter horses they load up with drugs, goaded onward by Norteño cowboys with spurs, reliving the epic races for the line they have with mounted agents of *la migra*. This is one race I would really love to see.

We bounce into town past the dusty cemetery, with its wrought-iron crosses and silk flowers, the first heavy drops of a monsoon storm drumming on the hood of my truck. In my haste, I had forgotten all about the rains. I drop Manuel off and drive to the Super El Coyote supermarket, which is my last best chance of picking up a raincoat. There's a crackle of thunder, and inside the store the only dim light comes from the refrigerators stacked with sodas. Sure enough, in among the usual migrants' supplies and paraphernalia I find a tightly folded plastic poncho. It costs $1.50.

We make our last stop in Mexico at a migrant center a few yards shy of the border crossing. While it was first established as a border police force, Grupo Beta has since morphed into Mexico's migrant protection agency. Its agents, many of them seconded from cities hundreds of miles away from the international line, cruise the borderlands in unmistakable orange pickup trucks, rescuing stranded migrants, as well as, controversially, distributing advice, maps, and even comic books priming them on how to make the journey safely.

El Sásabe is a lonely posting. As Robin and Manuel have an on-camera chat about migrant flows with the director of Grupo Beta in the front room of the single-story office—currently some five hundred people a day are coming up through the town and striking out over the desert—I nose around the project. I notice there is an old weight-lifting bench and a table soccer game in a back room, to help agents while away the weeks and months of exile in the desert.

A young woman agent from Mexico City lets us use the tiled floor of the front office to pack our bags, all the while playing with Tomás's camera, smiling flirtatiously. We divide up the supplies, taking half the water and an armful of cans each. I also get the *piloncillo* and the tortillas, although within a few hours I will be swearing blind that I can't find them anywhere.

U.S. Border Patrolman Gavin Wieden shines an infrared torch on a dirt road on the Mexican border near Naco, Arizona. The picture was taken through a night vision scope. (Courtesy of Reuters)

I also have a sharp pocketknife, a cheap compass, and one item that migrants making the journey will not have, although the drug traffickers might: a satellite telephone. Smugglers use them to stay in touch with spotters ranged on hills, some deep inside Arizona, looking out for U.S. border police.

We plan to use our sat phone to call in entries for a live Internet blog, and as a panic button to summon help if we get into trouble during the walk, which will take us out across miles of desert, alternately baking in the summer sun and, it seems, raked by lightning storms. It is good to know that we have it, and Manuel shows us how to use it. I am only half paying attention, as I am beginning to feel nervous, wondering what on earth I am doing there.

The border up ahead is marked by a rusty cattle fence and rusted vehicle barriers. While jumping over it like the migrants we are shadowing would present no problem whatsoever, we are going to cross legally through the port of entry, for a couple of reasons.

While I have a fair bit of wiggle room with my job that allows me to weasel around to get a story, I cannot break the law. It also strikes me as a discourtesy to the border police I deal with on a day-to-day basis to go behind their backs and try and sneak in. So, instead, I have written ahead to the Border Patrol in Tucson and told them what we are planning to do, where, and when.

I pull on my thin poncho, then heft the loaded pack onto my shoulders for the first time. As I step outside into the rain to give a stand-up on camera, I am struck by how heavy the bag is, and by how useless the waist strap is at taking the weight off my shoulders. I stare into the lens as large raindrops slap and crackle on the mike, and speak rather curtly to our Internet audience.

"Here I am in El Sásabe, the main point of entry through which hundreds of undocumented immigrants cross from Mexico into the United States each day. Ahead lies forty-five miles of searing Sonora Desert to get to our destination. We had expected to cross in one-hundred-degree heat, but what we have instead," I say, shooting an irritable glance skyward, "is a rainstorm."

It's time to go. I raise both hands and pump the air in a decidedly premature victory salute. Tomás has pulled on his rucksack and tugged a jaunty orange poncho over the top of it. He spins round nimbly, looking like a pantomime troll from the pages of Maurice Sendak. He snaps a farewell shot of Manuel and Robin, and we set off up the broken, muddy track for the border beneath a darkening sky.

Two hours earlier we had been soaked with sweat, changing a tire in desert sand hot enough to bake a potato. Now we are walking in cold, driving rain, caught unawares by this brutal shift in conditions. Closing the gap to the line, I can feel the rain soaking into my clothes. Like many of the broke Latin Americans making this journey, we are quite unprepared. This is it, we are going anyway.

TWO

Walking to America

The brightly lit redbrick border crossing up ahead is framed by a heavy gray cloud that reaches almost to the ground. It looks to me like a beach hut standing on the edge of a broad, dark sea, or the last stop on a railroad line.

Unsurprisingly, given the area's fame as a springboard for illegal entry to the United States, Tomás and I are the only pedestrians crossing through the port of entry itself. The other border crossers, dressed and poorly equipped as we are, are beating out east and west of the port.

As Tomás and I splash up to the building in driving rain, we are met by a border inspector dressed in a smart blue uniform, a pistol tucked into his holster. He asks for our passports, which we fumble out of the protective wrap of plastic bags stuffed in our soaked rucksacks. He disappears inside an office with them as we take advantage of a last bit of shelter from the rain. Beside us, waiting in the small patch of dry concrete, is a policewoman from Tucson who has a slightly strained expression on her face.

As the thunder crackles, she tells us that she has been cut off by flash floods while visiting Sasabe (the Arizona counterpart to El Sásabe) and now cannot drive back to the city in her patrol car because gushing torrents of water have severed the road. A police helicopter, she says, is on its way through the storm to rescue her.

"The highway's cut in at least three places," she says. "The water is hip deep, and the current is so strong that it will wash a car away, even if it's just in up to the hubcaps." She looks at us. We are bedraggled, and I clearly look woefully unprepared, dressed as I am in a transparent plastic poncho in place of a proper hiking jacket. It reaches barely down to my waist, with gaping slits for arm holes. Tomás looks a little more like a hiker in his poncho and new boots, although his camera bag gives him away as something of a dilettante. "You haven't got a chance," she says, sizing us up. "The water will just sweep you away."

It is a tricky moment. I honestly don't know what to say to her by way of reply. A lot of illegal immigrants who have made it this far up to the border line have traveled from southern Mexico, Central America, and sometimes beyond, walking and clinging grimly to the cars of a freight train for much of the way. Almost nothing would stop them at this point.

While Tomás and I haven't been tempered by that kind of hardship, we are committed to our odyssey and are not going to be derailed by the weather less than a mile into it. I don't really know how to tell the policewoman that we are going to press on come what may, without her worrying about our safety, or perhaps even feeling she has to stop us.

It is quite a relief when the inspector steps back out of the office and rather ceremoniously hands us back our passports. The moment is broken. As we set off into the driving rain, someone at the border crossing behind us can't resist a last little quip. "Hey! I hope you guys know how to swim!" We don't respond, and walk doggedly off into the rain driving across the darkening valley. The mountains look like gritty shovelfuls of dirt thrown down onto a prehistoric diorama. The way ahead is lit by frequent flashes of lightning from perhaps half a dozen separate thunder cells, and what I glimpse in the gloom breaks all the half-formed notions that I have of deserts.

My experience of deserts is limited to roaming a few lonely reaches of the Sonora Desert in my travels for work. While it is bone dry, at least for most of the year, it looks oddly like a coral garden. The towering saguaros seem like tridents; then there are the blazing green ocotillos, with their javelin-stiff branches that seem to float over the sand like weeds in an aquarium.

But the path that lies ahead of us through a translucent veil of rain is different. We can make out a stretch of broad valley carpeted with wild prairie grass and stunted mesquite, and much of it is, I can see, quite literally under water. Clay-colored fingers of water rake the valley floor, which is dotted with spreading pools and even small lakes.

Our plan is to knock out a couple of miles on the highway—mostly to avoid the *bajadores* that often lie in wait in the borderlands—and then bear right into the Buenos Aires National Wildlife Refuge, and make our way north through the wilderness for a dozen miles until we cross the main road from Arivaca to Sasabe.

After just a few minutes' walk, my cargo pants are drenched and my feet are sloshing around in my shoes as we follow the slick blacktop of Highway 286 up over ridges and down into flooded washes. We hear the helicopter coming to pick up the cop, although it is lost in the gloom.

The worst of the torrential floods have already leapt and cascaded through the washes in a foaming stampede of runoff, although we are frequently wading through water up to our thighs. I had never, not for a moment, imagined anything even remotely like this.

After walking for a couple of hours, our light introduction to the trail is over. It is now pitch black, dead dark, the night sky blocked out with clouds. We turn into a side road, heading east into the wilderness, ankle deep in muddy rainwater on a night without even a sliver of moon or starlight.

It is not only the water that seems out of place, there is also something wrong with the soundtrack. Out in the desert, I had expected to hear the excited yips of coyotes setting out to hunt in the twilight, as I frequently do in rugged South Mountain Park where I run in Phoenix. But here we are surrounded by an eerie and unexpected cacophony of frogs and toads. They are somehow making the most of the rains, and it seems that the lakes and pools that have just risen up in the desert are instantly teeming with amphibious life.

They create two rhythmic threads working in counterpoint: an intermittent caterwauling in the foreground, overlaid against a quieter, more continuous purring in the background. If I shut my eyes to imagine them, the sounds are not so much amphibian as like raucous, primal birdsong. It is loud, comes in waves, and is on all sides in surround sound.

Walking now in the pitch dark, I notice the bite of the heavy pack cutting into my shoulders. I also feel an incessant itch from my pants, soaked through from the successive dunkings and drenchings they have taken. We trudge on, chatting over the din in the darkness, stopping to shoot some video with night vision. I have the unseeing gaze of the blind in the playback, and look clearly thrilled by the strangeness I am presenting.

To try and ease the journey along, I am looking eagerly for the path that I spied on a map before we set out from Altar that morning. More in hope than conviction, I lead Tomás on one track that branches off north in the gloom, wanting very much to believe that it will lead us up through the reserve without having to strike off across country in the dark.

We follow it up and down and around, skirting washes and lakes. At one point it beckons us into a darkened stretch of water between tall clumps of reeds and grass. I continue, first into hip-deep water, then up to my chest. Tomás follows, and as we ease out of the swamp, his cell phone starts to ring. Who can that be? I wonder. And how have we got a signal way out here?

He tugs it out of his pocket, and it is dripping with water. Resting on his palm, it sputters and shakes, racked by random electrical spasms in its death throes. Finally, it cuts out, taking all our emergency numbers with it. We still have the sat phone, but don't have contact numbers for our backup team. If we get into trouble, we'll just have to hope someone thinks to call us.

The drizzle cuts out, the sky clears, and the large wheel of the full moon rises over the desert. We can now see the trail we are moving on and the outline of the fistlike mountains lying on either side of the broad plain. I look down and see more foot tracks on the muddy path. They could be migrants, bandits, or even drug mules, but somehow it's good not to be alone out here. Tomás, however, has pulled up, and is staring critically at the tracks and then back up at the mountains bathed in the light of the moon that has at last emerged from the clouds.

"Tim?"

"Yes."

"What side of the Altar Valley is Baboquivari Peak?" he asks of the sacred dome that is home to I'itoi, the mischievous creator god who brought the Tohono O'odham tribe's ancestors out of the underworld.

"West. It should be out on our left."

"So . . . what's it doing to our right?"

"What the . . . ?"

I look up, and sure enough the lowering, dimly lit peak is off to our right. Then it dawns on me. I have led us around in a large circle, and we have now been heading back south for some considerable time.

Not only that, I look down at the trail, and the full force of my idiocy hits me. The tracks that I have been blithely guiding us along are our own. Thankfully, Tomás has spotted it before I can take us around on another useless lap, delighting in the delusion that we have company.

It's a blow. We have lugged our heavy packs several unnecessary miles and lost a couple of hours. Completely crestfallen, I realize it is time to stop pretending I know where we are and break out the compass. I rummage for it in the bag. It's part of a cheap hiker's multitool that also includes a whistle and a thermometer that I had picked up in Wal-Mart for a couple of bucks the week before. I can barely believe my stupidity!

Breaking smugglers' rules, I momentarily flick on a flashlight and take a bearing. We will now have to follow the compass needle relentlessly in a straight line, just west of north, to get us back on course for Three Points. Following its path is not easy, as it makes no allowance for the lie of the land or for the erratic distribution of the clawing desert vegetation.

As we set off again in the dark, we find that you can't follow the compass cross-country in a straight line for more than a couple of minutes without stumbling into something in the dark. It leads us through clumps of sharp cholla cactuses, through thickets of catclaw bushes, and past the darkened forms of barrel cactuses with spines gleaming like a surgeon's scalpel. We dodge around them, always keeping just west of north, to keep us parallel to the highway heading up from Sasabe.

The compass leads us indifferently over the darkened rim of first one plunging wash and then another as we head north. We scramble up and down the steep gullies, splashing through the ebbing floodwaters, hauling ourselves up the far side on muddy, tangled roots. I keep thinking of the young man from Chiapas we met at the clinic in Altar who had gashed his knee in a sudden fall, and I find myself grateful for the moonlight.

We splash on, hour after hour, up and down the *barrancas,* walking as best we can on the slippery mud left behind by the rains, all the while slipping, sliding, and slamming our toes into rocks, as we walk through the night. Even if we wanted to, we couldn't stop for a break: There is not one dry square inch in this ink-black water world at our feet. Besides, the temperature has dropped sharply, and it is too cold to stop. Every time we slow, I get the shivers.

As we march on, chatting in hissed stage whispers, I am grateful for one mercy. We haven't stepped on the rattlesnakes, spiders, and scorpions that we were warned about, although I see in the dawn light that my left hand has puffed up like a ski mitten. Something has clearly bitten me, although it doesn't hurt. I figure I have been stung by some kind of a horsefly or perhaps nipped by one of the more benign spiders.

My groin is sore from walking in soaked underwear, and I notice I have a barreling gait like John Wayne. So does Tomás. He pauses, looks at me as I take a few painful steps, and starts laughing hard. "It's like we've been riding for days on a horse," he says in his very workmanlike English. "But the horse is gone, and we are still with the fucking legs wide open!"

We stand on the muddy trail in the dawn, our shoulders shaking with laughter. When it subsides, we take stock of the sharp shift in temperature as the day breaks. The sun is now up and it is starting to burn. I tug my cash headscarf out of my pocket and lay it over my head, catching a peripheral glimpse of fluttering greenbacks. The view ahead is fringed with riches.

I have on a long-sleeved gray T-shirt bought from Lourdes, back at the store in Altar, while Tomás covers up with a smart plaid shirt that he bought for six dollars. I catch sight of him as he fastens the buttons. He's a city boy, but with his shirt and rolling gait, he looks like he's morphing into a Norteño cowboy. We pick up the packs with a groan, and trudge on. I am feeling the pain, when suddenly I jump in surprise. Something is vibrating hard in my waistband. It is the sat phone, and I had forgotten all about it.

"Tim? It's Robin. Where are you guys at?"

I look around me at an unbroken horizon of mesquite and cactuses. "I don't know," I tell him, then have another stab at it. "I have no idea."

"How are you and Tomás bearing up?"

"We've been walking all night, we're exhausted, oh . . . and I think we lost the tortillas," I tell him, and then we lose the signal, and our link to the world.

With the dropped call, it is beginning to sink in that we really are alone and, if not completely lost, not sure in any real sense of where we are. We set off again in the early morning light, following the needle north by northwest, trusting like early navigators on the high seas that it will lead us out of, well, nowhere.

Then, without warning, as little as fifty yards to our north, I glimpse a ribbon of asphalt. If a car had sped across it in that moment, I would have leapt out of my skin. We have made it to the Arivaca road! We are now a good twelve miles due north of the border, although thanks to my errors, we have likely walked closer to fifteen or twenty miles since we set out. We still have more than thirty miles to go.

I look up and down the road. It is about eight in the morning, and there is no traffic to be seen in either direction. I lift up the rusted strand of barbed wire and Tomás scuttles underneath, briefly snagging his pack on the barbs. We swap, I follow him, and we scoot over the road and break for the wilderness on the other side. We are getting into our secret journey, and are perhaps turning a little feral.

We are off-road, away from any vigilance, and with a good two hours more in our legs before we have to break from the heat of the sun, which is fast driving out the shivers of the night walk, turning the chill into sweat. I glance at the thermometer on the back of the compass, and see that the temperature is climbing up through the nineties.

Pushing north, we begin to see animals out on the back trails. A dirty gray coyote trots ahead of us, pausing briefly to look back with disdain. As the sun climbs we see three deer springing lightly out of a shady creek bed, nimbly crossing our path and bounding on east across the valley.

Since we dived off the main road the night before, we have seen no border police apart from a helicopter that circled with a searchlight in the small hours, way off to the east of us. Nor have we seen any other border crossers.

After a couple of miles, we follow a cattle trail that leads up to an abandoned camp used by foot crossers to crash during the day. It is set in the shade of a few mesquite trees, and it is a melancholy spot.

There are discarded plastic water jugs cracked by the sunlight, rusted tuna fish cans, and a small lean-to shelter made of branches and brush, to block out the harsh heat of the sun. I look up at Tomás, and we are both sweating heavily. We need to get out of the sun ourselves, or we will be burning through our precious store of water too fast. The place is a little desolate, and we decide to walk on, looking for a shady, out-of-the-way place of our own to crash.

When we lower ourselves into the bottom of a wash, I feel a welcome cool as the remaining moisture from last night's downpour evaporates from the creek bed. We really shouldn't stop here. It violates the principal rule of desert hiking—not to camp in washes, because of the very real risk of flash floods in the monsoon season. But the spot is irresistible. The sand feels as cool as if it had been pulled from a refrigerator.

I have a friend from the Tohono O'odham nation who told me she used to take naps in washes walking between villages as a child, so I figure that if she could do it, we can get away with it. We drop our gear down in the shade of a wizened tree on the sandy stream bed, to rest after fifteen hours on our feet.

I pull off my wet shirt and socks, and drape them over a tree root in the harsh sunlight to dry out. Then I stand there, taking stock of my body. I feel like I have been pummeled with a sock filled with billiard balls. Everything aches, from my neck and shoulders to my arms and the backs of my legs.

As I stoop down to rest, I notice that I am moving agonizingly slowly and groaning. I look at my feet. There are no blisters, although to my surprise, the nail of my big toe is cracked and turning purple. I must have stubbed it in the night, although I was never conscious of any pain. I call out to Tomás.

"How are you doing, my old mate?"

"Hmmm . . . My shoulders feel like pulp and my feet hurt," he says, tugging off the new Caterpillar boots he bought specially for the trip. Mindful of Coello's advice to avoid blisters, he peels off his wet socks to hang them out to dry. I catch sight of his toes, and see that it's clearly too late for that to bring any real benefit.

His feet are a morass of angry welts and blisters that start at the heel, spread out along the soles, and finally nip painfully at the toes. Each of them looks like it has been deliberately thumped with an upholstery hammer. I take a swig of water and lie down on the cool sand, resting my head on my backpack in the patchy shade of the gnarled mesquite tree.

I gaze up at a small lizard on a branch, and stare at it blankly. It has a flickering pulse in its neck, and it seems to be doing a rapid sequence of push-ups, framed against the sky. I study it wearily for a few moments, and then it's as if someone had yanked the plug on a television set. Everything goes black.

With almost every siesta I have ever taken—even those back at home in England where nobody really takes a siesta—I dream of death. Sometimes it is little more than a sense of the last minutes of life ebbing away, although occasionally the dream is sharper, harder, more startling, though rarely as vivid as this nightmare I have before waking.

There is gray-green light, and a mauve sky of summer thunder. I am on my hands and knees crawling through long, wet grass. I feel the thrum of electricity in the air behind me, and then I see it coming: a ball of lightning curving in from the edge of my field of vision. It jolts me back to consciousness with a gasp. I blink, casting around me for consolation. What I see is a tree festooned with socks. Then I feel the pain of my body.

I raise myself up onto one elbow. I realize that I am stretched out, right out in the desert very far indeed from any comfort, perhaps ten miles from the nearest building. It's odd, but I feel, momentarily, as if I have woken up treading water far out in the ocean, and now can't see the beach.

I look over at Tomás, stretched out beside me. It is now midafternoon. He is snoring in loud, deep rasps. I call out to wake him, and then I start looking for our food. I don't have much of an appetite, but I know that we have to eat to keep going way out here in the desert.

I fumble for a couple of cans of tuna for a meal, and hunt again for the tortillas in an exhausted funk. I rummage around in my rucksack for a few minutes, but they remain hidden in plain sight. (Much, much later, I will find them as I unpack my bag in a hotel in Tucson. Some Red Bulls that I had also brought for the journey turn up in the back of my truck.)

Tomás, now awake and bleary, pulls out the last can of refried beans from his bag and passes it to me. I slip a swollen finger through the ring pull and tug it open. The beans carve up like dog food, and we eat them off the knife.

We have just over half our water left, with two-thirds of our journey to Three Points still ahead of us. Thirty miles. It is not just a daunting prospect, it is a harrowing one.

We have been out for not quite a full day, but already I am worried by our physical state. I try to stand, grimacing. It is all I can do to hobble around our small desert camp gathering up my clothes.

Tomás pulls a couple of anti-inflammatory pills out of his bag and offers me one. We swill them down and get dressed like old men in a post-op ward. I watch carefully as he pulls on his socks and prepares for the boots. As he slips them on, he winces as if they were cast-iron clogs tugged cherry red from a forge. It starts me thinking.

Migrants who are in bad shape often stagger out to Highway 286—the road that runs north to south through the Altar Valley—and simply wave down a Border Patrol truck and give themselves up. That is, of course, if they have the strength to make it to the road from the edges of the broad valley and, indeed, if they know it is there in the first place. I feel weak as a kitten and in considerable pain, and I look at Tomás hobbling in his new boots, cracking a brave smile. "Tomás, old mate," I tell him, "I think we need to head for the highway." We were determined to carry on, but staying close to the highway would be safer, in case we needed a rescue.

As we walk up the wash, the anti-inflammatory pills kick in and the aches recede. We have a mile or two to go, heading west, to where I figure we will meet the lonely blacktop running up through the middle of the valley; through the middle of nowhere, in fact. We reach it, sweating hard, but delighted to be walking up the road, and not dodging knife-sharp vegetation. The plan is to walk on until nightfall and rest up.

We knock out miles 16, 17, and 18 one after the other, meeting a Border Patrol agent who stops us, checks our passports, and asks us what we are doing. He has heard to look out for us, and offers us water. I take an extra gallon, and carry on marching north into the gathering dusk. My legs ache, and now my arms burn with the exertion of carrying the water.

I look back and Tomás is twenty yards behind. I walk on, look back again a few minutes later, and he is now fifty yards behind. As we stride up the road, I have come up with a plan, although I am not sure I have the strength to follow it through. I want us to push on and walk another fifteen miles through the chill of the night, and break the back of the journey, leaving us just a dozen or so miles for the following day.

At around 6:30 P.M., close to sunset, we arrive at mile marker 20, and slump onto the sharp stones of the shoulder for a breather. We don't know where our backup crew is and we can't raise them on the sat phone. I am desperate to push on and not lose momentum, but Tomás simply can't. Not only is he, like me, exhausted, his boots are seriously ripping up his feet. I am suddenly faced with a stark choice common to many illegal immigrants making the trip: Should I leave my companion to his fate and carry on, or should we give up together?

I am too exhausted to think or plan or talk, and don't want to make that decision now. I drop the jugs of water, throw down my pack, and slump to the ground. I rest my head on a coarse tuft of prairie grass, sprawling cruciform in the dust. I fall into a deep sleep again.

We both wake up at around midnight, shivering. The moon is up, and a chill wind blows up from the south. We have gone from baking hot to freezing in a few short hours. We can't walk, so how can we stay warm? We are miles from anywhere, and I am now wondering how best to survive the night. I roll over to start knocking out some push-ups when Tomás stops me. He reminds me he has a Mylar survival blanket in his pack.

We break it open and wrap it around ourselves in the dark. I tuck it back under me and anchor it in place with Tomás's red poncho. The heat comes back quickly, although I know now that we are done. We are helpless, drifting. We sleep on like babies. No thoughts of ants or scorpions.

"¡Despiertense, despiertense, amigos!" (Wake up, wake up, friends!) I open my eyes and see a couple of pairs of black boots. I look up and see two Border Patrol agents standing over us in the dawn light. They have seen a couple of shapes wrapped up under a poncho and surrounded by water bottles. Well, if it walks like a duck, talks like a duck . . .

I am suddenly tongue-tied and trying to think fast to stop them from arresting us. My English accent rings out in the cold desert morning, tinkling like a teaspoon on bone china. I stammer out the plans for our trip, and how we are trying to walk up through the valley, that we told the Border Patrol in Tucson that we would be out there. One of the agents asks for our passports, while the other looks at us slumped on the ground. He pauses a moment, and takes stock. "Are you guys all right?"

The question catches me off guard. I find I don't really know how to answer that one. We must look quite a sight. We're sunburned, have several days' stubble, and are covered in dried sweat and mud. I feel like I have taken a bit of a knock and I need a few moments. I tell them we are fine, despite how it looks, and they leave us sitting at the shoulder of the highway.

I look over at Tomás, trying to figure out what we are going to do. I can make it back onto my feet sure enough, although it is far from clear that I can manage another twenty-five miles. Tomás looks at his mangled toes hidden in stained socks, looks at his boots, and I can see he is close to tears.

He wants to carry on and finish the trip, but with his feet in the condition they are, he just can't. I feel deeply for my friend. We decide to flag down the next Border Patrol truck and beg a ride to the gas station and store at Three Points that was to be our journey's end.

We don't have to wait long. A few minutes later a Border Patrol agent speeding south in a Ford truck spots us, brakes hard, and pulls over onto the shoulder. After explaining to Agent Gonzalez that we are not what we appear to be, we ask if he will give us a ride up to journey's end. Sure, he says.

First off, he offers us the steel detention cage bolted to the back of his truck, then thinks better of it as we are reporters. He invites us to sit up in the extended cab with him. Tomás clambers painfully into the back, I sit in the front. I have slipped into a kind of fugue where I can see things clearly but not make much sense of them. I notice he has a pair of night vision goggles on the dash.

Agent Gonzalez speeds us over the remaining miles almost without conversation. I feel the same disconnect as a jogger stepping off a treadmill and finding himself hurtling across the gym floor at walking speed. I am astonished, scandalized even, at how fast the mile markers are rushing by as we tear up through the desert.

Tomás, I later discover, is regretting the dozens of missed photo opportunities he sees on the trail. In no time, we are rolling past several tall radio masts and into the sprawling hamlet of ranches and trailer homes that, until a few moments ago, had been two hard days' walk ahead of us.

We are set down outside the Chevron gas station with its half-timbered general store. It's a place where Border Patrol agents, state troopers, and uniformed cops from the Tohono O'odham nation stop for a Styrofoam cup of coffee and a sandwich as they head out on duty. To my surprise, my disappointment and tiredness lifts, as I get a kind of tunnel vision. It is breakfast time and I am suddenly ravenous.

I go into the store, swinging open the door like it's opening time at an Old West saloon. I am going to have a cup of fresh coffee and some breakfast. I have a broad grin on my face as I walk up to the steaming coffee percolator. I grab one cup. It's too small. I grab a larger one. It looks about the right size. I pour the coffee, grab a couple of bacon and egg croissants, and within moments we are sitting at a concrete table on the porch eating hot food for the first time in two days. It's now my eyes that mist up.

After an hour or so I am starting to feel human again. Tomás is, too. I notice he is taking pictures—anything he can snap without standing up—and I am taking notes for our blog. We have finally spoken to Robin and Manuel on the sat phone, and as we wait to be picked up we begin talking through the various possible outcomes for this desert odyssey.

Had we been illegal immigrants, there are three possible ways that it could have ended. For me, so soon after being rescued from the desert, the first of them hardly bears thinking about: Three or four days into our journey, by now broken and with no water, we could have simply lain down under a tree and gone to sleep. Scores perish that way here every summer.

Another very real possibility is that we would have been arrested by the Border Patrol, hunted down in a variety of ways that make up the heart of this book—by groups tracking on foot or on horseback, or speeding over the desert in helicopters cued by a sensor or an unmanned surveillance drone.

The other possible outcome is that, after marching over rough trails through the valley for another couple of days and chilly nights, we would have made it through this perilous no-man's-land and into the U.S. interior. Our best chance of success would have been with a paid guide, and that onward journey is an an adventure all its own. This is how it works.

The trip deeper into the United States begins when a coyote—like Carlos, jabbering on the banks of phones back in Altar—calls contacts in Phoenix, telling them how many people he has on the move north, the location of the load-out that they are headed for, and then the day and approximate time that they will need picking up and driving on to the city. One illegal immigrant, a working mother from Guatemala who now cleans homes in Phoenix for a living, talked me through the endgame that Tomás and I could have expected shortly after we made the trip.

Thirty-two-year-old Gladys had spent all her adult life in the United States, married a Guatemalan here, and raised their three daughters before she was picked up, jailed, and deported by Immigration and Customs Enforcement police following a surprise swoop on her home. Once back in Central America, a place she now barely knew, she set off back to the United States within a month with a group of eleven Guatemalan immigrants in a journey that cost her husband five thousand dollars.

Much of it was made on foot, and Gladys, a large woman, shed around thirty pounds in weight on the four-week overland journey. They made the last stretch hobbling over the desert at night, as Tomás and I had. The guide walking with the group pulled a cell phone from his pocket as they neared the load-out point on one of the highways leading in from the desert to Tucson. He needed to finalize timing of the pickup with two load car drivers. It was important that there would be no hanging around in an area that is heavily patrolled.

Border police say coyotes favor inexpensive load cars with as much space as possible. Heavy pickup trucks with a covered bed are popular, as are Econolines or Grand Voyagers, and even the more spacious sedans. The two young drivers who pulled up to collect Gladys and her group drove a Nissan they had prepped by taking the rear seats out.

They hissed at them to toss everything but their papers and bundled everyone into the back, leaving a pile of trash at the load-out.

"They knew of course that I was *gordita* [chubby] so they said to me, 'Gladys, get on the floor, the rest of you on top of her.' And that's how we went. All I could see were two other migrants on top of me, and then the roof of the car," she said. She told me it was a three-hour ride up to Phoenix, the first part over desert back roads, the last stretch from Casa Grande on Interstate 10. After an hour her limbs went to sleep and she switched with one of the coyotes up front.

The two drivers left the crush of migrants uncovered in the back, although it is more common for coyotes to try and hide the load from a casual glance by throwing a blanket or a rug over them. If a group is being moved in a pickup truck, border police say, a common ploy is to fix a piece of black-painted plywood over the bed, which makes it look as if the truck is traveling empty although the space beneath will then be crammed with people, packed like sardines.

The weight of the human cargo is substantial, and the sagging springs of the truck are a giveaway to law enforcement. To avoid betraying their cargo, the smugglers often limit the movement of the springs with a metal brace or by placing wooden blocks into them to stop the suspension from sagging suspiciously. The adapted truck is a ringer for empty, although it will handle like a pig, reaching a tipping point on the slightest of curves without warning, pitching into an often lethal roll.

Border police say the smugglers increasingly try to beat the odds by using scouts ahead of and even behind a load vehicle. These scouts will roll on up the highway spotting for Border Patrol checkpoints, or trail the load, carefully watching for patrol cars heading north that could pull it over and search it. If they encounter Highway or Border Patrol, the spotters have been known to set off at high speed, acting as a decoy to draw police, much like decoy go-fast boats drawing the Coast Guard away from a freighter packed with cocaine on the journey from Colombia. If the spotters are trailing a load car that gets stopped, they have been known to slip in and pick up *pollos,* as migrants are sometimes called, fleeing from arresting agents.

Then there are the bailouts. When Border Patrol agents challenge load car drivers to stop either at a checkpoint or out on the highways, the drivers are often career criminals and will do what they can to avoid getting thrown in jail. A common tactic is to make a feint, apparently complying with the order to stop. They will in fact leave the vehicle in gear, open the doors, and bail out into a roll while it is still moving, knowing the agents in pursuit will try and save the load car and other traffic on the road.

"At the back of their heads, they know how you think as law enforcement. What are you going to do? Go after the guy or try and save some people's lives?" says Mike Scioli, a Border Patrol agent who worked on one of the key hand-off areas up by Picacho Peak on the I-10 north of Tucson. "These poor people in the back of the trunk pounding, because they are afraid now, they don't know what's going on, they hear the sirens." The agents really have no choice.

Since any vehicle used in the furtherance of a crime is immediately forfeit, the wily smugglers will try and avoid that loss by using stolen cars or, strange as it may seem, cars made available in a form of criminal pooling program. An investigation by Arizona authorities in 2004 and 2005 found that many of the migrant-packed minivans, cars, and trucks that the smugglers gun up from the border had been acquired in a complex black market transaction that surprised even veteran investigators.

Cameron "Kip" Holmes is the chief counsel at the Financial Remedies Section of the Arizona attorney general's office. During a visit to his office several months before Tomás and I embarked on our journey, he explained to me how undercover investigators tumbled to the scam carried out by cash-flush coyotes. First they would walk onto a number of the bunting-festooned secondhand car lots that flank downmarket Van Buren and McDowell streets as they run through central Phoenix. "The smugglers tell the owner how many people they want to move up from the border, perhaps fifty in the course of a night, and then they walk around the car lots setting aside the vehicles that they will need to move them," Holmes explained, as I sat taking notes in his heavily air-conditioned office on one of the hottest days of a very hot summer, my first in Arizona.

They pay cash for the cars, but when the cars are driven off the lot, the paper trail worked up by the dealership for the transaction shows a lien for each vehicle. This lien automatically guarantees that if the vehicles are seized by the police in a run up from the border, they are not forfeit. They will be returned to the dealer as guarantee for the phony outstanding debt, then returned by the dealership to the coyote.

The smugglers pay about 15 percent over the legitimate market value of the vehicles, but in exchange for the high price they get a number of useful things: title in any false name that the coyote puts forward, at a false address; the omission of filing federally required reports relating to cash transactions over ten thousand dollars; the false lien on the vehicle; and, oddest of all, the right to rent space on the lot for the vehicle when it is not in use, allowing the smuggler to come to the lot anytime to pick up his vehicle and take it to the border for a load of people.

"These streets look like rows of used car lots, but in reality they are more like the National Guard Armory for coyotes. It's rows and rows of cars just waiting for coyotes to come and use them," said Holmes, who has investigated racketeering and money laundering scams in the state for three decades. "In between the times the vehicle is in use, it has no connection with the smuggler. It is not registered to the smuggler, it is not parked at the smuggler's home or at any place that is associated with the smuggler, and nothing that is in the vehicle indicates any connection with the smuggler."

Side benefits of this scam often include installation of heavy-duty shock absorbers to bear hefty loads, together with removal of the pesky rear seats to cram in more passengers, in the increasingly sophisticated scams being carried out by a new kind of career criminal.

Federal and state police that I spoke to say human smuggling, which was once a mom-and-pop activity, has attracted the attention of Mexican drug traffickers in recent years. They are drawn by higher profits as tighter security drives up smuggling fees the length of the border and makes the use of a coyote almost indispensable to an illegal immigrant.

The trade also appeals to the *narcos,* many of them from Sonora and Sinaloa, the cradle of Mexico's most notorious drug gangs, because human smuggling carries jail terms that are much shorter than sentences handed down for drug smuggling. As a line of criminal endeavor, it carries far lighter consequences if they are caught. It is also, curiously, a good fit in terms of business cycles.

Border police say dopers are busiest at the back end of the year, when they haul the late-summer marijuana crop north in tractor trailers and aircraft to stockpile within easy reach of the border, and then run onward to market. Many realized that they could smuggle illegal immigrants during the slow period of spring and summer. It is, I always thought, a bit like a ski bum realizing he can windsurf in the off-season.

Needless to say, the involvement of drug traffickers in smuggling people has had serious consequences, transforming it in the process into a more sophisticated, professionalized operation, and adding a whole new layer of danger.

Mexican drug cartels have always used violence, although in the past couple of years the killing has become almost baroque in its savagery. Cartel enforcers stab, shoot, strangle, and slice off heads, often posting videos of their grisly murders on the Internet. The threshold for these acts of hyperviolence is extremely low. They can be revenge killings or bungled kidnappings, or even simply to sow terror, and some of their bloody tactics are now routinely cropping up in human smuggling in Arizona.

The soft end of it begins with extortion and threats made to migrants on the drive up from the border. ICE agents and Arizona state and local police report rough treatment by load car drivers, who assault migrants as they try and shake them down for more money on the road up from the load-outs, and then in drop houses across Phoenix. Some end up in the emergency room in valley hospitals, beaten and even stabbed with screwdrivers. Then the mayhem jumps up a notch.

The drug cartel *bajadores,* or bandits, have long targeted rival drug gangs' marijuana loads south of the border, which they simply steal at gunpoint and then traffic north themselves. But now loads of people are in the bandits' sights. The thugs know that hefty smuggling fees are paid by migrants' families or sponsors stateside. These fees range anywhere from fifteen hundred to two thousand dollars a head, by fairly conservative estimates.

For the bandits, then, a drop house or a load car packed with twenty men, women, or children is like a security van or bank deposit box stuffed with thirty to forty thousand in cash, or, in this case, flesh-and-blood bearer bonds. All they need to do is go grab the human cargo and redeem each person for cash from anxious relatives in towns and cities scattered across the United States.

Police say *bajadores,* often acting on a tip from a snitch inside a rival crew, will bust down the doors of a drop house in Phoenix to steal migrant loads. They will also target loads in transit, when the cargo is already conveniently packaged up and on the move. While the theft is often intelligence-driven, sometimes it's pure serendipity. Armed coyotes have been known to prowl U.S. illegal immigration's principal highway, Interstate 10 between Tucson and Phoenix, looking for their own, as in one case in November 2003 that served as a shocking wake-up call to police of all stripes, showing them how far the business had shifted.

It was a fall morning, and a heavy-duty Ford pickup truck packed with twenty illegal aliens rolled up the interstate near Casa Grande, bound for Phoenix amid heavy commuter traffic, with a couple of coyotes up front. The truck flashed past a green Ford Explorer heading south, with two smugglers from a rival group looking for a likely load to knock off. What happened next unleashed a chain of events characterized by the kind of improbable hyperviolence more common in a Tarantino movie.

"A quick U-turn, and the Explorer, driven by the second gang of coyotes, locks on target. They home in quickly on the F-250 pickup, and, armed with a 9mm and a .38 caliber handgun, the hijackers in the Explorer are ready for action. They commandeer the pickup, replace its drivers with theirs, and shift some of the illegal migrants from the pickup's covered cab into the Explorer," read an account written by a federal police officer and posted on the Internet.*

"What the hijackers in the Explorer don't know is this: Hidden among the illegal aliens riding in the back of the pickup they've seized is one of the coyotes from the first gang. Now traveling undetected in the back of his hijacked pickup, mixed in with a load of panicked Mexican migrants, the smuggler takes out his cell phone, dials his criminal superiors in Phoenix, and reports that the F-250 pickup and its load have been hijacked. Rival gang members, he tells his superiors, are behind the wheel and the pickup is once more moving north toward Phoenix, traveling fast and in tandem with the other gang's green Ford Explorer."

The smugglers immediately dispatched a rescue team of their own, a group of smugglers driving a gray Dodge minivan who were bent not only on recovering the load, but on revenge. The rolling hit squad were armed with AK-47 assault rifles and an Intratec TEC-9 assault pistol, roaring south over the blacktop highway like avenging furies.

"When they encounter the green Ford Explorer and the pickup at mile marker 181 . . . the shooters open up with the AK-47s from the back of the minivan, spraying the Explorer and the pickup with fifty to sixty rounds. The pickup, riddled with bullet holes from front to back, veers off the highway and stops. The driver, one of the hijackers originally traveling in the green Ford Explorer, is killed, along with three Mexican migrants riding in the back of the pickup. The rest of the aliens, some badly wounded, stream out of the pickup and disappear into the desert on the east side of I-10."

The driver of the green Ford Explorer and another smuggler sitting next to him were also wounded in the hail of gunfire. The bleeding man in the front passenger seat heaved the driver out from behind the wheel, started the engine, and headed north again. "Illegal migrants in the back of the Explorer are wounded as well, but the vehicle continues to weave down the highway at high speed," the report said. The gunmen

---

*The account can be found at http://www.cbp.gov/xp/CustomsToday/2003/November/5coyoteGange Slaying.xml.

were eventually tracked down by a posse of stunned federal, state, and local law enforcement, and the shooters were arrested and charged with murder.

I spoke about the drama to a group of ICE agents almost three years later, and they were still shocked by what they had seen on the busy Arizona interstate—the kind of rip-roaring shootout, with maximum violence, that is not uncommon among drug cartels in Tijuana, Ciudad Juárez, or Nuevo Laredo, the most lawless of the cities south of the borderline. Here it now was in the United States, on one of the busiest interstate highways in the country, involving a violent new breed of human smugglers who left in their wake a bloody, thirty-mile-long crime scene.

The incident was the first of several murderous assaults by *bajadores* who in the intervening years have killed several more people in at least two bloody ambushes of load cars near Tucson. On these occasions, police say they were looking to steal drug loads. While the bloody attacks grabbed headlines, more low-key load stealing has become a frequent event both along the smuggling highways of southern and central Arizona and in a surge of home invasions and kidnappings recorded in the Phoenix valley, which has become the busiest clearinghouse in the United States for human smuggling.

Once they get through to Phoenix after an increasingly perilous journey in an often carefully prepped load vehicle, the illegal immigrants' violent ordeal is very far from over. They are driven to any of a hundred or more drop houses across the sprawling Phoenix valley, operated by men and women working for criminal organizations reaching back to Mexico and by men like Carlos the coyote in Altar. Some of the smuggling operations have an even larger reach, several having ties to networks in Guatemala or other Central American countries.

The drop houses are usually in the poorer Hispanic barrios in south, central, and west Phoenix dotted by Sonoran burrito restaurants, muffler shops with special offers in Spanish, and Mexican supermarkets. Detectives say the gangs usually pay double and triple the going rent for the use of an apartment or condo, making landlords a tempting offer that many are reluctant to pass up in the subprime meltdown, a time of soaring mortgage repayments and slumping home values.

Following a tip from the Phoenix police department one fall afternoon, I went to a drop house raid in progress in a small strip of low-rent condos and apartments in the avenues of west Phoenix. Twenty-one illegal immigrants from Mexico sat outside the fake-stucco apartment in weak fall sunshine, waiting to be picked up by immigration police after being held for four days in the two-room apartment.

I was eager to see whatever I could about captive life in a drop house, but found the windows were covered by blinds to stop prying eyes from peering in, and, I suspected, to stop the bolder migrants from looking out and spying an escape route to the sidewalk outside. Obligingly, Sergeant Joel Tranter took me around back to take a brief look in through the kitchen door. Outside in a storeroom I found their shoes, put there, I suspected, to stop them running off down the pathway in search of help.

Gently restrained by Tranter from stepping into the crime scene, I could nevertheless see inside the apartment, which had just two bare mattresses on the floor for the score of migrants. I could also make out a stack of Spanish-language DVDs and a spiral notebook on the tiled counter in the kitchen by the doorway. There was a list of the migrants' names scrawled in blue ballpoint, along with their destinations stateside—all, it seemed, were headed for "Kentuky." Beside each name was a telephone number of a relative to call for payment.

Police searching the drop house also found one other chilling item that spoke volumes of the incarceration. It was around the time of Halloween, and at first the red electric cattle prod seemed like part of a costume. The device had two prongs like an imp's pitchfork, and had apparently been used to keep the migrants in order during their detention. I imagined Tomás and me, barefoot, taking turns to crash on the bare mattresses, watching action films in Spanish, while being menaced with a several-thousand-volt jolt of electricity.

It was pretty grim, although I learned it was nothing much. Weapons of all sorts are, in fact, commonly used to intimidate and control

Sergeant Joel Tranter, of the Phoenix police department, stands outside a drop house in the city, where officers have just detained twenty-one illegal immigrants smuggled north by coyotes. He is holding a cattle prod that coyotes use to keep illegal immigrants in line while they anxiously wait for their relatives to send on the smuggling fee of between one and two thousand dollars.

migrants, and even extort higher smuggling fees from their relatives. ICE agents, Phoenix police, and the Arizona Department of Public Safety see it constantly, in scores of raids made to clamp down on this trade that goes on day in, day out, around the clock, seemingly unstoppably.

"They will call the family whose brother, cousin, or sister they are holding, and they'll beat them and sometimes even rape them, all the while leaving an open line to the families," said Tim Mason, a detective with the Arizona Department of Public Safety, who has taken part in numerous drop house busts, and is clearly sickened by the trade in people. "It is a powerful incentive to make them pay," he told me.

Even though I have worked on the border for several years, I am still surprised and disquieted by what I have seen in and around southern Arizona, and by the size of the human smuggling trade, the millions upon millions of dollars in turnover it generates each month, and by the constantly evolving wiles and tactics of the people smugglers.

As I sit down in the office with Cameron Holmes, I ask him whether he saw any evidence that human smuggling was being choked off with the buildup at the border, or that the tide had started to turn against the increasingly brutal human smugglers. He shakes his head.

"They are just getting started. Human smuggling has been growing exponentially since the 1990s, and what we are witnessing here is the birth of a new criminal industry," he says. "The ultimate draw is the United States job market, and until that is corrected, the phenomenon will continue to accelerate."

THREE

Welcome to Tijuana

I am standing outside the international airport in Tijuana on a sidewalk studded with tall lamp posts, each decorated with a vertical flag like a samurai banner. They stand across a busy six-lane highway from the U.S. border fence, and mark out the booming frontier city's Paseo de la Fama, or Walk of Fame. Each of the dozen or so flags carries the image of a prominent local figure distinguished in the arts, sports, or business.

From high up on one pole overlooking the airport terminal and the hangarlike warehouses of Otay Mesa in California comes the firm gaze of singer José Medina, who is the director of the Tijuana Opera. Medina has sung Mozart at Lincoln Center in New York, given recitals in theaters and opera houses across Spain, and staged operas by Verdi, Puccini, and even Donizetti in his hometown of more than two million people.

On a banner alongside him is Alejandro Amaya, a moody-looking bullfighter in a dazzling blue *traje de luces* who has the looks of a soap opera star. He grabbed a reputation for daring in Andalusia in his *alternativa,* or graduation fight, during which he was gored. He finished the *faena,* or final act, with a four-inch gash in his thigh and was awarded a severed bull's ear by the cheering crowd. Then there are other notables including the local singer Julieta Venegas and the winemaker Luis Cetto.

There is no doubt that these people are worthy and accomplished, although you could be forgiven for not having heard of a single one of them. The luminaries filling out the roster along the Walk of Fame were chosen by the Tijuana Image Committee, a civic group appointed by the mayor of the teeming border city in 2002 to try and counter one of the most appalling image problems ever experienced by a city anywhere in the world.

If anyone has heard of Tijuana, it is not for opera, bullfighting, or fine wines. The figures most readily identified with the border city are brothers Ramón and Benjamín Arellano Félix, the boyish-looking kingpins of a drug trafficking empire that became synonymous with the booming border city: the Tijuana cartel. The mug shots of the cartel's leadership were plastered over the approaches to the border crossings in the city for years, although most of the men are now either dead or behind bars.

It is the smugglers, naturally enough, that I have come here to talk to. I get behind the wheel of my pickup truck at the airport parking lot, slip French singer Manu Chao's anthem "Welcome to Tijuana" into the CD player, and head out across town for one of several meetings with drug traffickers and coyotes. I am hoping that the thumping reggae beat and chorus—*"tequila, sexo, y marijuana, con coyote no hay aduana"*—will ease me into the groove and quiet my nerves.

Since I started writing about organized crime, cartel hit men have killed several Mexican colleagues. The first was Francisco Ortiz Franco, an editor for an investigative magazine in Tijuana. The hit man sauntered up to his car in the center of the city and blasted him to death in front of his two young children. Then a couple of months later, more thugs kidnapped muckraking columnist Francisco Arratia in Matamoros, south of Texas, and smashed each of his fingers with deliberate hammerlike blows and pummeled him until his heart stopped beating.

Subsequently, other cartel goons blasted a radio reporter nine times as she arrived for work in Nuevo Laredo, and strafed a busy newspaper newsroom in the city where a friend of mine worked. From the get-go it was clear to me that investigating the drug trade is dangerous, and whenever I set out to do so, my stomach is tied up in knots. For me, like most people who cover the crime beat, it holds an awful fascination, and the fear that comes with it is just part of the job.

For the first stretch of the drive I follow the highway alongside the border fence that runs west from the airport to the Pacific Coast at Playas de Tijuana. Watched over by the U.S. Border Patrol with day and night vision cameras and lit by a blaze of stadium lighting, it carves its way up and down steeply raked canyons, covered with sprawling tin-roofed shantytowns created by massive inward migration that swells Tijuana's population by a hundred thousand new residents each year. It's quite a sight.

The city's newest colonies come like a breaking wave sweeping up the gullies and *barrancas* of the city, filling them with cardboard, wood, and cinder-block houses as migrants from across Mexico pour into Tijuana. Many arrive with hopes of crossing the border to California, but often settle instead for work in the city's export assembly plants, or *maquiladoras.* The *maquilas,* as they are known, provide thousands of jobs putting together plasma television components, car stereos, and even skateboards, among other things, in business parks scattered across the city, from where these products are re-exported to markets across the United States.

Some of the houses I drive by are perched precariously on the brink of ravines, and the foundations of many of them have been shored up with stacks of used car tires; the poor but inventive residents improvise their homes with whatever they have to hand. Months and even years later, the city authorities sweep back through the neighborhoods, awarding residents official title to the land, putting in sewers, asphalted roads, and power lines as they draw the new sections into the city's embrace.

Soon the shops and Oxxo convenience stores follow, and what was once a shantytown is now a new barrio. Some homes have a touch of the

A group of people looking to cross the border illegally scramble up a barrier on the border in Tijuana. The barrier, the first of two, is made out of surplus U.S. military aircraft landing mats, some of them dating back to Vietnam. (Tomás Bravo)

anarchic inventiveness unique to the border city, like one neighborhood shanty in the cleft of a valley where the homeowner sculpted a thirty-foot-tall naked woman in concrete, standing tall, proud, and voluptuous, a beacon to all, heralding a world fecund with possibilities.

I have arranged to meet Agustín (not his real name), a former drug trafficker, at the Autonomous University of Baja California, and I am a little jumpy. *Narcos* sometimes kill people for trivial reasons. One I know of in Tijuana planned to murder a fortune-teller after she gave him a flawed card reading advising him of a good time to cross a dope load. It seemed prudent to meet up with Agustín in a public place, in full view of dozens of people. We settled on meeting outside the refectory.

He greets me with a smile and a handshake. Something that immediately stands out is a large scar with ugly contusions above his right ear. Otherwise, with his glasses and baseball cap, he looks like any other mature student at the university. We shake hands and sit down on the low wall of a flower bed to chat.

Agustín is now in his midthirties. He ran drugs through Tijuana for the best part of a decade, and has agreed to meet up with me as a favor to a friend of mine. Aside from learning about his life, I really want to hear his take on what is happening in the city, where, at that time, scores of people were being gunned down, beaten, and tortured to death each month as rival cartels battled for supremacy in an all-out turf war.

Born in the city, he grew up in Colonia Libertad, a neighborhood flanking the border fence just east of the San Ysidro port of entry, which is notorious for smuggling. Back in the 1980s, the strip flanking the north of La Libertad was dubbed the Soccer Field. Most nights hundreds of illegal immigrants would gather at the spot, some of them kicking around a soccer ball to pass the time until they would charge north to the United States, swamping the vastly outnumbered Border Patrol in what were known as banzai runs.

At first Agustín and his friends would slip over the border to the scrub-covered hills just east of San Ysidro, in California, hunting for rattlesnakes and playing hide-and-seek with the *migra*. But by age twelve, he had graduated to running backpacks of marijuana for local drug traffickers for a payment of a hundred bucks a time. When he left school, he was smuggling hard drugs including cocaine and liquid PCP over the border, at a time when the Arellano Félix brothers had trafficking in the city tied up.

The cartel, like every drug gang south of the border, operated on the *plaza,* or turf, model, controlling a stretch of territory. Theirs wasn't just any border *rancho*. Tijuana was and is the jewel in the crown of Mexican drug trafficking, and the most valued *plaza* on the entire border. It lies just over the line from California, the world's sixth largest economy, at the top of the sparsely populated Baja Peninsula coastline, which is wide open for receiving drug consignments from South America by aircraft or boat.

For years the brothers managed a megabusiness that funneled tons of coke, pot, heroin, and amphetamines to California in cars, trucks, boats, and even by clandestine tunnels that they punched under the border in a trade worth billions of dollars a year. By some estimates, the Tijuana cartel—or Arellano Félix Organization (AFO), as it became known to police—imported around one-third of the drugs snorted, smoked, and shot up across the United States, through a corridor that stretched from Tijuana over the mountains to the fertile plains around Mexicali, south of Calexico, California.

Soft-spoken Benjamín, or El Min, ran the business, while younger brother Ramón, or El Comandante Mon, secured it. Tijuana residents remember Ramón roaring around town in a red sports car, trailing a posse of heavily armed bodyguards, unbothered by the police, whom they owned. He oversaw the murders of hundreds of opponents, from the cops who wouldn't take the cartel's dollar to rivals who failed to pony up *derechos de piso,* a fee for running drugs through the area, and sometimes, it seemed, they just killed for the hell of it.

One time, the cartel went after a local marijuana trafficker in a village near the resort town of Ensenada, pulling twenty-one of his relatives and neighbors from their beds in the middle of the night. The thugs lined everyone up against the brick wall of a house and raked them with machine-gun fire, killing eighteen. In another particularly audacious hit, they killed a Catholic cardinal whom they were believed to have mistaken for a rival drug lord as he arrived at the Guadalajara airport. They would, in short, stop at nothing.

Often the victims were beaten and tortured, their mangled bodies tossed in the streets. Others simply disappeared after being picked up by armed goons in a technique known as the *levantón,* or "big pickup." The bodies were dumped in the desert or, according to police I spoke to, occasionally even dissolved in barrels of hydrochloric acid found in local warehouses. The cartel had the city by the throat for years, until it all began to unravel one morning in February 2002 when El Mon set out for what must have been a routine murder by their exorbitant standards.

Accompanied by his goons, he set off to the port city of Mazatlán, where he was reportedly planning to shoot dead a rival trafficker from Sinaloa, Ismael "El Mayo" Zambada, during carnival. Instead, he and two other members of his death squad were gunned down on the cobbles by police who were reportedly protecting him. Stunned by the loss, his brother Benjamín immediately went into hiding in the colonial city of Puebla, near Mexico City, where he was arrested just a month later. The AFO was now effectively rudderless.

The final blow came four years later when Min and Mon's little brother, Francisco Javier, unwisely went deep-sea fishing in international waters off Cabo San Lucas in his boat, the *Dock Holiday*. After he was nabbed by the U.S. Coast Guard, newspaper photographs showed "El Tigrillo" stepping off the cutter in San Diego in a blue bulletproof vest and handcuffs, still wearing the Burberry check shorts from his fishing trip. The AFO as an ubercartel was now clearly finished, and the most valued *plaza* on the border was up for grabs.

"Right now, it's a no-man's-land—*territorio de nadie.* Everyone wants to be the leader . . . but no one has full control," says Agustín, who is now out of the trade and studying, but keeps in touch with the gangs. "They [the rival smugglers] see a shadow and they want to kill it. They have become paranoid. It's much more dangerous than it was," he tells me.

Isolated cells from within the AFO have continued to smuggle drugs through Tijuana, and have also diversified into large-scale auto theft and kidnapping, sources say. Past masters at the *levantón,* the cartel's death squads have proved particularly skilled at snatching members of the city's business elite off the streets for ransom, although it would seem that old habits die hard. Instead of releasing them on payment of the ransom, the brutes often execute them as before, many with a trademark *tiro de gracia*—a single shot to the back of the head.

At the time of writing, at least two other drug gangs are operating independently in the city. The most powerful of them is the wing of the Sinaloa cartel under the control of El Mayo, the man Ramón reputedly died trying to murder. Then there are the Amezcuas, the amphetamine trafficking cartel out of Guadalajara, which is also operating in the city.

Like a Mexican version of Mogadishu, Tijuana's various neighborhoods are now under the control of the different warlords. Agustín explains that there's El Ingeniero (the Engineer) who controls the upmarket Hipodromo suburb, and El Licenciado (the Graduate) who controls Otay Mesa, to name but two. When the Arellanos held the *plaza,* they negotiated directly with police, setting out who was operating and where, although that pact is now broken.

While the *plaza* has been disputed, more than seven hundred people have been brutally murdered in Tijuana in the past couple of years, including more than fifty federal, state, and municipal cops as the killers slipped the leash. In one incident in 2006, three cops from Rosarito Beach were kidnapped, tortured, and then had their heads sliced off and tossed onto an empty plot in Tijuana. In another, a policeman was shot so many times that first newspaper reports said he had been "quartered"— chopped into bits. Then, in 2008, they broke the last taboo.

In an unprecedented attack, killers shot dead a man they believed was a local police commander, and then pumped bullets into his wife and three-year-old son. In fact, they had gotten the wrong man. Realizing their mistake, they tracked down the cop they were looking for, blasted him and his wife to death, and executed their nine-year-old daughter. It was clear: They were now also targeting children.

While Tijuana is in free fall, one thing remains unchanged: The various factions operating in the free town are hauling the same huge quantities of drugs up to the border, if not more than ever. While tighter border security means that much is getting diverted into the local market—where hundreds of so-called *tienditas,* "little shops," sell rocks of crack and bags of meth to Tijuana residents—the cartels are continuing to hurl multiton quantities of all kinds of narcotics at the ports of entry, where seizures for everything but meth were up in the last year for which figures were available.

That last small step over the line to pay dirt is arguably the riskiest in the whole criminal enterprise, and the drug cartels don't like to play dice. To get the drugs over the border, the traffickers are looking to throw the odds in their favor in any way they can. One of the principal techniques for transporting drugs north is in cars heading up through the ports, usually hiding the bales of pot, slender packets of cocaine, and bags of meth from view in secret compartments in the innermost recesses of a vehicle.

The smugglers call the compartments *clavos,* which means both a nail and a code in Spanish, although the border cops who search for them around the clock know them, in prosaic police speak, as "nonfactory compartments." The secret hideaways are worked up in specialist chop shops, some of them at work right in the center of Tijuana, a few blocks from popular tequila bars and tourist stores on Avenida la Revolución. There, the mechanics craft the secret spaces to order using angle grinders, welding torches, and hammers.

Among the simplest compartments found by border inspectors are ones carved into the hollow quarter panels of a car or truck, which can hold a compacted brick of pot or a few briquettes of cocaine wrapped tight in plastic tape. Other compartments have been worked up into the roof space of cars, trucks, and even tourist buses, or set around the wheel rims inside a vehicle tire.

More ingenious *clavos,* some of which are knocked out by criminal artisans with electrical engineering skills, have included car batteries scooped out and filled with heroin. The batteries are then resealed with a much smaller cell from a motorcycle, which produces just enough current to start the car engine for its run up to the line.

Fashioning a *clavo* is just part of the job of hiding a load. Drugs have a vigorous, telltale odor that trained narcotics dogs swiftly pick up on at the border crossings. In an attempt to throw them off the scent, part of the art of creating a secret smuggling compartment is in disguising the odor, or at least trying to disguise it, in a process referred to south of the line as "curing."

Some smugglers sink drug loads into fuel tanks, surrounding them with gallons of reeking gasoline, to try and throw off the dogs. Others have wrapped loads in aircraft grease, which they suppose masks the scent, or even with items like mustard or chili peppers, which they hope will act as an irritant. Instead of picking up a whiff of drugs, the hope is the dogs will wrinkle up their snouts and scurry off with their tails between their legs.

Load cars need a driver, and in a bid to tip the odds in their favor, the cartels tend to choose people who would buck the criminal profile. They want to find the gray man or woman, the person who won't catch the border inspector's eye, police say.

Gustavo (not his real name) is one such drug runner. Tall, smartly dressed, wearing designer eyeglasses, he comes from a comfortable middle-class family in a solid suburb of detached homes with large patios, on the road to Rosarito Beach, south of Tijuana. In his late teens and early twenties he went out to bars, clubs, and parties in the city, leading a fast life that spun out of control.

As with Agustín, we meet at the university campus, this time over a soda. He remembers the period he spent getting loaded on anything to hand, from beer to dope, coke, and meth. Not coincidentally, several of the guys from the group he ran with were part of a small trafficking cell linked to the AFO.

Knowing Gustavo as a drug user and thrill seeker, one of the group made him an offer he would be unlikely to turn down: How would he like the thrill of driving a load car over the border and making a thousand dollars for himself in the process?

It was an interesting proposition. Driving a load car was somehow a natural part of a lifestyle of ever-escalating risk, a life in which he snorted and smoked drugs for ever greater highs, in a life sharpened by the danger of hanging out with members of a cartel cell that ran one of the *delegaciones,* or neighborhoods, in Tijuana.

"I didn't need the money. For me, running drugs was a challenge. It carried the maximum thrill of transgressing both the law and the frontier itself," said Gustavo, who is now in his early thirties, sober for a couple of years and studying for a university degree, as we sat chatting amid a knot of students in the cafeteria one cool afternoon in the fall.

After paying him five hundred dollars up front, Gustavo's cartel contacts told him the make and color of the car he would be driving, and gave him the location of a parking lot in the center of Tijuana. The late-model sedan had been packed with narcotics at a chop shop in the city center, and the driver had left the key under the floor mat on the driver's side. He got in and started the engine.

Swinging the car out into the afternoon traffic, he set off on the short drive past the grimy shops and cheap hotels to an approach road leading up over a tree-lined flyover that arcs around to the port of entry at San Ysidro, the largest border crossing—not just on the southwest border, but on the planet.

The two dozen traffic lanes, the scores of *ambulantes,* or street hawkers, the lines and lines of street stalls, and the long traffic jams give the crossing the feel of a small city within a city. Then there are the lines of booths staffed by border inspectors dressed in blue uniforms, and the apron out front patrolled by drug-sniffing dogs. As he drew closer, Gustavo felt the flood of adrenaline coursing through his body and relished the challenge of mastering his nerves.

Most handlers tell mules, or drug carriers, they are carrying marijuana, which carries a higher threshold for prosecution, pound for pound, than cocaine, heroin, or methamphetamine if they are caught. In purely practical terms, it reduces the anxiety of the load drivers as they pull up to the port and makes them less likely to give themselves away.

In a classic panic attack, the driver's breathing would have a short, hard rhythm, and he would clutch the steering wheel in a white-knuckle

The border at San Ysidro is marked by a set of steel studs sunk into the pavement a few yards in front of the primary inspection booths. Inspectors dubbed "rovers" patrol the slender apron of U.S. territory, searching for drug loads and illegal immigrants hidden in with the traffic. Rovers account for almost a third of all seizures at the port.

grip—a clear flag to a keen-eyed border inspector that the car and driver would need closer inspection.

What the most successful learn to do is relax: slow their breathing, ease their grip, and let go of their fear. That way the inspectors carry on looking down the line of traffic for someone or something else that arrests their eye, prompting them to slap a colored sticker on the windshield of the vehicle and wave it deeper into the port of entry for a secondary inspection. For Gustavo, winning meant concentrating, and riding that adrenaline wave over the border.

"The challenge for me was breaking the law and making out that I was doing nothing. It kept me focused," he said, beaming at the recollection. Rolling up to the inspection booth with his border crossing card in hand, he looked calmly up at the inspector with a studied look of cooperative ennui. The inspector took his card and asked him where he was going. Gustavo told him he was headed to San Diego to shop and slipped through into California.

The short hop ended in the parking lot of a McDonald's in San Ysidro, close to the point where the trolley car leaves for San Diego. Gustavo parked the car, stowed the key under the mat where he had found it, and headed back over the border on foot along a caged-in concrete walkway that sweeps pedestrians over the traffic lanes backed up at the border and into Tijuana through a line of turnstiles.

He was elated, soaring, walking on air, after winning the high-stakes wager with himself. "It was an incredible rush that you can't describe," he recalled years later, with a glimmer in his eye that made me question how well his recovery had taken hold. "I have never known a high quite like it!"

The run was also carefully thought out by his contacts. He knew nothing of the cartel's structure, nor of the other people involved in the carefully compartmentalized smuggling process. He did not know anything about the chop shop or the people who ran it, and didn't even see the short-haul driver who dropped the car off at the parking lot. He didn't know who would pick it up on the north side, or where they were taking the load.

If he had been arrested at the port and offered a plea bargain by savvy federal prosecutors, he knew too little about the operation to be able to rat anyone out to minimize jail time for himself. He only knew a couple of guys at a party. The cartel had largely protected its operations.

Clearly, not all drug cartel mules are well-off youngsters with a taste for adrenaline. But what they share is a tendency to buck a profile and tilt the odds in their favor. It is not uncommon for inspectors to find a young mother in a car with cocaine strapped to her children, perhaps even stuffed into their dirty diapers, or, as in one eye-catching case, an eighty-three-year-old lady with ten pounds of meth taped to her body. I mean, who would have thought?

As one border cop said to me, "If you are working on the assumption that you can just look for any profile, then you are being beat. Because if you are looking for Hispanic males of eighteen to twenty-five years of age, they are going to use anybody else they can. We have beautiful young women in new cars, flirting with agents, dressed provocatively, running loads of dope. But you can't just look for that; if you are looking for that for your profile, the next grandma and grandpa that come through in a motor home, the motor home's loaded with dope, while you are focusing on the two pretty girls flirting with you. They are now the distraction."

To improve the odds, part of the challenge for the cartel is knowing just when to spin the wheel in this game of border roulette. This is where the spotters come in, and they work at ports of entry the length of the border helping not just the drug cartels but also the people smugglers or coyotes decide when to cross a load, and through which lane. In Tijuana, they have it down to a fine art.

Every time I have crossed the border through San Ysidro, there are always one or two people dawdling on a stainless steel bridge spanning the two dozen traffic lanes, and hanging around at the foot of the steps outside the Discount Pharmacy, which is the last chance for day-trippers to stock up on prescription medication before heading back north over the border on foot.

Some of them are lookouts for the smugglers. They are joined by rogue *ambulantes* weaving among the lanes of idling cars queuing at the port, touting sodas and souvenir shot glasses and even joke T-shirts, some of which ironize law enforcement. One ubiquitous shirt is stamped FBI, which in Tijuana stands for "Female Body Inspector," another is marked DEA. The kicker? "Drunk Every Afternoon."

The spotters and street hawkers are equipped with radios or mobile phones, and either watch over the line of traffic lanes at the port from afar, or walk right to the border line, marked by a set of steel studs sunk into the road, a few yards short of the inspectors' booths. There, they send back real-time, actionable intelligence to the smugglers, detailing the movements of the inspectors. To the police who work there, it is a constant provocation reminiscent of wartime.

"The fact that someone can stand out there and pretend they are selling flowers on the Mexican side when they are really watching what goes on in lane twenty-three and reporting back, it's almost like a countermeasure in a time of war," James Hynes, the director of the San Ysidro port of entry, told me during one of several visits I made while researching this book.

"We do see the spotters come up, and they get quite brazen. They'll walk up into the pedestrian lines if there is a big queue, and they'll come up close and see what we're doing and then report back," he added.

The spotters are looking for any opening. It might be the dog handlers changing shift at the port, or an inspector known to be less vigilant than his colleagues coming onto the line. To take advantage of these fleeting windows of opportunity, the smugglers need to be close by with their load cars.

Investigators say they might be lurking in access roads to the port used by cops and emergency services, ready to roll, or, in some flagrant cases, they may even have thrown up the hood of the car in the approach lanes to the border crossing and flipped on the hazard lights, feigning mechanical trouble until it's time to go.

On one occasion, inspectors watched illegal traffic spike moments after a group of rovers—the inspectors who work on the slim apron of the United States between the port of entry and the line of steel studs marking the Mexican border—were reassigned to the other side of the port to work an operation in the southbound lanes funneling traffic from the interstate into Mexico.

"As soon as the spotters saw the officers shift, then we saw a big surge of alien loads coming across. So they just wait. I mean minute by minute. They will literally hold the vehicles at the border in very close proximity so they can get in line, so that they can get communication that will say 'Hey, try it now!'" said Adele Fasano, then U.S. Customs and Border Protection's field operations director in San Diego. Once they see that fleeting opening, the smugglers have one last way of tipping the balance in their favor, and it is chilling.

A big drug cartel like the AFO will receive loads of marijuana and also cocaine in multiton quantities, brought up from drug farms in central Mexico or shipped in from Andean producers. Once staged in a safe house in Tijuana, or for that matter any other town or city along the border, it will be broken down and thrown at the ports in smaller quantities so as to spread the risk of interdiction.

"Whereas in a commercial conveyance we tend to get loads of one to two tons in a truck, that's a risky proposition for the drug smugglers if they get apprehended, as that is a multimillion-dollar drug shipment," Fasano said, patiently explaining the wiles of the traffickers to me in one briefing. "So what they do is they break it down, and that's what we call shotgunning. Multiple loads in smaller quantities, so that if some of them are intercepted, they are betting on the fact that some will get through. It's less of a risk factor."

Fasano explained how the smugglers will often deliberately send three or four load cars at the same time, often with a decoy load at the fore. The small load of relatively low-value grass might draw the attention of the drug-sniffing dogs. The drivers or passengers may even be drilled by the traffickers to scream up a storm, resist arrest, or try and flee the scene and escape back into Mexico. The flurry of activity around the car deliberately grabs attention, creating a blind spot for the real load, in much the same way a magician uses sleight-of-hand to distract an audience.

"They make a spectacle and draw attention to one vehicle, or they may target a lane where they know that our officers and canines are with a small quantity—say, twenty to forty pounds of marijuana—and then target the other side of the port," Fasano said. "Because once we get a load, the officers will all converge on the vehicle, and it does take their attention away. The officers in the preprimary area will come and assist, especially if there are individuals that need to be handcuffed. That draws resources and our ability to screen remaining lanes. They know we do that."

I feel I am coming to understand how drug traffickers punt their narcotics over that narrow urban line and into the United States. I now want to meet a Tijuana coyote. I have an early evening meeting set up with a lady called Susana, across town near the beach in Playas de Tijuana. I am not nervous, as I don't know of a single incident in which coyotes have killed a muckraking reporter. In fact, I am looking forward to our meeting.

I park a couple of blocks short of the beach and head into Sanborns department store. I am already sipping a Diet Coke in the café when Susana arrives. She is a little nervous. Settling into the booth, she orders a paloma—a cocktail of tequila and grapefruit soda served in a salt-rimmed glass. She has gamely agreed to talk to me about human smuggling in this extraordinary city on the edge, in so many senses, as a favor to her niece, who is a friend of mine. A mother of three children, Susana has for several years moonlighted as a recruiter for a female coyote in the city who is known for her faded beauty and onetime ambition to become an actress in the deeply melodramatic soap operas known as *telenovelas.*

While human smuggling might seem a man's world, many of the most renowned coyotes in Tijuana are women. In fact, one I learned of casually one day had been arrested by immigration police at least seventeen times for attempting to spirit illegal immigrants through the local ports of entry and into Southern California, and would probably make a great subject for her own *telenovela.*

It is a puzzle. I have in the past mused about why women seem to thrive at shepherding migrants over the line. One contact suggested that it might be because women are extremely good at handling fractious children, a skill that is transferable for handling adult migrants, who are by turns helpless, needy, and defiant. I decide to ask Susana about it as an icebreaker. "Yes," she says, her bright smile fading as she gets serious. "That, and the fact that women are stronger than men."

Human trafficking involves a significant division of labor. As in Arizona, the coyotes oversee a network of helpers including drop house operators and drivers on both sides of the border. They also rely on a *talonero* or *gancho*—literally meaning a "hook"—to feed the high-turnover business with a stream of migrants chasing the American Dream. This is what Susana does. She takes a sip of her paloma and leads me into her world.

A lot of Tijuana's *ganchos* are freelancers who tout for trade at the airport or, more usually, in the *camionera central,* the bustling bus terminal across town where coaches pull up at the end of a crushing road journey from towns that can be two or more days' drive away in the Mexican interior. The migrants, it seems, are as easy to spot clambering off the bus as first-time tourists in New York, ambling through midtown looking up at the skyline.

"You can tell them immediately. They are humble country people, and they always look lost," she tells me as a waitress darts between the tables, offering refills of the store's famously weak coffee. "The *ganchos* walk straight up to them. They tell them, 'Yes, yes, we can take you to Los Angeles,' that they need to pay up front and so on. Although, of course, a lot of them are rogues."

One time Susana found a man walking the dusty curb of the toll road heading south from Tijuana toward Rosarito Beach. Clearly tired and lost, he explained how he had been picked up by a *gancho* at the bus terminal who took his money and promised to take him to San Diego. Instead, he dropped him off at the tollbooth, telling him it was the border crossing: "'It's the *garita*,' they said, 'you walk through there and you're in California.'"

That kind of misfortune can be avoided if someone back home in the village has the number of a smuggler who they know has successfully crossed another relative or neighbor in the past. When someone from the community wants to cross, they simply call the same *gancho,* someone like Susana, who then passes them on to a coyote for a kickback of a hundred to a hundred and fifty dollars.

Picking them up at the bus station or the airport, she drives them to hotels or drop houses, which she calls the *oficina* (office). These can be private homes in Tijuana, or cheap hotels usually in the Zona Norte area of the city, the so-called tolerance zone where brothels and street drug dealers do business within sight of the border fence. There, she hands off her charges to the coyote, who smuggles them over the line to San Diego for a fee of around three grand each.

Urban borders consist of fencing punctuated by ports of entry. One of the favored ways of getting people through is taking the *pollos,* or migrants, directly through the port with documents procured on a thriving black market in cities south of the line in Mexico. The black market in identity documents varies greatly on the north and south sides of the border, and it is worth taking a moment to look at the differences to understand the full complexity of the scam.

On the north side, in cities from San Diego to Houston, fake identity documents such as Social Security cards and green cards are widely available from forgers, who sometimes even provide more complex photo IDs like state driver's licenses. Usually all an illegal immigrant has to do is ask any friend with a job how they got their papers, and they can often put them in touch with an intermediary working for a so-called document mill. Federal police estimate that hundreds of people work the mills in Southern California alone.

The forgers, who can be anything from a husband-and-wife team moonlighting after their day jobs to larger criminal networks, are technically well equipped. Some use photo scanners to copy legitimate documents, which they will then adapt on a Mac or a PC. Others will work facsimiles up from scratch. Undercover investigators in San Diego have followed the forgers around as they go to office supply stores in the suburbs, buying up card blanks that they take home and use to churn out fake residency and workplace documents, passing them through a laminator to give them a satisfyingly official-looking veneer.

I once held a few score of the confiscated documents in my hands. Up close, the cards often contain errors such as spelling mistakes. One I held was a poorly reproduced Social Security card with spelling errors in the blue soubriquet on the reverse side, where tricky words such as "punnishable" and "inprisonment" were simply too taxing to copy straight. In others, copies of fingerprints are sometimes off-color as the toner has run out in the printer.

ICE say the forgers sell immigrants packages of ID documents for sixty to one hundred and twenty dollars, depending on how many intermediaries are involved, which illegal immigrants use to land a job or rent an apartment. Adequate as they are for residency, where employers are not duty bound to verify their authenticity under the Immigration Reform and Control Act, these kinds of forgeries are not good enough to beat border inspectors. In fact, the inspectors know them as "fifty-footers"—fakes so bad they can spot them from fifty feet away.

The coyotes know that something run up by a document mill stands very little chance of getting an illegal immigrant through the port of entry. Instead, they rely on a thriving black market in stolen border crossing cards dubbed *micas*.

The credit-card-sized documents are a kind of passport allowing Mexican border residents limited travel over the southwest border. They were introduced in 1998 to standardize the papers needed by Mexican residents from towns and cities the length of the border, and allow holders to cross north to a narrow strip inside the United States to shop or visit with family and friends for a limited period.

The high-tech plastic cards are issued by U.S. consulates in border cities, and more recent versions called "laser visas" carry a digital mug shot and a scanned fingerprint of the bearer. On the back side they have a bar code and a broad magnetic strip that makes them machine readable at the ports of entry.

On swiping the card, the border inspector has all the background information on the cardholder, and can also cross-reference his or her fingerprints with a digital scanner linked to the Automated Biometric Identification System, or IDENT immigration database. The only thing is that the inspectors don't always take that final step.

Border inspectors aren't just there to weed out smugglers and other criminals. They are also there to facilitate legitimate traffic and trade. Often, facing long snaking lines of thousands of people backed up to

The market for counterfeit ID papers in the United States is huge. This pile of fakes includes Social Security documents, so-called green cards, and even California driver's licenses, seized by ICE in San Diego. The ID papers are run up by "document mills" and are generally of poor quality. They are often sold as a package to illegal immigrants. (Courtesy of ICE)

cross over in cities borderwide, they may just swipe the card, glance at the picture, and look back at the cardholder. If there is an apparent match, and the cardholder doesn't look jittery or nervous, the person is waved through the line and into the United States. The coyotes know it, they watch for it, and they exploit it.

People smugglers in gritty towns the length of the border buy the *micas* on a thriving secondary market, paying up to three hundred dollars a time for the cards, from often cash-strapped holders. So large is the trade that more than ten thousand of the cards were reported lost or stolen in a recent one-year period in Tijuana and Ciudad Juárez alone, although the trade is also thriving in other border cities like Nuevo Laredo, Mexicali, and Nogales.

Mexican police say coyotes that specialize in the identity card scam often have decks containing dozens if not scores of the cards, which they then shuffle through to match up with the men and women that they have waiting in hotels and lodging houses on the south side while they are prepped to cross the border.

Once they find a reasonable facial match, marrying up age, weight, skin color, and the shape of the face, they have a good start. While generalizations are often problematic, it is fair to say that a lot of Hispanics have dark eyes and hair, which makes a match more likely.

One illegal immigrant from the Mexican state of Guerrero who crossed using the scam told me how the coyote worked it. The woman, Minerva, or Mini for short, worked as an office cleaner north of the border. "The coyote had about three cards that were a reasonable likeness," she recalled. "Once I had the match, they got me to cut my hair and make myself up like the person in the picture. Then they started the drilling," she added.

In the days before she crossed through the port of entry—in Mini's case through Nogales, Arizona—the coyote drilled her on details embedded in her card, including the cardholder's date of birth and her address. Some migrants also memorize other factoids including the names of streets in the barrio of the city they live in, and a backstory that includes parents' names and even their occupations, which they regularly jot down on a cheat sheet. It is, in fact, pure Stanislavsky: method acting, border style, in which the immigrants come to inhabit the life of the cardholder they briefly impersonate in transit.

While it is all very well knowing the layout of the border city where they supposedly live in Mexico, the *pollos* are also coached in details of the forbidden city they have never seen lying tantalizingly on the far side of a gleaming chrome turnstile in the United States. Mini also had to figure out what it was that she was planning to do once she got over the border line to downtown Nogales, and was given a briefing on the layout of downtown, with its money changers and redbrick bargain stores selling discount clothing.

"I was a few months pregnant at the time, and I was going to go shopping for tennis shoes in the Chinese stores on the north side," she told me as we sat chatting one afternoon at a house in Phoenix. "I had it all worked out by the time we went down to the border to cross."

The time the coyote chose to move her group of eight migrants through the port of entry was during the morning rush hour. She went ahead, while Mini and the group slipped in among the workers, shoppers, mothers, and schoolchildren shuffling slowly toward the blue-uniformed inspectors in a line that trailed back and out of the port.

"The coyote was going to use an agreed signal if she sensed there was a problem," said Mini, raising her right hand up to her head and twirling a lock of her dark hair. "If she made that sign, then we were to break out of line and walk back into Mexico."

Mini looked around her, assuming the air of bored resignation of the commuters inching toward the turnstiles. She could see the CBP agent. He was glancing at the *micas,* waving the crossers through without checking their fingerprints, and glancing back up the line that now had several hundred people queuing up.

She moved forward. Coyotes sometimes tell the *pollos* to hold the card between thumb and index finger, squeezing so as to bow it slightly. The pressure stops their hands from trembling. Mini, though, didn't need to do that. In a final act in building her role, she had found her motivation for the performance of a lifetime that she was about to give. "I just rubbed my belly and thought of my child inside me, and how I was going to find a job and care for her," she told me, with a centeredness, a kind of gravity now in her voice, as she recalled walking the last few steps up to the inspector's booth.

The inspector took the card, glanced at it, and glanced back at her. She looked at him calmly, pulling a slack smile. Moments later, she was in the United States. She held on to the card the coyote had loaned her until she had passed a Border Patrol roadblock on Interstate 19 south of Tucson, and then gave it back to the smuggler to be recycled. The cost of the trip? Three thousand dollars.

In the *mica* scam, border crossers take on someone else's identity. In another popular ruse, the *polleros* make them disappear, smuggling illegal immigrants over the line hidden from sight inside a vehicle, either in a specially crafted *clavo* or simply tucked in the trunk of a sedan or the back of a people-carrier.

As well as building *clavos* for the cartels, the rogue chop shops will also work them up for the coyotes to hide men, women, and children that they are trying to slip through the ports of entry. Their handiwork is notorious to the border inspectors at the ports of entry across Southern California, who come across hidden compartments in every configuration imaginable.

Border inspectors have found spaces in the dashboard, where chop shop mechanics have stripped air bags and ventilation ducts to create secret compartments. It must be a real shock opening the glove box during an inspection to find a leg, an arm, or even a human face peeping out. Among the worst of the *clavos,* inspectors agree, are the so-called coffin compartments, where migrants get dropped into the gas tank.

To make one, the chop shop mechanics cut down through the bed of a pickup truck or the floor of a minivan, into the fuel tank, creating a compartment large enough to cram human cargo in a space designed for twenty or so gallons of fuel. They then reroute the fuel supply, often to the reservoir for windshield washer fluid, which holds just enough gas to get the vehicle over the border line to a drop house. Fitting people into the space is quite a process. Once they are set inside, the compartment is closed up and then the vehicle is rebuilt around it. Carpets are refitted and then the seats are bolted back in, leaving the immigrants entombed inside in a nightmare out of Edgar Allan Poe. They will be there for the time it takes to drive to the port, queue up in the revving lines of traffic waiting to cross, and, if they are successful, reach a drop house on the other side.

It's a close call, but some cops say the most dangerous way of hiding illegal immigrants is in the cradles they find jury-rigged beneath a car. Often several migrants at a time are made to lie on a few planks suspended just inches above the road. It might seem harmless enough in the crawling traffic lanes up to the ports of entry, but once they are through the other side, the load cars slip directly into fast-moving freeway traffic. It is a harrowing thought for many policemen. "They're just lying in it, inches above the road," Hynes told me. "And if they get through, they will be inches above the road, doing eighty miles an hour. What happens if they hit a bump?"

Other *clavos* have included items carried in cars, among them a papier-mâché piñata that a young girl had been slipped into. The bottom of the figure was papered over, leaving the girl trapped inside for the journey through Tijuana's streets and up to the port at San Ysidro, where wait times on most days are rarely below forty minutes. Perhaps it is not surprising that coyotes sometimes give tranquilizers to children to stop them from bawling during these terrifying ordeals.

As a slight claustrophobic, I have occasionally tortured myself by imagining what it would actually be like to cross through the border in a *clavo* or in the trunk of a car. While researching this book, I came across a woman who had made the trip through San Ysidro hidden from sight.

Josefina is from a family of fourteen children who lived in a small town near Guadalajara, Mexico's second city. She was heading north to join relatives living in Los Angeles. The journey was brokered by a coyote who lodged her in a small hotel with a group of five men, just a few yards short of the border fence in north Tijuana.

The day he chose to move the group, the coyote pulled up at the hotel in a small sedan, picked them up, and drove them to a parking lot behind a supermarket. There, he ordered them all out and into the trunk. Josefina was stunned.

"The *pollero* told us we would be crossing over in a car, and I had assumed that he meant sitting up in the back. Instead, he arranged us head to toe in the trunk, like sardines," she said, reluctantly reliving the journey some years later.

She looked up at the coyote framed in a rectangle of daylight. Then the trunk slammed shut, leaving her bunched up in the close darkness with five men whom she didn't know. The car had moved off and was rolling into the traffic toward the border crossing when the wriggling started.

One of the men jammed into the trunk next to her started to move. The movement was slow, almost imperceptible at first, but became more rhythmic, more insistent as the journey continued in darkness. Her arms trapped and unable to move away from the stranger dry humping her in the dark, Josefina broke her silence for the only time. "*¡Hijo de tu pinche madre!*" she hissed. "Just you wait until we get out of here!"

She didn't notice the moment when the car passed through the port. Finally, it slowed, turned, and rolled to a stop. They were in the garage of a drop house somewhere in metro San Diego. Footfalls, then the trunk came open. Dim light and fresh air. "First, I sat up and thanked God," she recalled. "Then I slapped that son of a bitch!"

Sitting in the café with Susana as she finished off a second paloma, I had one last question. What determines whether a *pollo* gets to walk over the line with a stolen *mica* or ends up buried alive in the innards of a car or truck?

"It's simple," she says. "If they are brave and can control their nerves, they go across with the *mica*. If they can't handle it, then it's into the trunk."

The secret world of the Tijuana smugglers is a vast repository of tried and tested means used to beat the border. How do the border police at the ports stop them? It was time to head back to California to find out. There were two groups of border police I needed to sit down with: the Customs and Border Protection inspectors at the ports of entry, and then the Border Patrol agents who work the spaces in between.

FOUR

Where the Rubber Meets the Road

Meet Sonny. He is a four-year-old German shepherd. I am standing a few paces inside the United States, watching as he strains and trembles at the leash, whimpering to get out into preprimary, two dozen lanes of idling traffic between the inspection booths at the San Ysidro port of entry and the line of steel studs marking the U.S.-Mexico border about a hundred yards to the south.

A "canine unit," or simply "K-9" in police speak, he is one of hundreds of dogs at work around the clock securing the ports of entry from San Diego to Brownsville, Texas, as well as checkpoints on some inland highways. They are one of the most effective tools that the U.S. Customs and Border Protection agency has for weeding out the smugglers from the legitimate travelers heading north.

"These guys are incredible. He's able to find humans concealed in compartments and marijuana that's concealed in gas tanks," Sonny's handler Paul tells me as we stand chatting down on the line, a few yards from the lanes of commuter and tourist traffic, doubtless sprinkled with load cars hiding drugs and illegal immigrants.

"These guys are out there and they're trying to hide it any way they can. They'll try and wrap it up and disguise the odor of the drugs they are trying to bring across, but he'll go right past that and find the source," he says.

The secret of Sonny's success is all in the nose. The quivering black tip of his snout is the portal to a cathedral-like olfactory chamber equipped with more than five times the number of scent receptor cells in a human nose.

As so often in this type of equation, the math is a little more complicated than it might at first seem. The sensory advantage that it gives dogs is exponentially greater than the relative number of scent cells, and they have an acuity estimated at anywhere up to several million times greater than that of man. But what does that actually mean?

Every time they breathe in, the dogs can snare the faintest trace of any given substance, and, not only that, have the ability to mark each scent out from a vast library of other smells. It means that the K-9 units like Sonny can distinguish the smell of many more different molecular compounds than we can, and in minute quantities of just a few parts per million. Once they snag that target smell, they can follow the odor right to the source.

They can distinguish the odors of cocaine, pot, heroin, and methamphetamine on the breeze—in fact, what they are detecting is the precise chain of molecules that make up the compounds and flush the pleasure centers of the brain—and can also be trained to single out the signature scent of a variety of explosive compounds and even nerve gases. Then it gets stranger.

The dogs can also be trained to sniff out the colored inks used to print banknotes and aid in searches for bulk currency smuggled southbound through the port by drug cartels, and, almost with a sixth sense, can distinguish the distinct odor of smuggled illegal immigrants from the smells of regular, legitimate drivers and passengers sitting up in their vehicles.

Mystified dog handlers don't seem to know quite how they do it. Perhaps they pick up on the subtle cocktail of stress and fear that people exude when they are cooped up and hidden while waiting in lines of traffic. However, they can attest to how effective they are. "He'll walk right past a thousand cars full of normal people, but he'll alert to one that has someone concealed," Paul says of Sonny. "We'll find vans with compartments welded up underneath, people in trunks, or maybe ten or eleven people in the back of vans under a blanket."

Dogs are cross-trained to pick up on two classes of odors: in Sonny's case, those of narcotics and concealed people. So prodigious is their ability that just three dog teams are needed at any one time to cover the whole primary, a strip of two dozen traffic lanes—an area twice as broad as the widest freeways circling most U.S. cities.

Stories abound among handlers of their dogs' skills. One working dog at the San Ysidro port of entry caught a whiff of narcotics while it was working in lane 5, hauling its handler across nineteen lanes of traffic to a vehicle in lane 24. The car was ordered to secondary inspection, where a load of marijuana was found packed inside a tire.

Sonny's largest find in a three-year career was a load of cocaine that he picked up across several lanes of traffic, barking and wagging his tail, Paul recalls. "It was one hundred ten pounds of cocaine that was hidden inside of a Jet Ski," he says, looking at the dog with admiration clearly undimmed after years of working together. "It was all him. He discovered it."

Border police can and do use almost any kind of a dog on the line, from a mutt rescued from a pound to something with a pedigree. CBP currently favors one breed above all others, the Belgian Malinois. It's a funny animal. The dogs look for all the world like a small German shepherd, although it would be perhaps more accurate to think of them as condensed rather than simply downsized. The breed are so eager to get out and work that they are borderline aggressive, and have been involved in what one CBP official dryly described, in probably my favorite-ever euphemism, as "biting incidents."

A commonly held notion is that the dogs must be forcibly addicted to narcotics to give them the motivation to snuffle out drugs. The truth is simpler and more gentle: They do it because they enjoy it, and, when they hit pay dirt, they get to chew on a toy. "It's a game to Sonny. He likes to get out there in the lanes and just have fun. If he finds a load, this is what he gets," says Paul, the human part of the canine team. He reaches into his back pocket and tugs out a short, thick hank of rope that he gives Sonny when he hits on a load.

While dogs like Sonny may be the inspectors' best friend, they certainly aren't the smugglers'. In fact, quite understandably, the dogs fill them with a mixture of fear and loathing. There has been at least one case reported at San Ysidro of contraband "cured" with an unknown toxic substance that sent a dog into convulsions, although it subsequently recovered. There have also been more anecdotal reports along the border of "hits" placed by traffickers on particularly effective canines.

While some smugglers turn mean and seem to want to get even with the dogs playing high-stakes hide-and-seek with them, the sight of them snuffling through the lanes in preprimary, relentlessly tugging their handlers behind them, terrifies some smugglers to the extent that they break into a sweat when they see one heading their way. Some simply slip into a funk and bail out.

"I saw one lady not long ago. She was four cars back in lane twenty-three, a canine started heading that way, and she just got out of her car and ran back to Mexico," port director James Hynes told me during one of several visits I made to San Ysidro. "She just couldn't handle it, she just bailed. We watched her run, and as far as the eye could see, she did not stop."

Sitting at the table in a second-floor conference room, Hynes has his back to the window. Behind him, perfectly framed in bright sunlight, lie twenty-four lanes of traffic running up from Tijuana, the largest city on the Mexican side of the border. The lanes are backed up to the horizon and beyond with cars, trucks, and vans, their motors idling as they line up to roll through the most-crossed port of entry on the planet. The sight over his shoulder gives the impression of something between the emergency evacuation of a city before a catastrophe—I find myself imagining a comet barreling across empty space bound for Baja California—and, but for the slight, creeping, forward movement, a vast, gridlocked airport parking lot.

The massive concrete and steel structure of the port handles a huge amount of commuter and tourist traffic, and Hynes is the man charged with sorting out the legitimate travelers and trade goods passing beneath his office from illegal immigrants and mules carrying contraband narcotics—and, here's the really tricky part, all the while keeping those vehicles rolling.

He comes from Buffalo in upstate New York, from a family with a tradition of serving in law enforcement—"There are always a lot of guns and badges at family reunions," he quips—and he has a background in the U.S. Customs Service, which specialized in nabbing smugglers and contraband before it disappeared in a shake-up that created the giant Department of Homeland Security in 2003. In his career reaching back over a decade, he worked at more than half a dozen locations before getting to run the port at San Ysidro while still in his thirties.

He is sharp, a fast talker, and has a New Yorker's directness in describing what he and the hundreds of inspectors who work under him at the port are on the lookout for as they work around the clock in the vehicle and pedestrian lanes leading up from Tijuana. "It's bugs, thugs, and drugs," he says, gesturing at the window behind him and the traffic reaching back through the port, which handles up to 18 million vehicles heading north to California each year, together with as many as 50 million people.

The traffic is high volume and pretty much constant. One former inspector I spoke to said that it can at times be a daunting experience going on the line at San Ysidro. The inspectors are on their feet for most of a shift, and the lines of traffic, either through the pedestrian hall or the broad vehicle lanes, barely ever let up throughout the day.

Given the seemingly endless lines, Hynes explains that the challenge is to keep the inspectors sharp so that they don't space out due to the production-line nature of the job, and become less vigilant in their close-up duel with Tijuana smugglers, who are some of the wiliest not just in Mexico, but in the world. To be effective, the inspectors have to be at the top of their game across the line, around the clock.

"If you are a factory worker putting hood ornaments on a Ford Econoline van all day, that can get old after about an hour. The same analogy would apply here. You can only do so much of it, then you have to go and recalibrate your brain and come back," Hynes says. "Some guys like to detect fraudulent documents in pedestrian, that's their thing. Some of them are preprimary load guys, some guys like to work the permit booth, but they are going to work it all. We like to keep that movement going for flexibility and random enforcement."

Incredibly, given the size of the port and the variety of tasks to be done, the cross-trained inspectors are rotated to a new activity not just every day, or even every hour, but every twenty minutes throughout their shift. The schedule of rapid changes frustrates smugglers targeting an inspector they see as perhaps less vigilant than another, and seeks to curb graft by making it more difficult for potentially corrupt inspectors to pass on their schedule to Mexican smugglers. It also keeps them on their toes to spot the lawbreakers.

"Smugglers come in all shapes and sizes. There's no one modus operandi. We see sixteen-year-old girls with little kids, we see seventy-five-year-old men in wheelchairs, and everything in between," Hynes says. In the course of a shift, inspectors may be told to make certain stops, of all red pickup trucks for instance, to try and ensure a random element like a control in a scientific experiment. The inspectors also have to rely on a combination of behavioral analysis, technologies and information systems, and simple intuition to try and catch them out. "There's no one way to do it, and that's why these officers have to keep their heads on a swivel and be alert for anything that doesn't seem right to them. It's almost like a sixth sense," he adds.

Hynes leads me out of the conference room to take me on a tour of the port. We pass a rogues' gallery with pictures of illegal immigrants and narcotics nabbed by inspectors. The one standout picture, the one

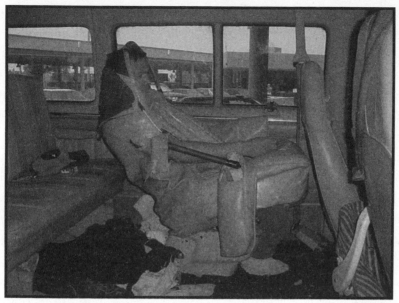

The picture of the "seat guy" is well known to police and reporters who work along the border. The illegal immigrant somehow worked his way inside the upholstery of a bus seat before crossing over to Southern California. What can it have felt like, and how did he ever think he would get away with it? (Courtesy of U.S. Customs and Border Protection)

that everyone comments on and remembers the length of the border, is the "seat guy"—a man who somehow worked himself inside the covers of a bus seat to try and slip through the port.

The man had jammed his arms inside the fabric of the armrests, but left his head poking out of the overstuffed vinyl seat back. It's a bizarre sight, and looks a little like he is being swallowed by an anaconda. The picture captures the desperation and sheer effrontery of some of the people trying to cross the border without the right papers, not to mention the strangeness that the inspectors come up against.

We head on down the stairs and out through the labyrinthine port structure. It has an odd kind of energy, a buzz somewhere between that of a busy police precinct and of a Greyhound bus station in a big American city.

Standing in the shadow of one of the inspection booths, Hynes explains the principal of "layered enforcement" by which police have three cracks at weeding out contraband and lawbreakers, starting with the preprimary area where Sonny and company work.

The no-man's-land, which is no longer Mexico but not yet the U.S. interior, is marked by steel studs sunk down into the asphalt, each the size and shape of a saucer. They are painted yellow, but the passage of millions of tires over the top of them strips off the color and buffs the steel to a dull sheen like a railroad track's.

The face of each saucer is cut by a raised line with the letters U.S. on one side and MEXICO on the other. This is the border line at the San Ysidro port of entry, the place where, quite literally, the rubber meets the road.

Aside from the dogs and their handlers, the preprimary apron, which is about the size of a football field sliced in two lengthwise, is policed by a rotating roster of inspectors known as "rovers," and they have a curious look to them. The men and women weaving through the lines of cars, pickup trucks, and minivans have the appearance of pit stop mechanics.

Driving through the port on dozens of occasions, I have seen some wearing kneepads of the type used by carpet fitters or Special Forces snipers, as they need to get down and dirty with the line of cars inching by them through the oil-specked traffic lanes bound for the booths. Then they have a tool belt with hammers to sound out the density of quarter panels and bumpers, and pole-mounted mirrors to peer under the vehicles snaking northward.

The rovers, or, to give them their full title, Anti-Terrorism Contraband Enforcement Team roving officers, weave in and out of the traffic, looking for a variety of telltale signs flagging a load car. It might be that they spot new paint or a recent weld on the bottom of an old gas tank, a clear sign of a *clavo* from a Tijuana chop shop. Or it could be that they simply spread their palms on the trunk of a car and lean heavily on it: If it gives a shallow, dispirited bounce, they know there could well be people hidden inside it.

The rovers work the traffic before it reaches the inspection booths. They are very effective, and account for almost one-third of all the interdictions made at the port of entry. They provide screening for the second line of enforcement, the inspectors at the telephone-booth-sized enclo-sures, standing sentinel before a traffic barrier that raises and lowers, controlling access to Interstate 5, and the freeways of Southern Califor-nia just beyond.

With traffic backed up in a wait that can sometimes be three or four hours on a busy weekend, inspectors going on the line at the booths are under considerable pressure. They have perhaps thirty to forty-five sec-onds to check the documents of border drivers and passengers and make an assessment about whether to wave them through. A key part of how they do that is in the way they frame a few brief questions to see if the travelers check out.

"You just hit them with things they should be able to answer," Hynes explains to me. "We are trying to gauge if it's a truthful or nontruthful response. Maybe you're looking at me or not looking at me. Maybe you're a little too friendly. The officer has to assess that whole picture, and it's often a gut feeling," he adds. "If someone has white knuckles and is sweating and won't look at you when he's answering the questions about going to Disneyland with his wife and three kids—why is he ner-vous about that? When people are under stress, their story only goes so far."

Aside from their questioning—the law enforcement equivalent of speed dating—they also have other systems and tools to check out the people crossing through the line. Inspectors have a screen hooked up to law enforcement and terror outlook databases, giving them a heads-up on terror suspects and criminals on the lam, from drug traffickers to kidnappers who might feasibly come through the port.

They also have canary yellow radiation portal monitors flanking the vehicle monitors in the traffic lanes, which are calibrated to pick up even trace quantities of radiation from people and vehicles crossing over the line. The rovers also have a key-fob-sized detector that will alert if it picks up radiation anywhere on the apron in front of the port in a pas-sive search for nuclear materials that might be used in a dirty bomb.

Should a smuggler with a crumbling story opt to floor the accelerator and bust past the booth to the road network, the inspectors also have one other gadget at their disposal. They jab a button in the booth and tire shredders pop up in the lane, disabling the vehicle before it can get through the port and onto Interstate 5 heading toward San Diego and Los Angeles. The system also activates railroad-type gates, red lights, and audible alarms.

Then, directly behind the line of inspection booths, is the third layer of policing, known confusingly as "secondary." It is the place to which inspectors refer the drivers and passengers they deem need checking out a little further, slapping a colored ticket onto the windshield at the end of their brief screening process to signal that they need additional examination.

Sheltered by the structure of the port and to one side of the busy traffic lanes, it's the crucible where the questioning ramps up and a traveler's story will either finally check out or fall apart completely. While the travelers are thoroughly questioned, the suspected load vehicles are meticulously searched and often pulled apart in a relentless search for nonfactory compartments. And here the inspectors have a remorselessness and skill that matches that of the rogue mechanics who artfully put them together in the Tijuana chop shops south of the line.

During several visits to the port, and having crossed through it dozens of times in a vehicle, I have watched rapt as the inspectors go briskly about their work, feeling that I was watching a Detroit assembly line in reverse. They swiftly take out spare tires, unbolt seats, and tug out trim, and seem to know the sweet spot to tap to pop out vehicle door panels. Within minutes, a vehicle, any vehicle, can be stripped right down to the chassis.

The search and disassembly process goes on around the clock, day in and day out. And in my visits to the port, I have seen some of the fruits of it: a *clavo* for dope discovered in the door panels of a battered green Jeep Cherokee on my first visit, and then a secret nonfactory compartment used to smuggle migrants in the trunk of a sedan on the most recent.

The space lay behind the car's rear seats, which had been carefully stripped of much of their padding. It was accessed via a trapdoor in the trunk that had been covered in carpet and mounted on black shop-bought hinges that created a few inches of space behind the rear seats to hide an illegal immigrant, who was subsequently arrested.

Another time, standing around on an escorted tour of secondary, I was intrigued to see an inspector kneeling on the grimy concrete inspection area, inserting a long black flexible tube into the fuel tank of a car. I took it to be some kind of siphon; it was in fact a fiber-optic cable hooked up to a video monitor, which he was using to search for packages of drugs he suspected were floating in the gas tank, although on this occasion he came up blank. The car was good to go.

The secondary crews also have other gizmos at their disposal for what they call nonobtrusive detection. These include handheld gadgets that measure density. The so-called busters reveal unexpected objects in spaces in cars where they would normally expect to find a void, such as the bumpers, door panels, or, another favorite, the bed of a pickup truck.

In addition, they have X-ray equipment (which actually uses gamma rays). The machines in use by CBP vary from portable systems mounted in a truck to a large facility like a drive-through truck wash. They can be set up to peer right through everything from very large vehicles, like a railroad car or a Freightliner truck, right down to a sedan or a pickup, carrying out an inspection in seconds. And the secrets they reveal in black-and-white can be startling.

The images show people packed into vehicles; they capture the ghostly outlines of packages of dope hidden in body and door panels, and even tucked into the tires and engine compartments of cars. The scanners, which are also used on occasional outbound inspections to Mexico, not infrequently show the shadows of bulk cash shipments, sometimes more than a million dollars in drug profits bound for the cartels south of the border.

The process of picking out the "bugs, drugs, and thugs" from legitimate traffic is, I always think, a little like using a threshing machine to separate edible wheat from disposable chaff, which is thrown away. It is a steady, relentless process accompanied by noisy hubbub, which, in the end, produces measurable results, like a pile of corn. At San Ysidro, the results are pretty remarkable.

On any given day, the inspectors working the three-step examination process at the port can expect to nab an average of 164 illegal aliens as well as 383 pounds of narcotics of all kinds, impounded in five separate incidents. They also arrest three people wanted on outstanding warrants, often for serious crimes like rape, murder, or armed robbery.

Aside from drugs, illegal migrants, and criminals, the layered searches also net other contraband, no less important to the port, including smuggled plants, animals, and foodstuffs, some as cleverly hidden as narcotic loads. One search using X-ray equipment at the Columbus port of entry in New Mexico recently revealed sixteen suspicious-looking packages hidden inside a truck that looked like a dead ringer for narcotics. A subsequent search turned up ninety pounds of soft Mexican cheese, destined for "people who wanted a taste of the old country," CBP spokesman Roger Maier said.

Then, perhaps strangest of all, some searches turn up live animals carried by border crossers. Inspectors at San Ysidro recently searched one man headed for California who had ten Amazonian parrots stuffed inside a duffel bag hidden in the back of his van. Other border crossers have carried finches taped in special pouches on their clothes, and in another find I heard about, a smuggler had filled a gas tank with heated fresh water, turning it into an aquarium to smuggle tropical fish into California.

All the animals seized at the ports get handed over to the U.S. Fish and Wildlife Service, which sees that they are cared for. For the criminals, illegal immigrants, and smugglers of various kinds that are pulled out from behind the wheel of a car or pickup at the ports of entry, or pulled out of the snaking lines in the pedestrian hall, there is a different fate in store.

People arrested at San Ysidro are walked back from primary or secondary areas and into the concrete and steel port building itself. It is here that the architecture of power kicks in. The shiny steel door into the facility from the secondary inspection area has a simple handle to open it from the outside. But once you're inside and it swings shut, there is no way out unless you have the codes to punch into a touch pad.

Inside there is a booking area with video cameras monitoring everything that happens. CBP agents pat suspects down for weapons and, such is the sheer volume of people processed at the port, give them colored wristbands so that they get streamlined according to their offense. Illegal immigrants get green bands, and criminals flagged by the port databases get an orange band, while drug smugglers get a red band.

"We just give them separate bands to keep track of them, it's our way of not commingling bad people," Hynes explains, as he leads me into the booking area where a dozen or more detainees sit around on benches, avoiding eye contact as they await processing. "Oftentimes we get separate groups in here. We can have nineteen illegal aliens with a van driver sitting next to a [wanted] criminal sitting next to a drug smuggler, and we don't want them getting commingled."

The task of finding out just who they have in custody starts with a simple interview where the detainees' names and other biographical data are taken down and run through criminal databases. Many, though, will have false names or some kind of cock-and-bull story about what they are doing, as they don't want their real identity to be revealed, usually because they are criminals on the lam, offenders sought on outstanding warrants from state and local jurisdictions, often many miles from the border. The easiest way to unmask them is to run their fingerprints.

The IDENT system, which anyone arriving in the United States by air will have seen at airports, checks the prints on the two index fingers against an immigration database. It is the first biometric system going down a path of ever greater investigation available at San Ysidro and other border stations and airports. Another system also in use behind the scenes at the ports is the Integrated Automated Fingerprint Identification System (IAFIS), a more thoroughgoing check that reads all ten digits and matches them against law enforcement databases.

I have heard so much about the IAFIS system since CBP got it a few years ago that I am fascinated to actually see one of the scanners sitting on the counter in the processing area of the port. It is about the size of a tissue box. I watch as one detainee's thumbs are run over rollers and held against a flat pane of glass on top of the box, where they are photographed by a digital camera. Then all four fingers on each hand are wiped and held up against the glass and are photographed in turn. The really clever part is in the software that then reads the prints.

Fingerprints evolved so as to give us better grip, and as is universally known, their configuration is unique to each person. The IAFIS program scans the unrepeatable sequence of nodes and intersections in each of the prints and transforms it into a numerical code. The results are then matched with data held digitally in a live crime database held by the National Crime Information Center that holds information from federal, state, and local law enforcement throughout the United States, as well as details on suspects, criminals, and fugitives sought by Interpol.

"Anyone who wants anyone will link that warrant into the system," said Hynes. "It doesn't matter if you're a sheriff or a federal agent, if they're wanted you'll get a hit." The system is one of those instances where high technology does everything that its developers and end users hope it will. It has led to the unmasking of thousands of criminals crossing over the southwest border each month, some whom have committed very serious offenses.

While I am touring San Ysidro with Hynes, inspectors detain a twenty-four-year-old from Tacoma, Washington, who was wanted on charges of second-degree murder, with a bond set at one million dollars. The inspector in primary found he was driving a stolen vehicle, and carrying someone else's Washington state ID. He originally told the inspector he was a U.S. citizen when interviewed at the primary booth, then when hauled into secondary he changed his story, saying he was a Mexican citizen, in the hope that he would simply be released back over the border under voluntary return. The stories all fell apart when his prints were scanned.

The system is also used at all Border Patrol stations to run the identities of all the illegal immigrants picked up in the spaces between the ports of entry. There are thousands of examples of its successes. One I found particularly striking came when the system identified three sex offenders picked up by agents in separate incidents in southern Arizona on the same day in August 2007.

One man, a Salvadoran nabbed in the desert near Lukeville, had been convicted of "lewd and lascivious acts" with a child under fourteen years of age. Two Mexicans were also picked up in separate arrests near Nogales. One was found to have raped his wife, while the other was found guilty of "oral copulation" while serving a jail sentence in San Quentin.

As well as being extremely accurate, zeroing in on offenders whose details are held in a database with more than 47 million names, it is also very fast. In the past, inspectors used to have to ink a suspect's prints and fax them to the FBI to process. Former INS inspectors said they sometimes wouldn't get a response back for as long as a couple of weeks, and then frequently a print would be smudged, and they would have to start over again. It was, particularly in the light of habeas corpus, far too slow for any kind of useful mass screening.

However, the IAFIS system usually comes back with a hit—if there is one—in anywhere between five seconds and a minute, according to inspectors who use it every day. The system is so effective that word has got out to criminals and fugitives south of the border and thinking of heading up to the United States, some of whom now routinely take evasive action to try and mask their identities and their secret histories as they sneak across the border.

One smuggler in Tijuana told me of a coyote who used a soft emery board to file off her fingerprints while she waited in line to cross through San Ysidro as insurance to help her beat the system if she was arrested. Border Patrol agents in Arizona told me they have caught people crossing over the deserts who have used Super Glue to gum up the telltale swirls on their fingertips or have even tried to burn them off with a candle flame or by dunking them in acid.

In another startling discovery in late 2005, inspectors at the port of entry in Nogales, Arizona, noticed a Jamaican man walking north with some discomfort. It was no wonder that he was hobbling. Closer inspection revealed that he had recently had a plastic surgeon remove the skin of his toes and graft it onto his fingertips, to try and hide his identity. He was wanted, it turned out, in connection with a money laundering investigation.

In the years that IAFIS has been in use on the border, police have seen it all, and if anything, such attempts at evasion only spur them on to find out who the person really is. "They know that if we put them through the system and there's something in their background, they know we'll get them," said Hynes. "Clearly someone filing their fingertips is doing that to avoid detection, so obviously that's reason right there to investigate them. We'll find some type of information to identify that person."

Once the agents get a hit and discover they have someone wanted on a warrant, they inform the relevant law enforcement agency, perhaps police in a city like Tacoma, or a county sheriff's office, so that they can send someone to the facility to pick the offender up. Meanwhile he or she is held in a detention cell.

Once they have arrested someone for a new offense, inspectors at the port have to then figure out what to do with that person. San Ysidro is unique in the country in that it has a prosecution unit comprising fifty officers. They take statements from detainees, create case files, and present about five hundred cases annually to the U.S. attorney's office for review to see if they want to take the case to court. The cases often don't go to trial, but straight to a fast-track system that pleads them out before they ever get to court.

The port has detention cells, each with heavy stainless steel doors and a toilet. The detainees get three meals a day while they are being processed. The complex also has a padded cell for rowdy, self-harming, or just plain violent detainees. The bare room has a floor of foam-backed plastic and soft, duck egg blue walls. It's an eerie place. You could be shut in here, raging and pounding your fists on the walls all day, occasionally looking up for an eye at the hatch. I found it quite chilling.

Working at the port of entry in San Ysidro serves as an unparalleled learning experience for the CBP inspectors assigned there. It presents agents in a few short months with anything that they are ever likely to see at any other port of entry in the country, as they are hit around the clock with some of the most brazen, bizarre, and creative scams imaginable. Within the CBP environment, officers say that once you have had your baptism of fire at this port, you're good to go anywhere within the system.

"I've been in seven or eight locations in my career and I don't think I have ever had the opportunity to work with employees as dedicated and capable as the ones assigned to this port. The employees here carry themselves differently, they are dedicated to their jobs, and they are very highly effective," Hynes said. "They see it every day, they love that environment and they thrive on it. I would put them pound for pound, one for one, against any other employee from any other port anywhere, and they will come up with more violations, more seizures, and more apprehensions, guaranteed."

The port at San Ysidro, and its companion crossing at Otay Mesa out east, are just part of the story of how this strip of urban border between Tijuana and San Diego is policed.

The rest of it, the long areas of fencing between the border crossings, is policed by the Border Patrol. Just as the Southern California ports of entry have been a crucible for developing tactics and practices for inspectors at other crossings on the southwest border, so the local Border Patrol has pioneered strategies and techniques for securing the line in built-up areas.

The San Diego sector of the Border Patrol begins at the Pacific coast, where the rusted metal barrier rises up out of the breakers and strikes out onto land. The spot is known rather prosaically on the north side as Border Field State Park, and on the south side as La Esquina de Las Americas—the Corner of the Americas, the point where Latin America, the Third World even, finally runs up hard against the First World's most prosperous nation, the United States.

The suggestive possibilities of that rather magical geographic quirk were briefly realized when human cannonball David Smith, Sr., set up his massive star-spangled cannon on the beach in 2005, and arranged to be fired over the barrier to California. He waved his passport before clambering into the barrel and being blasted in a fleeting arc over the fence to be caught in a landing net as the Border Patrol and a waiting ambulance crew looked on.

The spectacle was performed in front of a large crowd including mental patients from the Baja California Mental Health Center in Mexicali as part of a performance art project by Venezuelan artist Javier Téllez. Téllez told reporters the stunt was aimed at "dissolving borders" between the United States and Mexico, and between the mentally ill and the rest of the world.* For the rest of its run, the border is seldom so playful.

From the beach, the sector runs eastward for some sixty miles up over a mountain range to El Centro. The most heavily policed stretch lies along the fourteen miles separating San Diego and Tijuana. The distinctly urban nature of the San Diego Border Patrol's beat is captured by the sector headquarters, which is set back from the road in an area of Chula Vista filled with subdivisions and strip malls with outlets like Starbucks, Panda Express, and Target.

For a tour to see how this built-up stretch is policed, I meet up with agent Wendi Lee, one of the sector's public information officers. A Border Patrol agent for several years, Lee was raised by Mexican parents in San Ysidro, just across from Tijuana, in the 1980s. It was a time when the San Diego sector was the most-crossed stretch of the line, where struggling agents nabbed around half a million illegal immigrants a year, although the number that made it through was really anybody's guess. The area was, everyone agreed, pretty much in free fall, with people running across in the thousands, night after night.

Driving down the web of freeways to the border in a Border Patrol SUV, Lee points out the area where she grew up and went to school close

---

*Elliot Spagat, "Human Cannonball Fired Across U.S. Border," Associated Press, August 28, 2005.

to the San Ysidro port of entry, right in the thick of all that chaotic activity. She recalled the fear she felt as a child watching illegal migrants sprinting through the schoolyard while she was in class and knocking on the windows of her home day after day, often with agents running after them in hot pursuit.

"I remember being very frightened. My mother would put us to bed, and they [the illegal immigrants] would knock on the windows of our bedroom and tell us to 'open the door, open the door.' I was maybe seven or eight years old, we all had to go into one bedroom and all sleep together because we were afraid. It was daily, it was astonishing," she says of an experience that clearly shaped her choices when she grew up.

"I remember seeing the Border Patrol agents and thinking, 'Wow! You know, that must be a very, very tough job and also exciting.' I saw it as someone wanting to come into your house, and you wanting to keep them out," she adds, explaining how homeland and household security were pretty much indistinguishable for her growing up here. "This is what I have always wanted to do."

It is a beautiful morning in mid-April. Lee drives out through an area of grassland west of San Ysidro toward Border Field State Park and the Pacific Ocean. It is an area that was largely abandoned to border crime in the 1980s. It was one of two notorious spots where illegal immigrants and smugglers swarmed over the border every night, through what was an urban wasteland.

"Before, it was impossible to drive around and patrol," Lee explains, as we roll through an area where green fields now shade into subdivisions and a shopping mall selling cut-price Gap and Calvin Klein clothes.

"We were getting rocked, shot, and assaulted. You would see people gathering on the south side here . . . they would come across and get on the bus or the trolley bus," she explains, and head straight up to San Diego. They would also line up in the traffic lanes south of the San Ysidro port for what overwhelmed border inspectors came to call banzai runs.

"They gathered on the south side in Mexico, a group of twenty, thirty, forty at a time, and they'd run across through the port up the freeway. It caused a lot of danger not just to them but to the drivers. You just can't stop on the freeway when you are doing sixty-five miles per hour," Lee said. "It was a lot worse during the night shift as migrants would wear dark clothing, and it's harder for the drivers to see them until they are right on top of them."

That all changed in the mid-1990s, with Operation Gatekeeper, an enforcement push that marked a paradigm shift in border policing. Like Operation Hold the Line in El Paso, the push sought to seal the heavily transited urban corridor north of Tijuana, which at the time bore the brunt of illegal immigration to the United States.

It added more agents, deployed in three separate tiers back from the border line, and also gradually replaced the feeble old chain-link fence with an imposing-looking double barrier that we are now driving alongside.

The barrier consists of two fences separated by a patrol road, watched over by day and night vision cameras and lit up at night by harsh stadium lighting. At the time of writing, nine out of a total of fourteen miles have been built. It is an impressive-looking structure that has a geopolitical feel to it, especially lit up in a blaze of light after dark, when some Tijuana residents say it looks like the Berlin Wall or even a high-tech version of the Great Wall of China. The first time I saw it, driving along the line at night with Mexico's then commissioner for northern border affairs, I got goose bumps.

The new stretches of fencing, and the policing methods that now accompany them, have been taken as a model for urban border enforcement across the southwest. Lee gamely agrees to take me into the no-man's-land between the two fences, to give me a glimpse of how it works. We weave past McDonald's behind the San Ysidro port of entry, and head east over the tracks of the San Diego trolley, stopping on the far side short of a tall set of automated sliding gates that have the feel of the T. rex enclosure in the movie *Jurassic Park*.

The gate—called Roberto's Gate for a local Border Patrol agent, Roberto Duran, who was killed in a vehicle rollover while on duty in Arizona—carries a sign with a warning that you could be crushed to death if you get trapped in it as it closes. We roll forward into the strip, driving up a gravel track toward the area known as the Soccer Field, which posed one of the biggest headaches for police, wedged between the tall, parched, scrub-covered hills on the California side and Tijuana's teeming barrio La Libertad, where the shocking purple bougainvilleas are in full bloom. Once inside the closed system, it works like this.

The fence on the south side is some ten to twelve feet tall, made of rusted military aircraft landing mats, some of them dating from the Vietnam War era. Then there is a broad, well-lit, gravel-covered patrol strip watched over by camera poles thirty feet tall. Then there is a secondary mesh fence, standing seventeen feet tall, on the north side. The mesh weave, called sandia matting, is so tight that illegal immigrants can't get a fingerhold in it.

Looking at it, there is plainly something that sets it apart from a lot of fences surrounding junkyards, vehicle dealerships, and even private homes in a lot of U.S. cities. It has no electric fence or razor wire festooned along the top, threatening to snarl up, gash, or shock anyone who tries to cross it with a jolt of electricity. Playing devil's advocate for a moment, I ask Lee why not.

"There're a lot of issues behind it. We have had the suggestion of an electrical fence or barbed wire, but it would cause a lot of problems. Activists, humanitarians, a lot of people would get involved," she says. I look at it, and imagine the grim spectacle of Mexican immigrants dangling from rolls of barbed wire. It is clearly one that both the United States and Mexico, peacetime neighbors and NAFTA trading partners, want to avoid. The unadorned barrier brings into play a different philosophy and practice of policing.

The formidable yet ultimately harmless fence doesn't so much stop illegal immigrants and smugglers as slow them down in any attempt to push north. In order for it to be effective, agents have to watch the entire stretch constantly, around the clock. Aided by cameras, they are assigned a specific spot where they "sit on an X" for the duration of their shift, ready to respond to intruders.

This being Tijuana, the smugglers on the south side have also adapted and raised their game to try and beat the measure. Some go underground, burrowing shallow "gopher holes" that reach under the fence, or else they tap into existing infrastructure running under the border or parallel to it, including sewers and gas pipelines, and attempt to shimmy north on their bellies, and others, such as the so-called ladder crews, go over the barriers.

The ladders are knocked out in Tijuana workshops, and can come in various shapes, lengths, and configurations, although all share the characteristics of being light and highly portable. One I saw was made up of a central steel strand the width of a finger, with rebar treads welded horizontally at spaced intervals. It was made to be rolled up into a big hula-hoop-sized loop, thrown over the coyote's shoulder, and rapidly unfurled, not on the first barrier, which can be climbed unassisted, but over the taller secondary fence. To do that, they need to create a distraction.

The smugglers will often draw the Border Patrol agents' attention by sending a decoy over a section of the fence in a stretch they don't intend to cross. With all eyes on the decoy running around in no-man's-land, an agile smuggler will scramble over the first barrier into the fleetingly created blind spot, and quickly uncurl the ladder and throw it over the secondary fence. Most ladders are made with a hook so that they catch over the inclined lip. Now set up, he will run back over the strip to Mexico to fetch the group of illegal immigrants.

"Once they see the ladder is in place, they will push the group of five or ten through in a matter of seconds," Lee explains. "There has to be somebody holding the ladder on the south side of the secondary fence, as it's not stable at all. You have to hold on with all your strength or you will fall. They will climb up the ladder, stay on the slanted part [of the fence], and then make that long jump down" on the far side. They are then in Southern California, with a short dash down to the San Diego trolley bus.

Despite its limitations, the fence is a formidable obstacle to smugglers and illegal immigrants, and has succeeded in cutting the number of arrests in the area by more than two-thirds. It works because police

An agent for Grupo Beta rolls up an improvised ladder put together by smugglers to clamber over the border barrier separating the Mexican powerhouse of Tijuana from metro San Diego. The ladder, which is light and easy to carry, has been tailor-made with a sturdy hook to slip over the inclined lip of the tall secondary barrier. (Tomás Bravo)

have found the ideal combination of surveillance cameras, lighting, and barriers, watched over by agents who are ready to respond in moments. While it works very well in the urban San Diego–Tijuana corridor, Border Patrol agents and their political masters in Washington are divided about whether the model is an appropriate one to apply across the nearly two-thousand-mile line.

San Diego's Republican Congressman Duncan Hunter supports it, and would like to see double fencing constructed on at least seven hundred miles of the border. Homeland Security Secretary Michael Chertoff, however, takes a different view. He backs the use of such fencing in urban areas where illegal immigrants and smugglers need to be swiftly apprehended before they can simply melt into the streets of the towns on the north side. But he does not believe that the barrier would be appropriate in the vast empty reaches of the border.

The double barrier in San Diego works, at the end of the day, because it is very intensively policed. There are Border Patrol agents stationed every few hundred yards around the clock, ready to pounce on border crossers straying across their strip from Tijuana. There are a lot of them, and they have a great deal to do during their shifts.

However, some long, lonely stretches of the border running through Arizona and much of New Mexico have comparatively little traffic. Any agent sent to sit on an X out there would face the mind-numbing prospect of going perhaps days at a time without even seeing anyone, much less making an arrest. Then he or she would face a long drive back home to Yuma, say, or Tucson at the end of a shift, in a work pattern that could very quickly become demoralizing.

While smugglers and illegal immigrants in Tijuana could simply stroll a few paces to the southern reaches of San Diego and vanish into the streets and industrial parks, out in the desert wilderness in Arizona they may have to trek as many as fifty miles before they can, in any useful sense, feel that they are in the United States. That harsh, empty terrain calls for a very different set of strategies for policing, and has several highly specialized units tasked with securing it. I decided to head to Arizona and find out who some of them are.

FIVE

Horses and Black Hawks

Border Patrol agent Jim Weygand is from Brooklyn, a lifelong fan of the Yankees, the Jets, and the Devils. He tells me he always wanted a career in law enforcement, and had figured on joining the NYPD. Then one day his father pointed out a recruitment ad for the Border Patrol.

He learned Spanish working in landscaping with Hispanic immigrants in New York, which helped him when he moved out west to Tucson from Bensonhurst with his wife and family. "The only thing I miss is the food. The food is horrible out here. In New York they have horrible Mexican food, here they have horrible everything else," he says.

Weygand makes an unlikely candidate for an Old West lawman, but that is in a way what he is. We are chatting as we bounce along the Figueroa Ranch Road west of Arivaca, out into the Altar Valley, in the back of a Border Patrol truck towing a trailer with four horses.

He has calfskin gloves like a ranch hand and light-colored chaps that reach down to his ankles. In his belt he has a pistol. Like all agents, he practices being quick on the draw and firing from the hip. In fact, the only detail missing is the broad-brimmed hat. "Growing up in the city, I'm not comfortable in a cowboy hat. I have one, but I don't wear it," he says. Instead, he goes out on the trail in an olive green Border Patrol baseball cap, which soaks up the sweat.

His colleagues, though, look more the part. Galen Huffman is at the wheel. A quiet, soft-spoken man in his forties, he was raised in Bisbee, an old mining town in the Mule Mountains in southern Arizona, where his father was a barber and a sometime copper miner. He has a Marfa palm leaf hat, a kind favored by a lot of working cowboys over a Stetson, sitting on the dash beside him as he drives. He chews Fine Cut Winter-green tobacco, spitting gloops of juice out the window onto the frosty desert trail.

The last member of the team is Bobbi Schad, who sits up front beside him. She is the unit supervisor, and Old West skills run deep with her, too. She grew up in Tucson in a family of riders and began competing in gymkhanas and barrel races as a schoolgirl.

Some border police see the horse patrol as something of an anachro-nism: The unit seems to be just great for school visits and recruitment posters, although they question how cost- and time-effective they are as a policing tool. Others, such as one border rancher I spoke to in southern Arizona, believe there is something uniquely effective about what they do that makes them one of the most relevant units on the border today, as well as, in his view, one of the hardest working.

I am also buckled up in a pair of chaps. I am going to ride out with them for a couple of days as I want to see for myself what the agents do in this unit that reaches right back to the origins of policing the south-west border more than a century ago.

Mounted Inspectors were sent out to secure the border from Chinese illegal immigrants back in 1904, although the U.S. Border Patrol itself was not created until 1924. The principal problem back then was incur-sions by bootleggers hauling scotch from Canada, as well as tequila from Mexico and rum from the Caribbean through the Florida Keys, all to keep the party going during the dry era of Prohibition.

Recruits on the southwest border had to supply their own "hay burn-ers" and tack. Given a revolver, animal feed, and twenty-five dollars a week in pay, they were sent out to hunt down the *tequileros*—rogue

Mexican cowboys hacking up over the back trails on horses and mules loaded up with tequila and mescal and sotol, a rough, fiery drink made from the desert spoon cactus.

Now, more than eighty years later, contraband is still on the move over some of the very same trails ridden by the old bootleggers, only nowadays it's Mexican pot, thousands of tons of which are grown each year, and more than 440 tons seized by Border Patrol south of Tucson last year on its way to market across the United States.

The smugglers have been joined in the interim by hundreds of thousands of illegal immigrants who trek up each year from Mexico and all places beyond, the vast majority of them dirt-poor laborers looking for any kind of a job stateside, some of them with their families in tow.

While the horses are about as old-school as you can get, they are very far from being an anachronism. In fact, they are making a surprising comeback in the Border Patrol due to a variety of traits that they bring to policing in an era of unmanned drones, virtual fences, and other high-tech gizmos and gadgets.

As we are chatting in the back, Huffman is driving with one hand on the wheel, leaning out the nearside window in a southwest version of the Detroit Lean. He is looking intently at the edge of the sandy ranch road for tracks of people crossing north, to find a trail for the horse team to work.

Suddenly, he pulls firmly up by a cow trail leading up from the border some ten to fifteen miles to the south. The trail, which is just shaking off a light rime of frost in the wintry sunshine, carries the tracks of a group of more than a dozen border crossers. The mixture of imprints, made by shoes such as classic Chuck Taylor baseball boots, as well as New Balance and Nike athletic shoes, tells the agents it's more than likely a group of illegal immigrants. Drug mules favor hiking shoes and even knockoff versions of the Border Patrol boots, with tough Vibram soles.

The sign is good, less than an hour or two old, and it's time to get going. Weygand, the urban cowboy of the group, goes to the long white

Border Patrol agent Jim Weygand leads his horse Rocky over rugged terrain in southern Arizona. In the search for illegal immigrants and drug traffickers, the patrol favors muscular American quarter horses, for their stamina and agility. Some of the horses are confiscated from Mexican drug traffickers, who like them for exactly the same reasons. (Courtesy of Reuters)

trailer in tow to fetch the horses, already saddled up and ready to go. A clatter of hoofs on metal, and they are out on the trail, ears forward, eager to get moving.

I have been matched up with Flashy, an American quarter horse, or more precisely, a quarter-horse type. The breed are so called as they are fast over the quarter mile, and have, according to some reports, clocked speeds in the sprint at over fifty miles per hour. Not surprisingly, they are built like sprinters: squat, with powerful haunches, neck, and shoulders.

As well as being capable of short bursts of speed, quarter horses are phenomenally strong, and are famed for their stamina, almost like mules. Their relatively small size also makes them very maneuverable along the narrow cow trails they often follow, weaving up through mesquite. The breed also has a steady temperament, good stock sense, and a sheer eagerness to work that makes them the workhorse of choice for ranchers across the West. Those same qualities also recommend them to border cops and (here's the strangest of ironies) Mexican drug smugglers alike.

Most of the horses used by the Border Patrol are handpicked in private sales by experienced horse patrol agents, who then take them for a trial period. A surprising number, though—around a fifth of the horses in the unit of the patrol that I am riding with—have been confiscated from Mexican drug runners, who use them to run dense bales of pot that have been compressed in garbage compactors.

"Some of the smugglers have a good eye for a horse. They are good cowboys. They know the type of horses they are going to need. Most of the horses are coming from the northern part of Mexico, they are raised in the mountains, and they are good ranch horses," Schad says.

The smugglers, tough ranch hands and cowboys from Sonora, are often quite attached to their mounts. They are notorious for riding them hard over difficult terrain, often leaving them with open sores from chafing tack. But when the smugglers are caught, knowing that they are going to lose their horse is, for some of them, the most difficult part of detention.

Huffman recalls how the unit got two of their best horses from one seizure in nearby Green Valley, south of Tucson. The horse patrol tracked two dope smugglers up into the mountains by the Caterpillar plant, which is a local landmark. The agents had them surrounded when they were resting and the horses grazing, and rushed in before they had time to take off with one-hundred-pound loads of dope crammed into improvised burlap saddlebags.

"When we caught them, we got them off the horses and handcuffed them. The guy was telling the horse he was sorry, and was apologizing to his horse for putting on all that weight and taking him through the mountains. He kissed the horse on the nose and told him he was sorry. . . . There were no tears, but he was serious," he recalls.

That particular horse is called Hueso (which means "bone" in Spanish) and is one of the best working horses they have, a true poacher turned gamekeeper. Hueso and the other seizures are particularly good as they have experience of the mountains, and of getting over cut fences—details that spook a lot of other horses.

"Most of them are incredible horses, they truly are," Schad says. "They are the same quarter-type horses, they have the same build, and a lot of them have been traversing these mountains for a long time. They know the area, they are good already, they are good at crossing fences. The smugglers leave the bottom wire uncut and walk right over them," she adds, as she gets ready to move out.

I have ridden horses since I was a boy, though with no finesse and never anything fancy. Gathering the reins in my left hand, I slip a boot into the stirrup and swing up into the creaking leather saddle stamped with a Border Patrol logo. It feels like I am straddling a barrel on top of a stepladder.

Schad swings her leg up onto her horse, a bay called Freckles. Huffman rides a gray called Lobo, or "wolf" in Spanish. Weygand has Rocky, a highly strung newcomer to the unit. He has him on a tight rein champing at the bit, turning circles in the dirt road, eager for the off.

Huffman is the group's most experienced tracker, and he takes the lead, setting off at a brisk trot. I squeeze Flashy's flanks with my heels, and he breaks into a lope. The gait is powerful, implacable, like riding a freight train. It is also thrilling. Like every kid, I grew up watching Westerns on the telly, and now I am out riding with the closest thing to a posse that you are likely to find today.

We are covering a surprising amount of harsh terrain really fast, following Huffman up ahead, who is leaning out of the saddle to track, all the while chewing tobacco. I am struck by the expression of intense concentration on his face as he stares at the trail, almost like someone who has dropped a bunch of keys and is retracing his steps to find them.

Huffman leads us up and down washes, which the horses take steadily, weaving in and out of stands of cactuses and pushing through thickets of spiny brush that larger breeds would have to move around.

After a mile or two, the tracks strike out north across the prairie grass. It could be accidental, or it could be planned; either way it's a smart move on the part of the group of border crossers. Border Patrol agents call tracking "sign cutting." It is more difficult to cut for foot sign out here, and Huffman slides out of the saddle and starts tracking on foot, the reins gathered in his right hand, trailing his horse behind him. His rhythm is unbroken; he moves fast, his gaze fixed on the ground ahead, his eyes intent on a trail I can't see. He explains that you can follow tracks for quite some way without seeing any obvious sign, like footprints. "You see a little rock kick, or a flat little spot where they stepped. You can go a long way without ever seeing a footprint and still stay on it. It takes a lot more time and you go a lot slower," he says.

Huffman strikes out ahead. A few minutes later, he radios back that he has "bodies." As we head off down the hillside to join him, we learn that he had been cutting due north, having difficulty in seeing the sign. Finally he picked up on the tracks of one man and followed them. He has come up on a group of people, some of them hiding, some of them now scattering through thick brush.

By the time we reach Huffman he has a group of five or six people under arrest. They are dressed in thick sweaters, dark jackets, and woolly caps and scarves. He has led them into a sandy hollow and, speaking softly but firmly in Spanish, ordered them to sit down and take off their shoes, the Chuck Taylors and Nikes that we saw imprints of pressed into the trail.

They are compliant, exhausted by their trek and sleeping rough in frost. One man wrapped up against the chill says he is from Toluca, an industrial town near Mexico City. He explains that they have spent two nights walking the trail, sleeping by day, and adds that they are part of a larger group. It is then that I suddenly hear Weygand's horse whinnying, further up the trail in a maze of thick brush.

The tall New Yorker and Rocky are hidden in a thicket so dense that I am unable to make out anyone or anything in it, even from the vantage point of my horse. But as I come up on them, Rocky is clearly spooked and turning in tight pirouettes, churning up the sand with his hoofs.

Moments earlier, a number of footsore people dressed in dark clothing had begun to lift themselves up out of the brush on the desert floor, painfully, on blistered feet, and give themselves up to Weygand. It's curious, but it seems to be the horse that has found the group, and it confirms something I had been told before about horses.

One patrolman in Southern California had told me that, when he was spotting for border crossers at night with an infrared scope, he would often use a corral filled with horses on his patch of the border to alert him, in an early warning technique reminiscent of the way miners used canaries to detect gas in a coal mine.

If he saw the horses turning and looking off into the dark, he would, he told me, draw an imaginary line down one's neck and between its ears, and where it pointed, he would know to spot for illegal activity. Likewise, the agents I am riding with will later tell me they actively take cues from the horses' sharp ability to spot illegal immigrants in hiding.

The ability comes from the fact that horses are, in nature, prey animals that have evolved on the wide-open ranges by developing extremely keen senses to help them spot predators. Unlike people, who have eyes that look forward, horses have large, sensitive eyes set on the sides of the head, giving them a nearly 350-degree field of vision. Their keen eyesight, which is particularly good at night, is coupled with very sharp, directional hearing. The streaming sensory input is hardwired to a flight reaction, so that when a horse detects anything from an audio or visual cue, it shies.

These senses do not simply protect the individual horse. The animals in the herd work together to give the group even greater protection from predators. Huffman points out that when we are riding in single file on the trails, the lead horse is listening for any sounds on the trail up ahead. The horse in the middle, meanwhile, will have its ears to the sides, while the trailing horse will generally have its ears pulled back, listening, as they have since time immemorial, for that large cat that will leap from nowhere, or the pack of wolves that will snap at their heels. "They will usually see something before you do, especially at night. You feel their heart speed up, they tense up. . . . You feel it, you know to get ready," Huffman later explains.

Schad—who is one of the most experienced riders in the Tucson sector—explains a little more about the reaction of the horses. "Their sense of smell, sight, and hearing is so much better than ours. They will see somebody lying under a tree. They will look over to see it, and you look over and say 'Oh, there's a body under there,'" she says. "If you know your horse, you know its reactions. If they hear something at night, they will look up and see what it is. If it's like a deer or something, they will go back and whatever; if it's a group, they will focus in on it. . . . Today, they helped find the group under the trees."

That tensing reaction, combined with the Border Patrol's tracking skills, means that now the three agents have assembled a group of eighteen undocumented immigrants, who might otherwise have remained unseen, wandering up these rough back trails, beyond most other units' abilities to follow them.

We are, of course, in the middle of nowhere. The unit now has the task of getting the group back out over a couple of miles of rough desert to the ranch road, where agents with a vehicle are already heading out to pick them up. Once the arrest has been made, the stock management skills of their quarter horses come into their own, Schad explains. "It's what we call 'cow sense.' It's a herding instinct. We like these horses. It helps with their instincts to gather people, and if they run, to be able to chase them and have the desire to do that," she tells me as we are riding side by side at the end of a line of clearly exhausted men and women filing out of the desert.

The perspective I get from actually being on a horse is compelling. Flashy, without any encouragement from me, is eager to keep close behind a straggler, a heavily built man limping on sore feet. I notice that my horse moves to the outside, and appears to be trying to nudge the man down the trail with his muzzle. "It seems that the horse I am on, I'm not really trying to guide him, but he seems to be trying to round this guy up. Is that right?" I ask, truly amazed at what I am seeing.

"Yeah, they will," Schad says, with a guilty chuckle. "And when they want them to hurry, they are really bad, they'll start pushing them with their nose. If they were to take off running, we would go around them like you were herding cattle. The horses know that. They are used to going around them and getting them to stop, they are chasing down things, and around things, and through things . . . they are very active."

About twenty minutes later, we catch a glimpse of a white Border Patrol truck up ahead, with a detention cage on the back. It won't be large enough to hold this group. Soon, a second truck bounces down the ranch road, framed by the sugarloaf dome of Baboquivari Peak in the background—which of course brings back strong memories for me.

We file up to a flat area around the trucks, Huffman and Weygand in the lead and Schad bringing up the rear, with me tagging along beside her. The group are told to sit down again, while the horse unit members lend their colleagues a hand filling out the paperwork and processing the group.

Forms and clipboards come out as the agents start gathering names from each detained migrant, together with the full names of their mothers and fathers back south of the line. Voter registration cards and driver's licenses are checked, while the detainees are separated from their belongings. There isn't much room in the back of the paddy wagons. The group is told firmly to strip down to one layer of clothing—most are wearing two pairs of pants and several layers of pullovers and jackets—and place everything in the day sacks that each is carrying.

As they peel off their layers, I see several have images of the Virgin of Guadalupe on their undershirts, and it brings the day I spent in Altar with Tomás, Robin, and Manuel flooding back. The group are also stripped of their bracelets, chains, and amulets, the saints that have been keeping an eye out for them on the trail.

Finally, they are patted down as they clamber into the detention cages, heading off for processing. If they check out, and have no outstanding warrants or criminal records, they will be returned to Mexico later in the day, with all their belongings.

As the trucks drive off, I look at my watch for the first time since we started out from the stables around eight in the morning. It is now three in the afternoon and I am stunned at how quickly the day has flown by.

We ride out in bright winter sunshine to rejoin the trailer, which Huffman has already gone to fetch. Weygand puts the horses back inside, still tacked up from the day's ride, and we head back down the ranch road in the truck. Huffman is back at the wheel, and offers me a wad of his chewing tobacco. I take a pinch, slip it between my lower lip and gums. My mouth fills up fast with thick drool, and my lower lip turns numb. *This is what the West tastes like, then,* I think.

Weygand is relaxing, too, as we chat about the hidden world I have just had a glimpse into, miles from the main road. "It's not cowboys and Indians anymore, but it's cowboys and something," he says, musing about the job he clearly loves. "It's a classic. . . . It is hands down the best job I have ever had."

The agents who work the horse patrol like it because it is tactical, that's to say, they spend their time working the trails and not bound up with a lot of the pen-pushing that fills up the hours of many of the agents on this, the busiest stretch of the border, where around a thousand people a day are arrested.

The horse unit is a close-knit team with a good relationship with other agents on the trail, who support them in a number of ways. Their colleagues drive in to pick up the illegal immigrants, as they did today, and also pick up the drug traffickers and dope impounded by the horse unit out in the wilds. In addition, they share in the sign cutting, passing on and receiving tips.

The horse units' ability to reach remote areas, and the skills that their horses bring to seeing people hiding on the very periphery of their field of vision, and then rounding them up, are being increasingly recognized by the Border Patrol.

"They saw that more and more traffic was moving back into the mountains, so they decided to go back to old school, the old patrol. How did they use to catch everybody? Horses were a big factor in that," Schad says. "They realized we were so much better at controlling certain areas, so they said, 'Hey, let's keep utilizing an old-school tool and go back to the basics.'"

The Tucson sector now has around 150 horses and 87 mounted agents, four or five times the number they had five years ago. Horse units have also been boosted in Southern California—where they helped ranchers save livestock in the wildfires in late 2007—and in El Paso and Marfa in Texas.

What the units are doing, their members explain, is working to get control over a broad, empty strip of the border. As soon as the migrants and smugglers cross the line, the clock is running, and patrols have somewhere between a few hours and a few days to catch them before they slip into the cities and beyond their reach.

"We have more time than the Border Patrol working in the cities on the border. In the city there's all places they can hide, here there's a lot of space, but we get more time to track 'em and catch 'em before they get to roads and load-outs," Schad explains. "If we hadn't caught this group today, we could have passed it on to the next shift. You could say that's passing the buck, but it's good teamwork." Establishing control over this vast wilderness means getting onto a group, tracking it around the clock, and racing to bring it in before it can get north.

In the two days that I have ridden out with this unit, they have apprehended twenty-nine people in the wilds. The first group of eighteen took perhaps two hours to track and round up out in the far eastern side of the valley. The second group, eleven people detained on the second day I was riding with them, took about twenty minutes to find.

It is clear that if time is of the essence here in controlling these rugged borderlands, then horse units are clearly effective, working in combination with agents in four-wheel-drive trucks and on quad bikes, as well as with other technologies.

I have a sense of how they work to track and beat the smugglers. I am now curious to know what other ways there are of policing that vast strip of desert that is more than three hundred miles wide and some forty or fifty miles deep.

The best way, bar none, of covering that ground and getting to out-of-the-way places fast is in a helicopter. One type above all others gets there fastest: the Black Hawk, and it is ideally suited to holding this terrain. And I am off there next.

We will be flying out to intercept the group of intruders with the cargo bay doors of the Black Hawk helicopter open, and I have been told by pilot Rich Rouviere to loop my feet through the shoulder straps of my rucksack to make sure that it isn't sucked out into the slipstream by the rotors.

My bag firmly anchored between my feet, I tug two seat straps over my shoulders, two from down at my sides, and plug them all into a dial-like buckle that pins me hard back into the metal-framed seat. I can barely move an inch.

U.S. Customs and Border Protection air interdiction agents Tim Dybis and Todd Sager check me over and strap themselves in by the Black Hawk's gunners' windows directly in front of me, facing out toward the darkened runway at the military base on the outskirts of Sierra Vista in southern Arizona.

There is a whiff of jet fuel in the air as the two powerful turbines power up and start spinning the rotors. As it winds up to take off, I ease off my headset, slip out one of the foam earplugs, and wonder at the deafening howl as the blades thrash the hot night air.

The heavy military helicopter rises up and moves over the runway as if it were on rails, its rotors thumping as it gains speed and height as we head for the looming shoulders of the Huachuca Mountains in the dim moonlight. I can make out the brush and ridgelines as we climb, flying lights out.

Rouviere is wearing night vision goggles that flip down in front of his eyes from his helmet—decorated with marijuana leaves from a string of dope busts he has made. As he pulls them forward, the phosphorous screens blink on, bathing his face in an eerie green backlight, like the amped-up glow of a watch dial.

The flight crew of a CBP Air and Marine Black Hawk prepare for a mission at the Davis-Monthan Air Force Base in Tucson, Arizona. Later that evening they will drop into a remote area of mountains far beyond the nearest road and nab a group of nine illegal immigrants. Two will get away. (Courtesy of Reuters)

The Black Hawk and its crew are heading out to intercept a group of a dozen or so border crossers from Mexico, spotted walking up through the rugged Patagonia Mountains east of Nogales, likely heading for a load-out and a ride up to Tucson. The helicopter can respond to any call-out, ranging from injured migrants to armed drug traffickers.

In the cargo area directly in front of my knees, there is a medical station that is equipped with oxygen cylinders, a defibrillator to restart stopped hearts, and backboards to stabilize patients with serious spinal injuries.

Also tucked into the belly of the robust helicopter is a strip of road spikes to knock out vehicle tires in high-speed pursuits and an armory with high-powered assault rifles that can shoot through a car radiator and stop the engine cold. It is, essentially, a flying tactical unit equipped like a hospital emergency room.

As we pick up speed and hurtle over the mountains, Dybis and Sager gaze at the dimly lit terrain streaking beneath us, their feet resting on the sill of the gunners' window. There is something strangely serene about them as the chopper closes the gap on the encounter.

"We're three minutes out," Rouviere chimes in over the headset. Like other Black Hawk pilots in the Tucson CBP Air and Marine unit, he served in the military reserve, and, in his case, spent a yearlong stint flying with the military in Baghdad.

Sager, a former paratrooper, has a searchlight ready to flick on the intruders that we are pelting toward helter-skelter in the dark, and it's not just any spotlight. The Nightsun casts a 30-million-candlepower beam, and is, they say, like a theatrical spotlight on steroids.

"We're two minutes out."

I feel a sharp surge of adrenaline as the encounter nears. The CBP Black Hawk units are little known outside police circles. I have seen them streaking overhead down in the desert a couple of times, and now I am finally going to see how they work.

As the Nightsun strikes up and the heavy military chopper banks in the dark to circle around and land miles from any backup, I am glad I had a chance to get to talk to the crew, and learn what they do, while we were back at the base.

The office is brightly lit, in a prefab building on the apron of the runway at the United States Army base at Fort Huachuca, about twenty miles north of the border, and I am standing around chatting with the crew after our flight down from Tucson in the dusk.

Sager—he and Dybis are the two "backseaters" in the team—is the most chatty. He is short, stocky, and in his late thirties. Originally from Ann Arbor in Michigan, which he jokingly refers to as the People's Republic of Ann Arbor for its political liberalism, he has a solid military background.

He served in the 82nd Airborne during the December 1989 invasion of Panama to oust strongman Manuel Antonio Noriega, parachuting in to Torrijos International Airport in Panama City at night to take it from the Panama Defense Forces.

Just eight months later he was dispatched to the Persian Gulf in the first Gulf war, and then served in a long-distance reconnaissance unit for five years before switching to law enforcement.

His current role flying in Black Hawks came via beginnings as an inspector for the former U.S. Customs Service in Detroit and then working for the service's special response teams, or SRTs, which are the same thing as SWAT teams.

In the hour or two before we set out, I am trying to grasp what exactly it is that the crew do, and what sets them apart from the other units at work securing the most heavily trafficked section of the Mexico border. "How it differs from us and other specialized units is our rapid mobility. We can go instantly from a rescue, to bad guys that are running away, to helping an officer who is pinned down by gunfire," says Sager, who is dressed in combat fatigues and a flak jacket, and looks more like a soldier than a policeman.

When they reach a group they have been sent to apprehend, the backseaters can either be dropped off on the ground by the Black Hawk pilots, or, if the area is too mountainous or thick with obstacles for them to land safely, dropped in on a rope.

As they are often dispatched to work unsupported in out-of-the-way areas, part of the task going in is being able to read a fast-unfolding situation and be prepared to respond in a heartbeat. "You have to be able to scale it up or scale it down in an instant. You have to be ready to talk to someone or have a full-on fight to the ground. You can't go out there thinking about the new shoes you bought last night. When we get into a mission, it's usually something bad, and you have to have the right mindset," Sager says. "You try to stick together, you don't want to go running off by yourself most of the time, but sometimes it ends up that way. So the struggle's on and you just use the tools that you have on your belt to help you make the apprehension."

To get a sense of how Sager does his job, I ask him to talk me through the broad array of tools that he wears strapped down tight over his fatigues, enabling him to move fast and unhindered. First, he has on a bulletproof vest, inside which are pouches filled with dozens of rope handcuffs made of nylon with a cleated zip tie, which all CBP air enforcement officers carry to cuff large groups of illegal immigrants. The footsore immigrants are usually cooperative after a sapping couple of days on the desert trails, although they occasionally get runners who peel off from a large group in the dark and flee on foot, so they sometimes need to cuff them together.

Sager also reserves two pairs of shiny steel handcuffs for the drug traffickers he encounters out in the mountains and desert wildernesses, who will often have a lot of fight in them. "The cuffs have a sweet spot to them," he says, showing me how to clap them down briskly on the top of the wrist. "You bring them down there and they snap right on."

Sager wears a blue signal light like a button. It can be used as a flashlight to illuminate darkened paths, and works as a strobe that identifies him clearly to the Black Hawk, which will usually be circling and watching his back while he works. He also has several flashlights for backup, tucked into a variety of pockets and pouches.

As well as extra ammunition clips for his pistol and long rifle, he carries a Leatherman multitool with a good set of gooseneck pliers. I have seen the same tool with the horse patrol. "The main thing I carry this for is to pull cactus needles out of my legs or hands, and from the bad guys we are chasing who sometimes end up falling into them," he says, explaining that the chollas, strange-looking plants like waist-high monkey-puzzle trees bristling with barbs, are the worst.

"It comes off in balls, and if you have one on you and you go to grab it, now it's stuck on your hand. When you go to throw it, usually it rolls off and sticks in your leg, and that's why you carry the multitool. The barbs are like fish hooks. When you pull them out, your skin comes out with it," he says, to laughter of commiseration from the flight crew.

The biggest problem confronted by the Black Hawk crew is not the illegal immigrants trekking up through the wilds, but the smugglers who traffic narcotics through the desert corridor south of Tucson on foot, on horseback, and in vehicles. They are anxious to avoid jail time, and will often fight, and occasionally even kill, border police who try to stop them as they make a run for the border.

Looking around the room at the flight crew, I try to imagine for a moment what it can be like to be dropped into the mountains on a rope, at night, to arrest half a dozen desperados who are ready to do whatever they have to in order to stay out of jail. I am at a loss, and ask Sager how he handles it.

"The aggression you show on someone puts the fear into them. Even if it's a little guy, and he's aggressive, they know he means business," he says. "If someone acts up, take them to the ground and put cuffs on them. If you don't they will take advantage of you, they'll punch you and run, knock you down, or push you off of a cliff. I try to let everybody know that we are there to get the job done and that we mean business. Of course, be nice to the people that are nice, but if they are aggressive, show them that aggression back."

When they start swinging for you, what do you do? Dybis and Sager have a whole armory at their disposal, from pistols to shotguns and their pick of assault rifles. Working way out in the desert, often in the dark and without support, the easiest and safest option would, I figure, be simply to reach for the firearms.

To my great surprise, Sager is committed to using nonlethal force to tackle even the violent border crossers he encounters, at least as a first option. His first tool of choice is a rigid, telescoping baton that he carries in his belt, which has several uses. Fully extended, it can be used as a lever to pry the arms out from under resistant border crossers, who sometimes tuck them in close to their bodies to avoid being handcuffed. It can also be used as a simple blunt instrument to strike smugglers who want to fight.

"Have you got a lot of use out of it?" I ask him, referring to its thumping role.

"I have gotten a lot of use out of it, as a matter of fact," he says, flipping it so that it extends with a heavy, metallic clunk. "Everybody knows you are not going to shoot them, but when they hear that thing come out, they know that pain is coming. . . . You can't stand back and let the guy know you're weak, you've got to just attack, go in and get the job done quick."

Of all the smugglers that they tackle, Sager says that the dopers on horseback are the toughest. He describes one incident when he tackled a drug cowboy whom they had chased down in the Black Hawk as he made a desperate run for the border, galloping hard on his horse along a scrub-lined wash as a Border Patrol team closed in on the ground.

The rider was finally unseated when his horse refused to jump a barbed-wire cattle fence. Sager, who teamed up with the ground agent, lunged at the Mexican cowboy, who was committed to fighting for his freedom with every ounce of his strength.

The smuggler got a first surprise kick in, and Sager fell to the ground. The Border Patrol agent jumped on him as Sager got up and ran over again, taking another kick in the knee that knocked him off his feet. "I just happened to run up from a bad angle, through cactus and trees, and went straight into the feet. I got a couple of strikes in. He was swinging and we were swinging, he was bloody, we were bloody. Finally we got the cuffs on him."

The scene is like something pulled from a Wild West novel, or the kind of vivid comic book sold on Mexican newsstands. It is, though, real life, and happens time and again, far from the public gaze. And it is not just the horse packers that they tackle in these out-of-the-way spots.

The Black Hawk units also have become specialists at stopping drug traffickers who speed over the desert from Mexico in pickups crammed with bales of pot, often driving fast at night with lights out and wearing night vision goggles of their own. There is no manual for this kind of arrest, and it is something that the pilots and backseaters figured out with practice. Rouviere tells me how they do it.

The helicopter flies at the speed of the car and to one side, in a highly prominent position where the driver locks eyes with the pilot as he speeds along a desert wash or trail, driving as fast as he can back south toward Mexico and safety.

What he doesn't know is that the Black Hawk has already dropped a two-man spike team two miles farther down the trail that is getting ready to throw a strip of sharp, hollow prongs across the path to punch holes in his tires. They are positioned in the perfect spot, hidden in a dip that is not visible until the last moment.

"I fly next to the guy for two reasons: I want him looking up at me and I want his attention off the road. The other thing is, we don't need a lot of communications on the radio," says Rouviere. "The spike team see the aircraft and they know I am alongside of the vehicle, that's how they know that it's coming up on them."

The backseaters out on the trail are waiting for a truck driving without headlights up toward them over a dirt road at eighty to ninety miles per hour in a situation that is now fraught with danger. "You're not like a regular police officer who has a vehicle to hide behind, you just have a bush, and they swerve to hit you," Sager says. The very real danger was made crystal clear in early 2008, when a fleeing Hummer packed with drugs swerved to avoid a spike strip set out on a road west of Yuma, Arizona, killing a senior Border Patrol agent, Luis Aguilar.

Knowing how exposed they are, and how the driver may well try and run them down as he flees hell for leather for the border, Sager explains, one member of the Black Hawk team will have his assault rifle trained up the trail.

If the driver sees the trap and swerves to run the agent down, his colleague will shoot with the assault rifle, which can fire on fully automatic or in rapid three-round bursts that will punch right through the radiator and stop the engine. If that doesn't do the trick, then he will shoot the driver.

As they are closing the space down, the ground team is ready to pull the strip of spikes out on a cord; the driver and the chopper pilot are eyeballing one another. At the last moment, the backseater pulls out the strip when the driver is committed and can't stop.

In the incident they described, the hollow spikes, like metal porcupine quills, stuck in the front tires. They shredded them within a couple of miles, leaving the driver to carry on flat out, running on the wheel rims until he lost control. Then the agents rushed in and arrested him.

The improvised technique works like a dream. In the first six months that the units started using it in the Tucson sector, the Black Hawk crews spiked thirty-four smugglers' vehicles, a work rate that surprised even the product's manufacturer. "When we called Stinger, they said, 'What in the heck are you guys doing with all those spikes?'" Sager recalls, with laughter. "They said, 'You use more than any other agency in the country.'"

I am beginning to grasp who the backseaters are and what they do, but now I want to understand about the very businesslike black helicopter, with the CBP Air and Marine logo picked out in gold on its side, which is parked on the runway outside the office. Rouviere is a font of information.

Now in his forties, he tells me that his one dream as a boy was to fly. He earned his private pilot's license when he was still in his teens. Later, he became a Border Patrol agent and learned to fly helicopters while serving in the Arizona National Guard, flying Black Hawks, an aircraft used as the military's workhorse, but rarely used by police.

The military helicopter, Rouviere explains, is well suited for its role on the border. First off, it is the fastest chopper in the CBP Air and Marine fleet. It can speed over the borderlands at up to 180 miles per hour, meaning that it can get to most of the places it needs to from the unit's base in Tucson within twenty minutes. It also carries some armor, a plus in this violent desert corridor. "The Black Hawk is a military aircraft. It comes standard with armor plating. It's bulletproof in a lot of ways, so that's a great advantage for what we do," he says.

The robust Black Hawks weigh in at about eleven tons. The pilots' seats are lined with Kevlar, although the armored plating that extends through the cargo area in the standard combat models has been taken out, making the helicopter lighter and effectively extending its operational range over the borderlands.

Unlike other lighter helicopters used by the CBP Air and Marine, such as the A-Star (which is also used by police forces including the LAPD) the hefty Black Hawk can put down pretty much anywhere in the uneven desert terrain, studded with spiky plants.

"With the other smaller aircraft . . . it's really easy to hit small bushes and shrubs and things like that with the tail rotor," Rouviere says. "We have poked holes in the bottom of them, but believe me, it [the Black Hawk] will take a lot more than one of those smaller helicopters."

Powered by two powerful turboprop engines, the Black Hawks can carry more payload than other choppers in the fleet, even in the searing hot summer weather like the late summer night we are flying. The helicopter can take seven or eight people, rather than three or four like the A-Star. The extra payload capacity means pilots can use it to evacuate illegal immigrants in a medical emergency, or transport detainees from extremely remote areas, or, and this is common, to fly seized bales of marijuana often totalling hundreds of pounds in weight out of the desert.

When they are transporting a group of people, the pilots set them down at a hospital, or at a point the Border Patrol can reach on the ground in vehicles. Sometimes they even fly footsore Border Patrol agents out of the desert after they've been tracking a group of border crossers for hours on foot.

According to Rouviere, "Sometimes when these guys get caught, it's after agents have tracked them literally for hours and hours, and once they catch them, hey, everyone is exhausted, so we fly them, as it is sometimes almost physically impossible to hike eight hours back towards a vehicle with a bunch of prisoners."

Curiously, in their hidden world way out in the borderlands, the units also occasionally meet Mexican drug backpackers who have walked up a dope load, dropped it off at a desert load-out, and are now looking for a ride home to Mexico.

Standing on a hilltop, they have been known to flag down the Black Hawks, knowing that, while there are a lot of incriminating clues that mark them out for what they are, there is nothing sufficiently damning to land them in court. The Black Hawk crews will set down, and pick up their adversaries.

"We know by experience from their clothes and their demeanor, and the fact that they are not carrying their little school backpacks, that they're packers," Sager says. "You can see the red marks on their shoulders [from carrying the heavy loads], they wear certain necklaces, their shoes, they don't carry wallets like the average illegal. . . . You know they are carrying."

The crews fly them out to be processed by the Border Patrol like any other illegal immigrant. Then, if they have no prior record or outstanding arrest warrants, the smugglers are simply driven back down to the border and released back into Mexico like any voluntary returnees.

The drug traffickers are in no doubt that the Black Hawks are among their most feared adversaries in terms of policing, as intercepted radio communications between drug trafficking organizations from Sonora show. While they are wary of all border police, they particularly dislike the fast, heavy military helicopters flown by Rouviere and pilots like him.

"That aircraft is pretty intimidating," he says. "When we show up, people are running. I don't think they want to stick around and stand and fight, I really don't. That's not a personal feeling, because I have been working in this office for eight years and I haven't seen anybody yet," he said. "I think it is the whole package that is intimidating, I think it's the aircraft, I think it's the color, and it's the fact that they know that we can land it just about anywhere, they know that we bring our own firepower with us—not just guys with automatic weapons, but highly trained guys that we can actually drop off."

The units are cued to go out and work by alerts sent in by an array of hidden sensors set out in the borderlands, intelligence from the Border Patrol, or a tip-off from the latest state-of-the-art drones that wheel out over the desert.

As we are chatting at the base, the cue to scramble comes in. A group of eleven people has been spotted walking out over the mountains to the west of us. We break off and trot out over the darkened runway to the Black Hawk. It is time to see it in action.

In less than ten minutes, the helicopter is out over the target coordinates. It banks sharply out over the desert brush, its rotors kicking up a blizzard of debris as it circles above the ground, losing height on the turn.

Rouviere and pilot Wade Koontz are wearing night vision goggles that give them a clear, three-dimensional view picked out in shades of green. While they also have the night vision kit, Sager and Dybis prefer to use the Nightsun as, they explained, it picks out colors in clothing, helping them to distinguish the people they are there to arrest from their natural desert backdrop.

Following the beam as it skates over the terrain, I suddenly see it: a flash of red in the brush below. It is a man's jacket. Then I see a figure, then another figure, a group, and then it's like Rouviere said: Everybody is running. We circle once more as Sager tracks the fleeing group of illegal immigrants with the spotlight and the helicopter throws a circle around them, cutting off their escape.

The Black Hawk settles on a sandy rise in the dark and Sager and Dybis are out the doors. It takes off again and circles the scene. I can make out the two agents by their flashing strobes, running through the brush and mesquite rounding up fleeing members of the group. They look suddenly tiny and very alone.

As they gather up the group, Sager briefly flashes a light in their eyes, momentarily messing up their night vision and making it harder for them to flee in the uneven, dark area, studded with mesquite and chollas.

The helicopter circles, keeping in touch with the backseaters, gathering a tactical view of the scene. Within three or four minutes they have arrested nine out of the eleven border crossers, and now have them sitting in a group. There are too many detainees to fly out of the wilderness area in the Black Hawk, so they will have to hold the group until the Border Patrol agents arrive on the ground.

The helicopter continues to circle to try and spot the two who have fled, and all the while Rouviere and Koontz are also watching the backs of the agents on the ground. After about twenty minutes, I see the lights of two quad bikes rising and dipping as they close in over the rugged landscape, as the Border Patrol backup arrives.

Dybis and Sager hand off to their colleagues, who will walk the group out and down to a road to book and process them. Rouviere sets down the helicopter to pick them up, and we set off back to Tucson in the dark. It has been stunning, and, together with my ride with the horse patrol unit, flying with them has given me a vivid sense of some of the ways the deserts are being secured.

It has also left me with the desire to know what other special units are in the borderlands, far from the public gaze. There are two more on my list.

SIX

Crack Units

The parking lot at the desert grocery store is filling up. I'm perched on the tailgate of my pickup truck, watching the cars as they roll in and gas up at the pumps, then park outside the rough-timbered store. A sheriff's deputy walks in purposefully, sauntering out a few minutes later with a Styrofoam cup of coffee and a bag of doughnuts. He sits down on a stone bench on the porch to spend his break in the shade.

A rancher driving a Chevy truck rattles onto the concrete apron, bales of hay and salt licks for cattle tossed into the back, and he heads in to shop as country music blares out onto the forecourt through loud-speakers.

It is four o'clock on a baking Saturday afternoon in August at Three Points, the cleft fork in the road southwest of Tucson where Highway 86 comes in from the wilderness, the very spot where Tomás and I once shared breakfast. I am watching everyone that pulls into the parking lot quite carefully as I'm waiting to be picked up. And it is a strange and unequal rendezvous. The people who are coming for me know my name, the make and color of the truck I am driving, and even the plate number, although I have no idea who I am looking for.

They are members of a discreet law enforcement SWAT team that are rarely in the public eye, a fact that they seem to be very comfortable with. A shadowy unit within the Border Patrol, they are reputed to have a whole range of weapons right out of the special forces' armory and tough, backwoods tactics.

They have been deployed alongside Drug Enforcement Administration agents combating the cocaine trade in the high Andes of South America, on the streets of south central Los Angeles to quell the 1992 race riots, and entrusted with the mission of snatching back Cuban youngster Elián González from his guardians in Florida a few years ago. They are currently engaged in a little-reported hunt for the hardiest smugglers trekking over out-of-the-way trails that crisscross the southwest border with Mexico.

I take a pull on my water jug, wipe the sweat from my eyes, and look at my watch. It is almost 4:20 P.M. They are twenty minutes late, and I figure that now they won't be coming. It looks like I will just have to head back down the highway to Tucson, nursing my disappointment at being stood up. It took more than a year of negotiating with Washington bureaucrats to green-light the visit and now it's . . . "Mr. Gaynor?"

The voice comes from my left. I jump half out of my truck. Parked right next to me is a large brown Chevy Suburban that I hadn't even noticed pulling up. The paintwork has been dulled by the sun, and it has no law enforcement decals down the side. Inside are two men in full battle dress uniforms, wearing rangers' caps and wraparound sunglasses. "Get in the back," the driver tells me. "I'm sorry we're running late." If stealth is part of their arsenal of tactics, then this is definitely round one to Bortac.

Jim Volcsko and Pete Sanchez introduce themselves as they pull away from the store and head down across the desert at speed toward the Mexico border, forty-five miles to the south. All I can see is the back of Sanchez's head as he drives. He is soft-spoken, with a deep voice that sounds very much like the actor Vin Diesel's—an impression reinforced by a strong jawline I can just about glimpse, and by his physical presence that reaches into the back of the truck.

Volcsko is taller and slighter in build, and has a courteous and yet reserved formality as he swings round to field a barrage of my questions.

I ask about their truck, which is clearly not standard issue for law enforcement. It has a satellite navigation system stuck to the windshield on a rubber sucker, which can tell the team where they are to the nearest few feet. Tossed in the back are khaki sleeping bags and a couple of pillows, and behind the front seat is an M-4 assault rifle and body armor. Also in their equipment are night vision scopes, as well as state-of-the-art thermal imaging gear used by the military, and flash-bang grenades developed for the British Special Air Service. By the look of it, I'd say we are going camping in a war zone.

Each of the Border Patrol's nine sectors along the southwest border has its own SRTs, or Special Response Teams. Like Bortac, which is a federal team deployed in the United States and around the world, members are volunteers, who must pass fitness and aptitude tests. They then go through special weapons and tactical training at a center at Fort Bliss in El Paso, with yearly refresher courses, to prepare them for a close-up battle to secure the border. It takes place along the trails and pine-topped mountain ridges of the southwestern deserts and the remote banks of the Rio Grande, in areas that are far from the public eye and sometimes scores of miles from the nearest road.

The units can be deployed anywhere from San Diego to Brownsville, Texas, to hunt the hardiest smugglers on the border. Some of the time they will go after illegal immigrants taken over remote trails by coyotes betting that Border Patrol agents will not try to make it up and into the areas. But much of their effort goes to combating tough Mexican drug runners who deliberately target the emptiest and least-visited stretches of the border between the ports of entry, to avoid the relentless probing of sniffer dogs that can root out narcotics across more than a dozen lanes of traffic, and the penetrating gaze of X-ray cameras that can now show up drugs hidden not just in door panels and car tires, but even tucked discreetly into the engine manifold of a car.

"We are paid to hunt people," Volcsko says, glancing back over his shoulder as we hurtle down the highway. "If the operation calls for us to target illegal aliens, we will target illegal aliens; if the operation calls for us to target narcotics smugglers, we do that."

The sun is now dropping behind the dome of Baboquivari Peak to the west of us, casting long shadows over the cactus-strewn desert where the teams operate. Loaded up with food and equipment, Volcsko explains that they often hike up on back trails into an area they are going to work, to set up camp in the wilderness as they prepare a stakeout that could last for days or even weeks. They are also sometimes dropped in by helicopter.

"In order to get to these people, you have to go up to the remote areas where they cross, whether it is through the desert or through the mountains, and you have to be comfortable working out there, far from all comforts, often for days at a time. It takes a certain kind of temperament," he says.

A little later he goes into a revealing explanation of how to catch, kill, and skin a rattlesnake, and the three different ways he has found to prepare its meat in a bush kitchen: blackened, pan fried, or plain barbecued. Listening to him, I can see that he is not showboating, but in fact perfectly at ease in this harsh environment. I ask him if that's right, and he nods. "If you don't like roughing it, this would be a miserable existence."

We finally reach Sasabe, one of the loneliest crossing points on the whole border, and an area that is a headache for police. It is set into a vast tract of remote desert, reaching over to the empty reaches of the Tohono O'odham lands to the west, and another rough, mountainous tract of wilderness stretching for miles toward Nogales to the east.

It is an area too rugged to build an access road with a drag strip like the ones the Border Patrol use to patrol other parts of the border, and in fact, I discover, it has no barrier at all in many areas, just a few cast-iron obelisks set on rocky promontories to mark the line. In short, it is a physically brutal terrain that is very tough to secure.

On the south side lies El Sásabe, in Mexico's northern Sonora state, with its low-slung brick and cinder-block homes. It was once a ranching town and a backwater brick-making hub, and it is where Tomás and I came up through on our trek to the United States. The town, which has a booming strip of flophouse hotels and gaudy bars to cater to the traffic, is also a key staging area for dope smugglers preparing to haul literally tons of bulky and pungent marijuana north to Arizona from clandestine farms across northwest Mexico.

The lights blink on in the desert border crossing as the twilight deepens. We are in what news photographers and television crews call the golden hour: a time of lengthening shadows where the sun's ebbing rays draw out the rich red and golden tones, turning often the most ordinary-looking towns and cities into places of magic.

This corner of Arizona is adding to that tonight, throwing two rainbows across the sky as gathering monsoon storm clouds rumble across the horizon. On the south side in Mexico, the single-story houses are also aglow, and the few streetlights wink into life as the migrant smugglers and dope runners weigh up their chances.

They are figuring where to snip through the seven-strand barbed-wire cattle fence marking the border, and what path to run north to the load-out points in scattered villages south of Tucson and in the Tohono O'odham reservation near Sells.

We swing abruptly off the road and bounce along a sandy track running parallel with the border that is fringed with cactus and mesquite trees. Sanchez studies the GPS satellite navigation device on the windshield as it tracks our course yards north of the international line. We cross over washes that could fill with foaming flash floods at any minute as the storm rolls in over the desert with a distant crackle of thunder.

It is difficult for me to gauge distance as we carve up and down over the ridges and washes. We reach an area about ten miles east of the town that the unit has already identified as a smugglers' trail. The area we are heading for is marked on the GPS, and there is already a scout team set up, carrying out surveillance from a rocky knoll just a few yards north of the border line.

Sanchez pulls up in a deep crease in the terrain—an area that cannot be overlooked from Mexico—and switches off the engine. The team puts together their scopes, guns, and body armor, as I gather up my pens and a recorder. I have dressed in dark clothes, as I sensed they would be appropriate, and have a dark blue hat jammed down over my ears to keep any lingering light from catching on my bald head.

The unit is spotting for a band of drug smugglers who are likely to push across tonight on foot with rucksacks full of dope, and possibly guns. "If we have to go in, one of us will wait with you," Sanchez tells me. "You are to remain on the ridge." I nod.

Ducking under a fence, we head up the hill. Volcsko and Sanchez have their rifles and a range of night vision and thermal optics tucked into webbing belts. Their radios link them and their two colleagues, relaying their soft-spoken commands to an earpiece as if they were a Secret Service detail.

Volcsko cautions me to keep an eye out for the black tarantulas the size of a child's hand that are now swarming out of their burrows, and the rattlesnakes that also come out to hunt at night. "You won't always see them or hear their rattle," he warns. The climb is not too tough, and soon we are a couple of yards below the brush-topped ridgeline. Sanchez gestures for me to keep low.

The team has chosen the area carefully. The knoll we are crouched on is backed by a larger hill behind us, which prevents movement along the ridgeline from being thrown into stark relief. "If you raise just the top of your head over the ridge, they probably won't be able to see it," Sanchez says, beckoning for me to come forward.

He passes me some binoculars and tells me to look closely at an area just below the summit of the hill opposite our own, which lies no more than two hundred yards south, across the line in Mexico. I scour the slopes of the hill. At first I can't see anything but scrub and the heavy forms of the barrel cactuses. Then I gasp and nearly drop the binoculars.

Just below the ridgeline are five men, sitting motionless in a row. They are wearing black garbage bags—"Mexican Gore-Tex," Volcsko quips—and they are staring back north over the hill toward where we are hidden, silently watching the area with binoculars.

"They are spotters working for the smugglers," he tells me. "They are looking to see if the trail is clear, probably so that they can run a narcotics load across later on."

I raise the field glasses and take another look at the opposition. They sit as still as cactuses and are all but invisible in their makeshift black capes. They are so close I could call out to them without raising my voice.

I think of the Allied and German troops who paused the First World War on Christmas Day 1914 to play a game of soccer in no-man's-land. I wonder about the forces at play that make us adversarial, that have turned those few yards of separation into a gulf. I ask Volcsko whether he thinks they have seen us. "Not unless they have a spotter already on our side of the border, watching the blind side of the hill," he says, matter-of-factly. "It happens."

It is striking to actually see them. I have dropped into a world where smugglers and cops are on a par, sparring right out in the desert to win operational control of the borderlands. It is a battle that is waged up close, yard by yard, night after night, by opponents using surprisingly similar equipment and tactics.

The spotters, I later learn, often camp out like Bortac for days at a time, lying up on promontories, sometimes miles inside the United States, which are chosen for their commanding view. The scouts smudge out their presence with desert-pattern camouflage or by disguising their hideouts with mesquite brush. They watch for Border Patrol day after day through binoculars, calling in their movement on two-way radios, cell phones, and even satellite phones, which the best of them keep charged up using portable solar panels.

Dropping back down the ridgeline and out of sight, my two hosts relax, waiting for dark. I explain that I have been out with Border Patrol agents on other ride-alongs, but this operation feels different. We are not cutting sign—looking for telltale signs of intrusion and following a trail as I had with the horse patrol unit. We are watching and waiting. I get the feeling that we are setting a trap. Volcsko nods. "We will sign cut, but what we like to do is to find an area and go watch," he says, speaking softly despite the far-off rumble of thunder. "We will typically go up into an area that we believe they are planning to cross through and secrete ourselves. Often we will sit in the brush, and the battle dress uniform will take care of the rest—but what we really like to do is to work at night."

They carefully choose a place to stake out, melt into the landscape with camouflage, and then they wait in silence. A few weeks before, I had seen a praying mantis perched on a branch beneath a streetlight in Douglas, a small border town in southern Arizona. It was beguilingly still yet somehow had all the tension and danger about it of a set snare. I am beginning to sense that here.

The first stars are winking in the sky. It's strange to imagine, but soon we will be able to see perfectly. The team has two different kinds of sophisticated night vision optics. One is a straightforward battery-operated scope that renders the pitch-dark world in shades of green. It is the sort of device that shows up the bedroom antics of participants on *Big Brother,* and is familiar to almost anyone with access to a television.

Volcsko flicks it on for me, and the darkening world becomes quite clear. I can see the hills, the ridgelines, and the stars peeping through a caul of cloud. The other device he calls the Raytheon, for the Massachussets-based defense contractor that makes it. It is a bulkier infrared thermal imaging scope that picks out anything emitting heat, from a warm vehicle engine to a body.

Sanchez switches it on, and its monochrome screen blinks into life. He tells me not to be startled by the dozens of glowing bodies I will see ranged like sentries on the opposite hillside. "They are barrel cactuses, not people," he says. "They retain the sun's heat after dark."

As the darkness thickens, the operation begins to unfold. The unit consists of eight men. Two slip down into the valley floor on the border line, and stake out a path that any smugglers will have to use to walk north. Stealthy and unseen, the agents will stay hidden, watching and waiting, keeping constant, whispered contact with the rest of the unit by radio.

The element of surprise is vital to the operation, as the people they are looking out for are unique in the smuggling world, and present a physical challenge every bit as difficult as the terrain they march through. I first heard about them from a Mexican narcotics cop working under-cover at a migrants' shelter in Nogales, Mexico, two years before. The story was so fantastic that at first I could barely believe it.

The cop had been seconded to the shelter from the Sonoran state capital, Hermosillo. Chatting quietly in Spanish, he told me an anecdote about a different kind of dope mule. They were strong local ranch hands, aged between eighteen and twenty-five, who carried packs of up to ninety-five pounds of marijuana on their backs in handmade burlap rucksacks that fit their shoulders like a worn glove on a hand.

The smugglers, he said, were in such good shape they could heft the loads for distances of up to forty miles at a time, much of it at a trot, and were often cosseted by the Sonoran drug lords. "The *narcos* train them at their ranches, and feed them up on steaks and vitamins," he told me, his eyes widening. "They treat them like racehorses." He actually said that: "like racehorses." Could it really be that there were *narco*-athletes working this section of line?

I ran the story by cops working on both sides of the border, all of whom confirmed versions of it. "They are usually very hard to appre-hend," said one helicopter pilot with the then Border Patrol air wing, now CBP Air and Marine, after taking me on a white-knuckle flight over the Baboquivari Mountains close to the area we were now staking out. "They are in incredibly good shape with maybe three to four per-cent body fat. They carry huge bundles of narcotics on their backs, and they literally traverse the mountains and go for days and days at a time. They climb to the top and then they just stay on the ridgeline down the whole mountain range to avoid apprehension," he told me.

As the smugglers pick their way along the darkened paths, they some-times leave a trail of energy drinks and tuna fish cans in their wake, an indication of how seriously they take performance nutrition. One Bor-der Patrol airman told me they had even been known to leave unfit stragglers literally dead in their tracks. "They were just trying to keep up with the rest of the people in the group and they couldn't do it, their hearts exploded," he said. "That's how hard they work."

I learned there is also a clear division of labor within a smuggling crew. While the wiry mules carry the dope loads, one man on the team is delegated to cook and carry the provisions, and a further one or two men are assigned to work as a security detail, armed with anything from a knife or a handgun to a hunting rifle or a Kalashnikov assault rifle.

As they stalk north along the darkened trails, the minders patrol like a trained military unit. "A lot of times they will do a bounding movement where either the armed escorts or the scouts will go forward to clear the way for the group," Sanchez says. "We've seen the armed escorts flanking the group, and even doing box searches out front."

Encountering a bandit with endurance training, and armed with an assault rifle, on a darkened trail is obviously bad news enough for any cop. However, the danger dials are ratcheted up a further few notches by the fact that many of the smugglers are cranked up on drugs. In a bid to boost their stamina and heighten their alertness, the traffickers routinely give them stimulants to make them fly along the back trails.

Sometimes it may be nothing more than ephedra, the metabolic stimulant that coyotes occasionally give to migrants to speed up their work rate on a long trek over the borderlands, and which I had tried to find in the pharmacy in Altar. They are, however, also given cocaine and, most problematic of all, methamphetamine, which is widely cooked up in megalabs across central and northwest Mexico.

Usually snorted rather than shot up out in the desert, the drug is rapidly absorbed into the bloodstream, causing a cascading release of neurochemicals that raise the heartbeat, eliminate fatigue, and hone mental alertness. The rush is physiologically identical to the fight-or-flight reaction provoked by the nervous system in situations of extreme stress, and meth has a long and ill-starred history with the military.

During the Second World War, Nazi chefs laced chocolates with the drug, distributing them widely among elite forces, tank crews, and fliers of the Third Reich. Like the *Fliegerschokolade* ("flyer's chocolate") or *Panzerschokolade* ("tank crew's chocolate"), the crystal meth fed to drug runners on the border makes them bolder and more aggressive, and gives them greater stamina.

"We found one group who had a time period to get to the area [where] they were going to get picked up," Sanchez says, recalling a string of arrests reaching back over more than a decade that he has spent with the unit. "They were given methamphetamine by the gentleman that dropped them off to help them on their way. It makes them braver. When somebody's on a drug like that, it gives them like a Superman type of feeling. And when you have the adrenaline dump of being apprehended at night, then I'm sure fight-or-flight kicks in and they are probably more apt to fight at that point," he adds.

It is a mixture as volatile as gasoline spilled on sun-baked asphalt, and understanding how to control the situation involves entering into the mentality and methods of special forces units. Chatting with a former member of the British SAS while researching this book, I began to understand a common set of principles for approaching danger, whether that be working undercover in Northern Ireland during the Troubles, or guarding a news team in present-day Iraq, or springing an ambush in the darkened borderlands.

First, the minders find good local information about the place they are working in, such as the ways in and ways out of an area where they are on an assignment. Then they assess the levels of risk posed by the people they may run up against. Are they likely to be armed? If so, with what? What kind of training do they have, and what is their modus operandi? Once fully apprised of the local conditions, and with a clear sense of whom they are up against, they decide on a course of action. And here's the thing: They commit to it, right to its ultimate consequences.

The degree of evaluation and the severity of that commitment became clear to me while chatting with the British soldier about his work minding a TV news crew in Baghdad. Having worked there since shortly after the U.S. and coalition invasion in 2003, he had watched the security situation as it slipped into a tailspin. It became clear to him within a year or so that scouting the ground out and working with good local information was no longer enough to keep people safe.

Insurgents were now targeting Westerners and, in some grim cases, beheading them on camera. He began carrying a Kalashnikov tucked into a bag that he kept on the floor of his SUV, and he was absolutely clear about how it was to be used. It was not for gunplay, nor for threatening potential assailants. "If the weapon comes out of the bag," he told me flatly, "I start killing people."

Out on the border line, Bortac shares a similar set of principles, but with the aim of bringing everyone home alive. After identifying an area to work, they will trek up into it and become familiar with the routes in and out, often setting up video cameras or infrared motion detectors that will give them a heads-up on the smugglers as they come on up the trail.

They know the smugglers, how they are armed, and what they are likely to have taken. To spring the trap, they have to have the same calm, surefooted commitment to outcomes with which the SAS man would reach into the bag for the AK-47. If the smugglers stumble into the trap they have carefully prepared, the agents will spring it. If the smugglers choose to fight, they will meet overwhelming force. In a strange irony, that combination of surprise and unquestionable authority is often just what's needed to bring everyone home alive.

One of the best tools that Bortac has at their disposal is the flash-bang grenade, a kind of powerful firecracker with a bright, momentarily blinding flash, which was developed for the SAS. They used it to spectacular effect when they stormed the Iranian embassy in London in 1980, throwing a group of armed Iranian militants off guard to rescue hostages including a British policeman. Out in the desert, the stun grenades can be pivotal in throwing armed intruders off balance, and turning a situation around.

"In a situation, we'd say 'Okay, when they pass this point here, I'll deploy the flash-bang,'" Sanchez tells me as we look out over the darkened gully leading up from Mexico. "We wouldn't actually throw it at them, but in the direction they are traveling. When you hear something in the rocks, you're going to look. They look, the noise and light distraction device goes off, and it stuns them for up to a second or so. It gives us a little bit of lag time to apprehend them. Even if they have weapons, those few seconds will turn a lethal situation into a nonlethal situation."

One man in the group gives the orders throughout, so there are no conflicting instructions, and they are barked out clearly in Spanish. *"¡Bájense! ¡Todos al suelo!"* (Get down! Everyone on the ground!) "If you have a guy step out, and he's very authoritative, and he gives commands very forcefully and confidently, and he tells you to get on the ground, and he doesn't give you any leeway, you are going to be very reluctant to try anything," Sanchez says.

Once the group is all facedown on the trail, they are ordered to cross their legs and place their hands behind their heads. A second agent will search each of them for guns and knives, and will place cord cuffs with a plastic one-way cleat swiftly over their wrists. It is game over. They have gone from strolling along in the silent darkness to being trussed up, facedown, and under arrest in a matter of seconds.

In several years on the job, Sanchez and Volcsko have subdued fit, armed groups of smugglers on scores of occasions, and even on one occasion a group of ninety illegal immigrants—without ever once having to fire their weapons. It is, given the circumstances ranged against them, and the often trigger-happy culture of many police forces, a quite remarkable record.

After spending just a few hours out on the trail with them, I can see how their preparation, teamwork, and total commitment to outcomes have worked for them. Also, out in the dark, miles from anywhere, and with God only knows who preparing to jog across the line in the dark, I feel quite safe. It is a very good feeling, especially as the units are likely to play a greater role in securing the line in the months and years ahead.

Increasing attention to border security in the wake of the 9/11 attacks has boosted policing resources at the ports of entry and the spaces in between. The move has thrown a tightening chokehold on dozens of ports of entry from San Diego to Brownsville, in an effort to weed out smugglers from legitimate travelers, while barriers have been reinforced around all cities on the border.

Security has also been gradually ratcheted up over the mass migration routes and smugglers' runs through the easier-to-reach areas of southern Arizona, California, New Mexico, and Texas, as more Border

Patrol agents and even, for a time, National Guard troops are put out on the trails and unmanned surveillance drones take to the air to monitor movements.

While there are clear successes, all precedent suggests that determined immigrants will not give up trying to cross, but will instead head out into the more remote, less watched areas to press north. It is almost certain, too, that the drug smugglers will also work the back trails, as they raise their game to match tighter security. Combating them will likely mean putting more Bortac units with men like Sanchez and Volcsko out on the line.

With years of training, sitting out and waiting in the inky blackness of the border line, they feel they are ready for the challenge. "We get paid to hunt people," Sanchez says of the larger role that likely awaits them in the future. "We just have to be smarter than them."

Not far from where I met with Sanchez and Volcsko there is another special police unit that hunts in a very different way. If Bortac could be likened to a praying mantis, this group hunts like a wolf pack.

It's a cold, blustery morning in February on the Tohono O'odham reservation southwest of Tucson. I am sitting in an SUV with Immigration and Customs Enforcement supervisory agent Kevin Carlos. He pulls swiftly out onto Highway 86, steps on the gas, and the truck surges down the blacktop toward the west desert with a throaty roar.

He flicks on the siren and we pick up speed, barreling across the vast, empty landscape of saguaro cactuses, mesquite trees, and creosote brush at ninety miles per hour to get to the small village of Pisinemo a few miles north of the Mexico border. Carlos brings me up to speed.

An ICE agent on a quad bike has been tracking a group of pot smugglers riding up from the darkened international line on horseback since before dawn, and has come across a second set of foot tracks leading out of the wilderness. Both converge on the lonely village in the south of the nation.

"He's been on the tracks since four o'clock this morning, and now they're bringing them in," says Carlos, without taking his eyes off the highway as we streak over the desert. Olive-skinned and in his late thirties, he is dressed in a leather jacket and slacks, and wears the shiny agency badge tucked into his belt. At first glance he looks Hispanic. In fact, he is Native American, a Tohono O'odham, and the supervisor of an elite group of American Indian trackers that works the vast desert nation. The Shadow Wolves, as the unit is known, has fewer than twenty members. But they have become something of a legend on both sides of the rusted border fence for their prowess at hunting down drug traffickers.

Set up under the U.S. Customs Service in 1972, the unit originally comprised a handful of former Indian cops and military veterans from the Tohono O'odham reservation, a broad sweep of wilderness that straddles the Arizona border. The tribe's traditional lands extend south into Mexico.

It is stark, rugged, and extremely hostile terrain for outsiders, who often feel uncomfortable there or even fail to appreciate its spare beauty. One guidebook to the area cautions that "the only reward in driving the one-hundred-mile width of the reservation is [to be found] in its utter desolation."

But the Tohono O'odham see it through different eyes. They, and their ancestors the Hohokam, have lived there for well over a thousand years—some say right back to the time of the Pharaohs—and have very deep ties to the lands on which they have thrived.

Their tales tell of I'itoi, Elder Brother. He made the Tohono O'odham out of clay and gave the land to them as they were the only people who could survive on the tract of desert, where water is scarce and summer temperatures soar to 120 degrees and winter nights can be bitterly cold.

For long generations before the U.S.-Mexico border was ever drawn on a map, members of the tribe farmed squash and gathered cactus fruit, and trekked across the Sonora Desert to fetch salt from the Sea of Cortez in what is now Mexico. They also hunted for deer, javelina, and jackrabbits, drawing on tracking skills and a deep knowledge of their lands honed over the centuries.

When the U.S. Customs Service came to the tribe for help in keeping

narcotics out of the country, it must have ranked as one of the most as-
tute decisions ever taken in policing. Tracking quarry down in that particular corner of the parched borderlands was written in the Tohono
O'odham's genes from the ancestral hunt for meat. When they were set
after drug traffickers, the results were, by any reckoning, dramatic.

Stealthy, fast, intuitive, and utterly relentless, the group formed
around a core of seven officers soon accounted for almost half the drugs
seized by the service in the busy high desert smuggling corridor southwest of Tucson, using an innate gift for tracking. It didn't matter whether
the traffickers were trekking north over the vast cactus-strewn wilderness on foot, hacking up on sturdy pack horses, or driving in trucks, the
Tohono O'odham trackers would find their trail and run it to ground
before their quarry could make it off the Connecticut-sized reservation.

What seemed to set the agents apart was both their tracking ability
and their stealth. One of the first of them, Stanley Liston, was known as
the Shadow Man. He got the tag for an uncanny ability to move silently
up a trail and slip in among groups of smugglers while they slept. "He
was so good, he could sneak into a camp of the bad guys and take an
article of clothing, or some matches or cigarettes from an individual,
and come back out of the camp and explain to everyone this is where
everyone is sitting or laying," Carlos says, talking as he speeds to the latest drug bust. "Then they'd go in and capture them."

A retired agent told me that the "wolf" part of the name was given
them by the smugglers south of the line in Mexico. They had been
tracked by agents of the Border Patrol, but these people, they said, were
different. They would follow you sometimes for fifty miles, never just
one of them, and they would never let up. It wasn't so much like having
a cop on your trail, they said, but a wolf pack.

The trackers became the Shadow Wolves. Soon the unit was opened
up to other American Indian tribes across the United States, maintaining as a minimum requirement that agents have at least one Native
American grandparent. At the time of writing, the unit has fourteen
members, both men and women, from eight different nations. Aside
from the Tohono O'odham at its core, there are Navajo, Sioux, Kiowa,

Blackfoot, and Cherokee agents, all using sign cutting techniques either learned on their reservation or taught them by the old hands in Sells, the dusty capital at the heart of the Tohono O'odham nation.

To try and understand what it is that they do, and how they do it, I had sought out one of their former supervisors a few weeks earlier. Marvin Eleando is an O'odham in his midfifties. He joined the unit shortly after returning from service in Vietnam with the U.S. Marine Corps, and then spent twenty-seven years tracking with them.

He was famed for having once crept stealthily up a trail behind a group of drug mules until he was right on their heels. With his sense of mischief as sharp as his tracking skills, he drew his pistol, reached up, and tapped one of them on the shoulder. "It made him jump pretty good!" he tells me when we meet up for lunch at a casino on the I-10 south of Phoenix.

Eleando is broad-shouldered and wears a USMC baseball cap with evident pride. His face is creased from years out on the desert, tracking in harsh sun and bitter winter winds, and has a broad smile.

He tells me he used skills in the manhunt that he had learned tracking deer over the desert and mountains with his cousins and grandfather. They taught him to read the hoof trail, the scat, and the meanderings of the deer. He learned to read the rhythm of the hunt, the pauses to eat, the herd's time for rest. It was the same, in fact, hunting people. "The trail itself that we are tracking these people on, it's telling us a story," he explained. "It says to us, 'This is what we are carrying, this is where we are going. If you can find us, find us.' You have to have that feeling in you, like you know where they are going. You have to put yourself in their position, and think like them, like 'Now where am I going? Where do I need to go?'" he says.

The Sonora Desert has a broad and largely soft surface of sand and loamy soil, dotted with rocky outcrops and clawing brush and cactuses. I learn that everything from a mustang to a tarantula will leave a trail scribbled across the desert floor, or snared in the barbs stretched out across the wilderness like a long line for tuna. However, tracking the smugglers is no easy task.

Most of the drug mules are mestizos, the descendants of many of the same Sonoran Desert tribes as the Tohono O'odham. And much as the Shadow Wolves could be said to have tracking in their genes, this tough caste of Sonoran smugglers have evasion in theirs. They have dodged the Border Patrol since it was formed in the 1920s in the era of Prohibition. The smugglers also know about the American Indian trackers and they have raised their game, trying to hide their tracks in any and every way they can. Eleando has pretty much seen them all.

"The illegal aliens have got women in there, kids in there, they just walk out there like they own the place. They don't carry anything except maybe some food and water," he says of their guileless wanderings in the desert maze. "The traffickers are different. They don't want to be found, they are trying to fool us," he says, relishing the challenge that they would throw down to his team.

Some smugglers will bind foam or carpet remnants to their feet, to leave a faint, ghostly trail. On some parts of the border they have been known to put their shoes on backwards to make it look like they are going in the other direction, or take their shoes off and hop from rock to rock to leave no trace.

Other common scams involve carrying boards to lay over ranch roads so as to cross without leaving tracks, or using a mesquite branch to rake over their tracks. For Eleando, it's child's play: You simply track the brush out.

Another ruse the mules for the Sonoran cartels use is to beat out ahead of groups of immigrants, hoping that their heavy, load-bearing tracks will be buried or lost among the stampede of men, women, and children who will follow on behind. There, you look beneath the sign, for the heavy step with the incised heel and toe point. That is your smuggler.

Other smugglers making the journey sometimes step carefully in the footprints of the person in front, to try and mask the number in the group, or they will cross over the line into a thicket of dense brush where they think no one will be willing to pick up on their trail.

One tale that Eleando tells catches the intimate knowledge that the smugglers and the Shadow Wolves have of one another. He says the dope mules would gingerly pass burlap backpacks stuffed with dope across to Arizona, to ensure that they didn't leave telltale drag marks on the ground.

"They used to just drag their backpacks, until they found out that we could pick 'em up easier that way. Now they hand the backpack over the fence to the other guy on that side, that way they leave no imprints on the ground. But once in a while they mess up," he says. "Their backpack will hit the fence line and it's got those little stickers [barbs] and they'll catch some of the little fibers from the backpack, and we'll see it," he adds. The Shadow Wolves now have their sign, and start to pursue it.

For the trackers, it is not enough to think like their quarry, they also have to run the smugglers down before they can pass out of the reservation, which stretches up over seventy miles to Casa Grande near Phoenix, and is bounded by Gila Bend to the west and Three Points to the east.

To do so it's vital to be able to tell how long beforehand any group—whether they be on foot, on horseback, or in a truck—has passed along up the trail, so as to be able to determine whether their tracks are fresh enough to be worth pursuing. If a foot trail is more than a day or two old, the group of backpackers will very likely have dropped their dope off at a load-out, and will be back in Mexico. Tire tracks, on the other hand, are old in an hour.

One of the key allies that trackers have to help them is moisture, which provides a variety of clues to age a trail. One of the most obvious forms it takes is the rain itself. A sudden desert storm will brush out old tracks like a cloth sweeping over a schoolroom blackboard. Anything that ventures out onto the dampened trail afterward will leave tracks lying "on top of the rain"—dating their passing to the cloudburst's last sputtering drops.

Trackers also have other allies that help give a trail a timeline. Eleando explains that nocturnal animals like kangaroo rats, rattlesnakes, and scorpions also help chronicle elapsed time, as they set out on their restless search for food after sundown, overlaying any foot tracks with telltale "night sign."

Among the most exact timekeepers are the tarantulas. The giant furry spiders are fastidious and house-proud nest makers, who immediately repair damage to their homes. "If the nest is broken, it takes about an hour to rebuild it," says Eleando. "If it's not fixed, then we know that whoever we're tracking passed by less than an hour before."

Once the Shadow Wolves have established that their quarry has passed by recently enough to pursue, the pace and rhythm of the hunt picks up as they race to run them down within the boundaries of the nation.

As they are closing in for the arrest, the trackers' other senses now start to come into their own. They listen for the sounds of the smugglers' voices on the breeze, and start to use their noses to snare a telltale trail of scents. "People that smoke, you can smell them even if they are a ways from you, if the wind's right," Eleando tells me. "If they are moving along sweating a lot, you can also smell that body odor, too. Sometimes they change their socks. They take their shoes off on the trail, and you can smell their dirty feet out there."

Then there is the dope itself. Mass farmed, with stalks, seeds, and all tossed in, it has the rich, heady reek of sun-dried hay out on the desert trail, rather than the sappy odor of top-of-the-range skunk or hashish that is popular in Europe. The pungent smell alone can guide the agents in the final few steps to a load, often hidden in a wash or area of brush away from a desert campsite, so as to break any incriminating chain of evidence to the smugglers themselves.

The Border Patrol has many good trackers, men and women who can do everything that Eleando and his team do. Other units under the old Customs Service (which has now regrouped under ICE) could as well, and on at least one occasion, so one former agent told me, challenged the Shadow Wolves to a competition.

But if there is one anecdote that truly sets the group of Native American trackers apart from their colleagues and rivals in the somewhat competitive interagency field of tracking, it was the time they were called in on a search when everybody else had tried and failed. They were the last resort, facing the one moment when they had to reach deep inside and make everything that they knew count.

It's a situation that a handful of people experience, perhaps a Navy pilot, low on fuel, who has one last pass to land a jet on the heaving deck of a storm-tossed aircraft carrier, or a free climber caught on a narrow ledge as a thunderstorm rolls in. The thrum of electricity at his back, he dips his hand one last time into the bag of French chalk and climbs as if his life depended on it, as indeed it does.

For the Shadow Wolves that lonely moment came late one night near the hamlet of Covered Wells, in the heart of the nation. It wasn't their lives that were on the line, it was more serious than that: A child's life was in the balance.

Slipping his carergivers, the five-year-old boy had wandered off alone from the village toward the rugged mountains that loom ominously over it like giant furniture covered with a musty green tarp. The rescue services came out but were unable to find the youngster wandering among the brush and boulders, despite the help of tracker dogs. The Border Patrol, meanwhile, who are themselves no mean sign cutters, also turned up a blank.

It was after dark, and the boy now roamed the back trails with the nightwalkers—the mountain lions, coyotes, rattlesnakes, and scorpions. When the Shadow Wolves were finally called in, the gravity of the task at hand was clear to Eleando and his team of American Indian agents. "I told them, 'You got to stay on this no matter how fast or how slow you go with it, but you got to stick with it,'" Eleando says, the smile now gone and a note of steel coming into his voice.

The agents went out in pairs, one looking hard at the trail almost in a trance, and the other standing back, open to the broader landscape of rubble and hard, bare rock. "Sometimes you concentrate so much on what you are looking at on the ground that you will miss things even if they are right next to you, because you are focused on the tracks," he says. "I've seen people walk right by a rattlesnake just a couple of feet away, and they don't see it. That's why we have the backup guy."

Finally, at six in the morning, they came upon the small boy sitting in a wash. He had a dog from the village that had followed him along the trail, and stood watching over him throughout the night. The unit brought him home.

I ask Eleando how they did it. What was it that led them across rock to a child weighing no more than forty-five pounds? He is silent for a moment, and then the simplicity of his answer seems touched by something mystical, almost a kind of sixth sense. "You look around on the sides. Everything is in place, except for where he is walking."

So, fast-forward to that cold February morning on the road to the drug bust in Pisinemo. After the master class that Eleando had given me at the casino where we met for lunch, distilled from his years on the back trails, the takedown itself seemed quite straightforward.

We roll through the village, with its Trading Post store and tin-roofed mud-brick homes, many of them ringed with live ocotillo fencing, and out to a ranch home in the windswept wastes on the south side of town. A squall blows in over the sand, and it seems forbidding somehow, like the British coast in winter.

Carlos takes us out to meet the Navajo tracker with the unit, Harold Thompson, who has chased up five horses over a trail leading up from the border. I look down at the hoof marks. They are laid "on top of the rain" at his feet and stand out as clearly as trowel marks in a window box. They lead to a stash of twenty-five hefty bales of marijuana, bound into pairs with thick yellow nylon rope, ready to be picked up and driven north to market in Tucson or Phoenix. I have never seen so much pot in my life.

The bales have been spray painted black with an aerosol to take the gleam off them in the dark and make them more difficult to spot with a flashlight in this borderlands game of cat and mouse.

"It's good to put it on paper and use it for the stat sheet," Thompson quips, standing over his haul, dressed in a camouflage battle dress flak jacket with U.S. CUSTOMS POLICE picked out in yellow on the back. He is wearing steel-rimmed glasses that make him look more bookish than tribal.

Looking down at the trail in the loamy, ocher-colored sand at his feet, he finds a second, fuzzy set of tracks laid by a group of carpet walkers, the smugglers who bind carpet scraps over their shoes. They are faint, meandering footfalls, the imprint of light sand laid on light sand, in a cunning ploy to throw the pursuers off. They weave their way out of the mesquite and creosote brush just to the south of the village. I can only make them out with difficulty, although to Thompson they couldn't be clearer if they were scribbled in Magic Marker.

Calling on the help of an O'odham colleague, Charmaine Harris, they swiftly run the meandering scuff marks a few hundred yards north across the desert toward the village. I tag along with Harris, looking closely at the ground, trying to coax the story from it that Eleando assured me is there.

As we draw close to the village, the sign is written over by other tracks laid by villagers, tires, the padding feet of dogs. It is as if the faint clear signal laid in the dirt is drowned out by white noise, like static.

Harris looks down at the trail, and then up to a greasewood tree alongside it, and pulls a clawing frond up to her gaze, scanning the tiny barbs for clues. "Burlap. You see it?" she asks, calling me over. I look closely and then I see a single slender fiber no larger than a suture, snagged from an improvised backpack. We are still on the trail.

We push on, following the ghost tracks toward an adobe cottage surrounded by ocotillo trained into upright bars. The tracks bunch up at the gate. The story is coming strong now. I see a group of weary smugglers with heavy burlap rucksacks jostling to get into their sanctuary. The Shadow Wolves have brought the trail home.

We stand around outside the humble adobe home in the weak winter sunshine, waiting for a search warrant. One of the agents passes me a plastic crate and places it in front of a high window under the tin roof, then beckons for me to step up. Standing on it, I raise my head and snuffle. The smell of felled hay is rich and unmistakable, and so much stronger than I could ever have imagined. How much dope can there be inside? And how many people?

The homeowner, an old O'odham man in his early seventies, is ada-

Shadow Wolf Charmaine Harris, a Tohono O'odham, studies a thorn bush to see if drug traffickers have passed by. It yields a single burlap thread the size of a suture—proof that backpackers hauling pot have brushed by it in the night. She follows the tracks up to a house in the village of Pisinemo. (Jeff Topping)

mant at first. He will let no one inside without a warrant. Eventually he relents and several agents file in. They swiftly arrest four men, two tribal members and two weary-looking Mexicans dressed in fatigues and T-shirts, who have trekked thirty miles with their feet wrapped in buff-colored carpet slippers held together with four well-placed twine stitches. The agents bring these shoes out of the house, and I slip them on and tread lightly around the yard, searching for the compelling sense of empathy that I had felt, fleetingly, on the trail. Walking a few yards in the smugglers' shoes is strange. They seem to be of the ground, neither leaving nor touching it.

The agents also impound more than a dozen bales of marijuana—wrapped in burlap sacks marked DUTCH POTATO FARM, SASKATCHEWAN, CANADA, in an ironic snapshot of the underbelly of NAFTA. The haul brings the one-night total for the unit to more than 1,200 pounds of narcotics. The work rate that they have set for themselves is such that it is not a record, but merely a good average.

Talking with Eleando, and then following the Shadow Wolves out on the trail to Pisinemo, I had gotten a fairly clear sense of the quite extraordinary tracking skills that they have. But there are also other factors that make them an even more effective police unit.

One of them is their ability to combine the truly ancient skills that follow their own unique cadences and rhythms with totally contemporary technologies. Standing by a quad bike used for tracking, and with a radio and a satellite location device hanging from her uniform, Kiowa agent Sloan Satepauhoodle explained how the high-tech and the no-tech come together. "We use GPS, we use our radios, we use all modern technologies possible, in addition with what can't use technology. We have to get out here and just look. You have to strap that backpack on and walk it up, it's all part of it," she says.

For agents like Satepauhoodle, a Notre Dame graduate who has been with the Shadow Wolves for six years, the combination of the tribal and the contemporary is important. Rather than being assigned to a theme park world of the ancient, they are also allowed to embrace modernity on their own terms. "It's like both worlds. It's like both worlds working together. I like it a lot, it doesn't stagnate us, it helps us progress," she tells me.

Their adept use of technologies sharpens their tracking skills, makes them faster and more precise in what they do, and also boosts morale among members. Another factor that boosts the Shadow Wolves' keen sense of motivation is the context in which they work. A T-shirt on sale in various tribal nations in the Southwest shows a black-and-white photograph of a rather stony-faced group of Native American warriors in full battle dress. Beneath the pictures is the legend PROVIDING HOMELAND SECURITY SINCE 1492.

While it ironizes the whole notion of borders, and what it means to be an American, the message also speaks to the powerful motivation that many members of the Shadow Wolves bring to their jobs—which are about providing security in a very up-close-and-personal way to their homeland.

Charmaine Harris is Tohono O'odham, and her personal experience exemplifies this. She grew up on the nation, where she worked as a tribal cop in the capital, Sells, before becoming a Shadow Wolf. She sees stemming the chaos that spills over the borders from Mexico with the migrants and drug traffickers as a powerful and personal reason to get her out on the trails.

"I see a lot of the destruction it does. I grew up going out into the desert and being in the mountains. Now I go up there, and I see all the trash," she tells me as we stand waiting outside the ranch house in Pisinemo. "I also see what the drugs can do to the people. A lot of them have a lot of potential to be something, but a lot of them don't because of the drugs. They see easy money that way. In a way it's personal," she adds.

The combination of ancient skills, modern technologies, and a powerful motivation is a winning one. The success that the Shadow Wolves have had in securing the wild stretch of the border has brought the unit greater attention in recent years. Under a border security bill passed by Congress in late 2006, the Shadow Wolves were brought to work for ICE from the Border Patrol, and were authorized to form units to operate on American Indian lands elsewhere in the country. With congressional backing, the unit is helping to train American Indian trackers to use their formidable skills to secure parts of the porous border with Canada, more than five thousand miles long, which is frequently crossed by both cigarette and dope smugglers and is also seen as a weak spot in U.S. homeland security. There they are working with the Blackfeet tribe, whose lands straddle the largely notional northern border between Montana and Alberta, in Canada.

As well as playing a bigger role domestically, the Shadow Wolves are also being sought out by a number of governments in countries from Europe to Central Asia who are beating a path to their door to seek help to train police units to secure their own borders. Members of the unit have taught tracking methods to border guards securing the frontiers of the new Europe—in Latvia, Poland, Estonia, and Lithuania—and at the time of writing, they are planning a trip to Croatia and Macedonia in the volatile Balkans region. Agents from the unit have also been to Turkmenistan and Uzbekistan in Central Asia, to teach police there how to track groups, some perhaps with links to Islamic extremists, slipping over their borders.

The unit's boss in Arizona, senior ICE agent Alonzo Peña, was visiting the nation the day I went. Standing by more than half a ton of pot scooped up in one night's work in the secure yard of the unit's headquarters in Sells, he made it clear that they had a key role to play both at home and abroad in the future.

"They are highly talented . . . and the eyes of the world are now on the Shadow Wolves," Peña said, as two agents weighed the bales of pot on a portable scale. "They are known throughout the world for their skills, and it's really important that they can utilize them to help others."

With the recognition of the valuable role that American Indian trackers play, there is every chance that more of them will be out on the borders, both in the United States and around the world. Intruders hauling drugs, guns, migrants, and who knows what else over the darkened frontiers probably won't even tumble to the fact that they are being followed. The first time they'll know is when they feel that hand on their shoulder and spin around to see an agent with a pistol in hand. For them, at least this time, their border adventure will be over.

SEVEN

Predators

It is late dusk in November, and the last rays of the sun slip below the rugged mountains east of Nogales in southern Arizona as five wiry young men walk north from the border line. They have put together backpacks out of burlap held in place with straps made from a soft rug, making light of the loads of between thirty-five and sixty pounds of marijuana that each one of them carries.

They march in single file behind the leader as they head up into the Patagonia Mountains near the small town of Lochiel. It's the best way to move over a darkened desert trail, lessening the risk of blundering into a cactus or stomping on a rattlesnake. Moving swiftly, they close down the miles to the load-out area where they will hand off the dope to a driver before setting out for home.

The team of burros, or drug mules, work for the rugged cartels in Sonora state—a border strip that was at the time dominated by Los Números, or The Numbers, a violent band of cowboys who operate in the dusty towns on the south side that are protected by drug kingpin Joaquín "El Chapo" Guzmán, one of Mexico's most-wanted men.

They are lean and fit, and they know full well the best ways to beat border police and deliver their pungent, densely packed load of grass. This year, the rain-soaked highlands and plunging canyons of Mexico's Golden Triangle have produced a record crop of the drug over the summer months, which the cartels throw at the border in any way they can.

They choose the steep paths over the mountains as they know the Border Patrol can't follow them even in their sport-utility vehicles, and can only track them with difficulty on horseback and quad bikes. As they head for the ridgeline in the dark, they know to listen for the clatter of the Black Hawk helicopters of the Customs and Border Protection's Air and Marine service, who are just about the only cops that can reach them up there.

The first winking stars come out over the darkened trails, and it is silent. The march is hard going, and the group pauses on the trail for a break. With the weight off their shoulders for a moment, their tension eases. As they sit in the gathering darkness they are in their comfort zone, as these things go, only this time they are wrong. Dead wrong.

Slender and powered by a quiet turboprop engine, the aircraft is flying 15,000 feet above the ground. The lights on its wingtips blink discreetly, and are barely visible at five and a quarter miles away. Combined with the low airspeed, the lights give the impression of a much larger aircraft flying at an even greater distance.

Stealthy and all but invisible, the plane is flying in a loop known as a racetrack pattern. The aircraft is one used by civilian contractors working for the military and the CIA as they scour the mountains of Afghanistan and Pakistan for Al Qaeda and Taliban leaders. The drug smugglers are in fact being tracked by a state-of-the-art Predator B drone.

In a ground control station on the other side of the Huachuca Mountains, CBP Command Duty Officer Dave Gasho studies the steady, sharp, highly magnified infrared images streaming in from the optical "ball" on the belly of the drone, and he has a very clear idea of what he is looking at.

Back in the 1990s, the thirty-nine-year-old pilot flew Citation jets packed with surveillance equipment out of Howard Air Force Base in the U.S.-held Panama Canal Zone. These State Department–assisted missions were to track narcotics shipments in source and transit zones across South America and the Caribbean.

Later, based in Peru, he followed drug flights packed with cocaine as they sped low over the Amazon jungle from clandestine drug labs on the first leg of a journey to market. Years on the job have made him a specialist at spotting, tracking, and interdicting drug smugglers by air.

Now, he looks at the heat from each of the smugglers' bodies picked out in black on the screen, and the cool, bulky rucksacks standing out starkly in white. He studies the group as they sit chatting in the darkness, reading their body language like an open book. "They have no idea they are under surveillance," he says. "If they thought they were being watched, they would hide in a tree."

Gasho picks up the radio in the windowless trailer parked on the grassy corner of a landing strip at a U.S. military base more than thirty miles away. Using an open channel relayed by antennas on the drone, he speaks directly to the crew of a CBP Black Hawk helicopter that is just finishing up a mission helping Border Patrol agents to apprehend a group of illegal immigrants.

The Black Hawk is flying over desert south of Tucson. Gasho gives pilot Rich Rouviere the GPS coordinates of the drug mules, and he wheels the helicopter around in the air and starts closing in fast over the mountains toward the group as they traverse the remote trail.

It is one night after the full moon, and the mountain landscape scrolling beneath the Black Hawk is bathed in ambient light. This is ideal for night vision equipment, which gives him a clear, three-dimensional view.

The copilot sits beside Rouviere in the cockpit. There are two air interdiction agents wearing flak jackets and flight suits in the belly of the chopper. They have handcuffs and sidearms, and they know from the radio traffic they are going to have to jump out and arrest backpackers. The adrenaline is flowing, as they know from experience that they will likely have to belly into the fit young drug mules like linebackers.

Sound travels much more clearly over the desert at night. On the chill hillside, the silence is broken by a low bass rumble. The smugglers look up, scared. They recognize the deep thump of the rotors drawing closer to them across the now ink-black desert floor. They know that it isn't the sound of a Border Patrol A-Star helicopter. It's the heavy military workhorse with the SWAT team in the back.

They pause, listening hard, waiting and hoping for the closing aircraft to veer off and sweep away over the mountains to pick up some of the thousand or more people who trek over the border into Arizona each night from Sonora. But it doesn't. In fact, the sound seems to be coming straight toward them in the darkness.

They break from the path, ditch their drug loads, and scramble for cover beneath a mesquite tree as Rouviere closes the gap implacably, watching the unlit ridgelines slide beneath him in sub-aqua shades through his night vision goggles.

Two minutes out from the target, the sensor operator back at the ground control station types a command into the computer keyboard in front of him, and the word "LASE" blinks up on the monitor screen.

The CBP drone locks on to the group with a laser illuminator that can't be seen by the naked eye, but for Rouviere, looking ahead through night vision equipment, the target area ahead of him is now bathed in a blazing pool of light. "These guys are lasing it now, so as I get close, I'm telling Dave 'I've got the spot.' Not only do I have the spot, I can see the guys under the tree with my night vision goggles. It is lit up like daylight," he later tells me, pausing to give each word emphasis. "It looks like a spotlight on those guys."

He flies right up to the tree, looking down at the group huddled in the dark, their heads bowed. The sound of the Black Hawk is deafening now as it hovers, the vortex of its downdraft thrashing the branches of the mesquite like a flail and whipping up a tornado of dust and debris. Rouviere sets it down lightly.

The smugglers have been looking down at their feet all the while, but now one of them looks up. His expression has all the bewildered candor of the sightless in the dark, and Rouviere and the copilot glance at each other and start to laugh.

"The guy looked up and he went 'whoooah!' It was kind of like 'How did you know we were here?' They were absolutely stunned," Rouviere tells me. "The guy I'm flying with, we look at each other and start laughing. Because we know what's going on next. We know these guys are done, and they know it!"

The air interdiction agents tear out of the back of the chopper, and pounce on three of the men and quickly subdue them. Two other mules take off at a sprint down the darkened hillside, oblivious to the bumps, rocks, and cactuses scattered across their path, in a bid to make it as far away from the helicopter as they can.

Running hard, one trips and plunges headlong down the slope, and in moments an agent is on top of him in a clinch, snapping metal cuffs on his wrists. The other smuggler runs on, blind, picking his feet up as he barrels down the slope, trying to avoid tripping. He runs to a tree. He clasps its trunk, finds hand- and footholds in its low branches, and starts to climb. Further down the slope, several Border Patrol ground agents have arrived on the scene to assist. They set off up the hillside with a tracker dog, searching for a scent as the Black Hawk's rotors churn the air.

The trackers and their dog pass beneath the tree, looking for the fugitive smuggler, unable to locate him as he perches just feet away from them, breathing hard in the darkness. But through the drone's powerful infrared optics, Gasho can see him clear as day. He guides the agents back around to the spot, and they make their last arrest.

All told, from the moment that the drone first spotted the mules to the arrest of the last man, just thirteen minutes have elapsed. Gasho, who has overseen and directed the whole operation from the ground control station, allows himself a smile. Later, he will tell me: "This is textbook. It's as good as it gets."

I speak to Gasho in depth later, when I visit the U.S. Customs and Border Protection drone program, tucked into the corner of a military airfield in the shadow of the Huachuca Mountains, a couple of hours' drive southeast of Tucson.

A klaxon sounds in the chill December morning, and the heavy doors of the tall hangar at the U.S. Army Intelligence Center and School at Fort Huachuca inch back. The space inside echoes like a basketball court, and has the low thrum of sodium yellow lights. I stand on the threshold staring in at the drone.

It is full-sized, with broad wings tall enough to walk under without stooping. It has a sleek gray carbon-fiber fuselage with a slight bump housing the electronics on the nose, which gives it the disquieting look of an eyeless dolphin. Its strange appearance is enhanced by the fact that the aircraft has two sharply raked tail fins instead of a rudder, and, rather than being pulled along by a propeller, it is pushed by a powerful three-bladed turboprop engine mounted in the rear.

As I stand there staring at it for a minute or two, I find myself thinking that if a group of aerospace engineers had been specially tasked to design an aircraft to look stealthy and sinister, they could not have done a better job. The General Atomics Predator B drone looks every inch a spy plane.

The aircraft is flown not by CBP but by civilian contractors, one of whom walks me around the aircraft. In an environment dominated by men in uniforms, Cassandra Hunt stands out, dressed down in jeans and a sweatshirt.

The Colorado native knew from the time she was in junior high that she wanted to be a pilot. With a bachelor's degree in aeronautical science from Embry-Riddle Aeronautical University, she graduated with a commercial pilot's license. Graduates from the specialist school usually go on to have careers in commercial aviation or with the military or even as astronauts working for NASA. But Hunt opted to go into flying the surveillance drones for the San Diego–based General Atomics, and the job is an unusual one.

Rather than soaring into the skies, Hunt heads to a boxlike trailer with no natural daylight. Once inside the dark, enclosed space, she has a virtual cockpit from which she flies the seven-million-dollar aircraft so

Civilian contractor Cassandra Hunt stands in front of the General Atomics MQ-9 Predator B drone she pilots for the U.S. Customs and Border Protection Air and Marine service. Sleek, stealthy, and carrying powerful state-of-the-art optics, it is used to search for intruders in Arizona. (Jeff Topping)

new that, at the time I visited the program, the United States military didn't even have one.

Sitting in the hot seat, she has a video monitor set out before her relaying images from a camera in the nose cone of the drone. To take it up and into the air, she has a joystick and throttle controls on either side of a computer keyboard, as well as rudder pedals tucked on the floor beneath the panel, and hand controls to raise the undercarriage.

The virtual cockpit also has instruments giving her an artificial horizon, as well as information on bearing, airspeed, altitude, and so on, although it doesn't convey what it actually feels like to sit at the controls of a real aircraft. Aside from what their instruments tell them, pilots feel climbing airspeed from the deepening vibrations in the airframe, and they sense a banked turn from the increased g-forces that sink them deeper into their seats. Not here, though.

"You get the same feedback and response from the controls. The only difference is that you can't feel it in the same way, and the camera is just forward-looking, so you don't have peripheral vision," she explains, taking a slow walk around the drone as it stands in a corner of the hangar.

Patiently she points out the gray carbon-fiber dome housing the computers that fly the plane. She indicates the camera lenses fitted into the nose that relay the forward view to the trailer, and the stubby antennas that receive her commands as the aircraft wheels high above the darkened desert corridor.

Then there is the optical package, which is slung beneath the forward section of the drone, packed into a hemisphere that the crew refer to as "the ball." To my eye, it looks a little like R2-D2, the robot from the Star Wars movies, turned upside down and retrofitted in the truly alien-looking craft, and I half expect it to start whistling and beeping.

Hunt actually flies the drone from behind a locked door in the trailer, dubbed the ground control station in the CBP's quasi-military parlance. Locked inside with her is a ground crew directed by the command duty officer, who is one of a roster of active duty pilots for the CBP's Air and Marine wing.

The two officers in charge of the program while I am down there are Gasho and Rouviere. Gasho works a week at the base, then spends a week flying fixed-wing jets for CBP. He swaps with Rouviere, who steps out from behind the controls of the Black Hawk and works at the base for a week.

"When I'm out here for the week, he's back flying a Citation jet; when I'm back at the branch, I'm flying a Black Hawk helicopter. This way we are maintaining our currency as pilots, but more importantly, we stay connected with what's going on in the field," says Rouviere, wearing a camouflaged flying suit and a leather jacket against the chill of the high plains morning.

It is an important detail, he explains, as they are in charge of the law enforcement missions flown by the drone. "We decide where the aircraft goes, why it goes there, what it's going to interdict, and how it's going to

interdict. We manage the ground and air assets [involved in the search],"
he explains.

There are other members of the drone crew working in the command center. Alongside the pilot and CDO is the sensor operator. Another civilian employee, he sits beside Hunt, or the other General Atomics duty pilots, and uses a joystick and keystrokes to control the drone's highly sophisticated spy optics and laser designation system.

The optical ball beneath the drone swivels and turns independently of the aircraft, rather like the protuberant eyes of a chameleon. During taxiing and takeoff, the lens is tucked protectively up underneath in stow position, to stop it from getting chipped by pieces of grit kicked up from the runway.

Made by Massachusetts-based defense and aerospace company Raytheon, the ball comprises a multispectral targeting system. It has a daylight television camera providing streaming video images and an infrared camera that picks up heat as a clear dark image appearing against a cool white background.

The optics have powerful magnification, and can clearly pick out individuals from an altitude of 15,000 feet and a distance of five miles. The package also includes precise instrumentation that displays the aircraft's altitude, direction, and exact location. At the center of the screen are two crosshairs marking the target. Display information shows where it is, and how far it is from the drone in nautical miles, as well as data showing the angle of elevation of the camera.

When I see it in operation, I am taken aback by both the quality and stability of the rolling images shot by the camera. It is like movie footage. The sequence is shot not from above, as I had expected, but at a low angle more than five miles off to the side as the pilot flies in a racetrack holding pattern. The image is crisp, clear, and very stable as the ball effortlessly tracks the target.

Finally, there are two electronics technicians in the closed box environment, who monitor the health of the aircraft. They sit scrolling through data on laptops, checking on the thrum of the turboprop engine, the functioning of the ailerons, and so on, throughout every second of the flight. Seeing them going through their paces, I am reminded of Formula One pit engineers checking on the pitch of a Ferrari engine throughout at a race at Monza, only the crew are keeping a surveillance aircraft up over one of the most heavily crossed land borders on earth. It is a recent deployment of a technology that is only just coming into its own.

The first Predator drones were developed to fly reconnaissance flights in the mid-1990s over the battle-scoured villages of Bosnia and Serbia during the Balkans conflict. The pilotless aircraft had the advantage of being able to fly above the flattened homes and blasted bridges for hours at a stretch, providing real-time battlefield intelligence without risking NATO pilots' lives—an important political consideration following the bloody intervention in Somalia in 1993, in which eighteen U.S. troops lost their lives.

Despite the fact that three of the drones were lost over the Balkans combat zone—two were shot down and one iced up and crashed—the intelligence they provided proved their worth to the military, who in less than a year ordered more than a dozen more to put to work.

The slender aircraft, with its powerful engine and broad carbon-fiber wings providing plenty of lift, had considerable payload capacity, and its essentially passive role morphed into a lethal one after the September 11 attacks. The military, working closely with the CIA, retrofitted the drone with Hellfire antitank missiles bolted to hard points on its wings to give it a "hunter-killer" role in the new and open-ended War on Terror.

Not only could it spot for targets in new theaters of conflict, but it could also take them out. The first opportunity came in late 2002, when a pilot in Djibouti, in the Horn of Africa, flew a drone over Yemen, across the Gulf of Aden, in a CIA-led hunt for an Al Qaeda bomber believed to be behind the attack on USS *Cole* two years earlier.

A tap on a cell phone identified the voice of Qaed Senyan al-Harthi. The drone located him as he drove over the desert with five companions. The crew locked a laser designator onto the vehicle and blasted it with an antitank missile designed to rip into armor. Needless to say, it blasted the truck apart and killed all six people on board.

The drone's systems were later deployed by the CIA and military flying over the high deserts and mountains of Afghanistan and in the tribal areas of northern Pakistan. There the drone broadened the range of its operations, which were monitored in real time by CIA specialists half a world away at Langley, Virginia, providing in one instance close air support to one group of Rangers pinned down by counterinsurgents.

The evident utility of the program did not escape the U.S. Department of Homeland Security, the catch-all government agency tasked with safeguarding the United States from terrorist attacks. If the systems had demonstrated their abilities overflying the rugged redoubts of Al Qaeda in the Middle East and Central Asia, what could they bring to securing the similarly harsh terrain of the Arizona borderlands?

U.S. Customs and Border Protection got its first drone—they in fact prefer the term Unmanned Aerial System, or UAS, to signal its unarmed civilian mission—in the summer of 2004. The first UAS wasn't a Predator, but an Israeli-built Hermes 450 model. The aircraft was rolled out amid a certain amount of fanfare at Fort Huachuca.

As reporters wrote about spy planes making their debut on the border, the program created quite high expectations about what it could achieve. Its subsequent adaptation has been an object lesson in the subtle interplay of trial and error, as the cutting-edge technology is brought in from the military and intelligence services and set to work on the border line.

Working in Mexico at the time, I drove to Fort Huachuca with a colleague from the BBC in a long haul from Monterrey, via El Paso, in the withering heat of late August. We were looking to find out as much as we could about how it worked. Greeted at the main gate by a Border Patrol media liaison agent, we were whisked out to a runway where the aircraft was standing on the tarmac in the gathering dusk.

It was tended by a rather secretive Israeli ground crew who didn't want to give their names, and who offered few insights about how the aircraft was used back in their own country. I asked a technician if they flew it over the disputed Golan Heights or used it to watch over Palestinians in the West Bank, and she simply shrugged, sphinxlike.

The few Border Patrol agents assigned to the program at the time stood aloof in the twilight as the ground crew prepared to take the plane up, and had little positive to say about the new tool sent their way by their overlords in Washington.

The agents I spoke with had a lot of misgivings about the drone. Some of their reluctance to embrace the program seemed Luddite, a kind of lurking suspicion that the new technology might somehow usurp their jobs. The other complaint was that the aircraft made far too much noise—and it was true.

Standing on the grassy fringe of the runway, I looked on as the ground crew powered up the aircraft, which was about bar-top height and the length of a telephone pole. To my surprise it sounded like a very noisy weed whacker laboring to chop down heavy brush in the backyard.

The noise was still audible when the plane was several thousand feet above the ground, and largely destroyed the stealth factor that was so key to its effectiveness as it circled above the darkened mountain and desert borderlands, when even small sounds can travel a lot farther in the still quiet of the desert night.

"It made a lot of noise, even when it was quite high up, and the aliens crossing through the desert know to listen out for it," one Border Patrol agent told me, a detail I corroborated talking with a Guatemalan illegal immigrant who had made it over the trails and through to the Mexican barrios of south and central Phoenix during the trial period with the drone.

The Guatemalan, who now works as a warehouseman in the sprawling state capital, explained how smugglers leading the migrants through the harsh, sun-baked wastes from Sonora had dubbed it *el mosco,* "the fly," for its buzzing overpasses.

Preparing to set out on the trail north, the coyote had schooled the group of Mexicans and Central Americans to listen for the distinctive sound of the aircraft approaching, and drilled them on how to scatter and find cover, creating their own routine of countersurveillance and evasion.

The tips, in fact more mythic than helpful, included painting water jugs black to reduce their visibility to the drone's all-seeing eye, and even, in one totally contradictory instance, advising immigrants to cover themselves with aluminum food wrap from head to foot, to foil the heat signature sought by its infrared cameras. (Note to smugglers: The oven-ready technique is effective at masking some radio emissions and can, for instance, help shoplifters steal clothes fitted with radio frequency identification chips. It is largely useless, though, at stopping significant heat seepage, although seeing a migrant wrapped in foil gives Border Patrol agents a thigh-slappingly good laugh that they will remember years later.)

Another problem with the Hermes drone was the fact its undercarriage remained permanently extended throughout the flight, hanging beneath the slender body of the aircraft as fixed and immovable as the legs of a billiard table.

Aside from any limited aerodynamic or aesthetic hindrance—it really didn't look as sleek and stealthy as a kick-ass spy-plane should—the arrangement also created three permanent blind spots for the surveillance ball cradling more than a million dollars' worth of precision optics.

Rather than having a 360-degree field of vision over the desert landscape, the operator's view was constantly interrupted by the undercarriage, an effect a bit like having a child clap his or her hands over your eyes when you are trying to watch TV: Not only are you unable to see what's going on in the show, but your concentration is broken and the smooth rhythm of your viewing is thrown off.

The Predator B drone, though, has these problems pretty much beat. Its sleek Honeywell turboprop engine winds up like a small jet engine, spinning the propeller slickly and quietly. Some say the slender aircraft is largely inaudible after gaining more than a mile in height, giving it back its vital stealth factor.

The new aircraft bucks the expectations of smugglers pushing through the desert below, many of whom are still listening out for the distinctive horticultural drone of *el mosco,* and are still unaware that it has been superseded. It is this passive role that makes it invaluable in revealing the secret life of the borderlands in all its rich candor.

The Predator B also has the advantage of having a retractable undercarriage that sweeps up after takeoff and tucks into the fuselage, giving the sophisticated optical package an uninterrupted field of view over the desert and mountain landscape below.

Now the crew can get a fix on a group of intruders from several miles away at an altitude at which the drone is all but silent, and coordinate an interception in a way that is almost textbook. However, the process of getting it right has involved one very expensive mistake.

A few months before my second visit to Fort Huachuca, the CBP agency had lost one of the new Predator B drones through human error. It was on a night flight over the desert region south of Tucson, flown by a civilian contractor operating out of the GCS trailer set up alongside the runway at the base.

The pilot and the sensor operator sitting in the hot seats that night were trying to fly the aircraft in an environment full of distractions. At the time, the trailer doors were unlocked. Border Patrol agents and other ground personnel could walk in and out, chipping in advice and making observations in a kind of open arrangement that, if it were a live TV show, would be known as "zoo format."

While it had proved workable for months, the situation led to serious and expensive problems that night in April, as the drone sliced through the dark night far above the babble of conversation and comings and goings in the control room. Newspapers reported that the pilots lost contact with the vehicle at 2:50 A.M. as it patrolled the border region at a height of 12,000 to 15,000 feet.

The unreported story of what happened reveals a cascading series of missteps, triggered by a simple computer crash. Just as a home computer or laptop computer sometimes freezes and requires rebooting, the computerized flight controls of the UAS suddenly froze in a case of "rack lockup."

It shouldn't have been a problem. The aircraft system was designed with backup systems that allow the pilot to switch seats and resume control from the sensor operator's seat alongside. The contractor, perhaps distracted by the interruptions, failed to follow operating procedure, and reset the controls of the drone to the positions it had before the rack froze. When he got back in contact with the drone, the trim and throttle settings were all out. Worse still, he had unwittingly switched off the fuel supply.

The aircraft coasted for a while, losing height as the pilot and crew frantically tried to restart the fuel-starved motor from the trailer. It swooped lower like a paper dart over a schoolyard, finally plowing into the side of a wash at the Morning Star Ranch at around 3:30 A.M., in desert a few miles north of Nogales. Seven million dollars' worth of composite materials, engines, and spy optics were smashed to pieces, although fortunately no one was hurt on the ground.

The costly error revealed several problems at the heart of the program. First off was the fact that it was directed by Border Patrol ground agents who had no direct experience of flight operations. The mission was now given over to CBP aviators with years of experience flying a fleet of both fixed-wing aircraft and helicopters. They set out to treat the operation from beginning to end as what it is: a flight mission.

When operations started up again, Rouviere and Gasho were placed in charge as the CDOs. One of the first moves was to ensure that the ground control station remained free of distractions by locking it from the inside like a civil airliner cockpit in the years since the September 11 attacks. All nonfliers are kept out in a second trailer, parked alongside like a police mobile incident room, connected by an intercom with the fliers.

"This is a sterile cockpit up to ten thousand feet. No one can come in and out of here. The only people that are allowed in here are the pilot, the sensor operator, the command duty officer, and the electronics technician, who monitors the health of the aircraft," Rouviere explains. "The Border Patrol guys are seeing the exact same feed from inside the trailer, and they start coordinating the ground interdiction," he adds, referring to the second trailer, from where Border Patrol ground agents watch the streaming images on a forty-two-inch plasma television.

From there they can watch to their hearts' content, discussing what they are seeing and offering their often invaluable insights to the cockpit through an intercom. If their chatter is too distracting, the flight crew can simply switch the intercom off, shut them out, and get on with their job.

Losing control of the drone also highlighted a need for fully redundant systems operating as backup. When I visited the base, the UAS pilots had a separate ground control station set up in the back of a Humvee parked outside their trailer, which remained fully powered up by thick, hoselike electricity cables, and was ready to go in an instant throughout the UAS flight.

Then there is the issue of ground safety. While the area overflown by the drone is largely unpopulated, it takes off and lands on the outskirts of Sierra Vista, a sprawling boomtown a few miles north of the border, and flies near other remote towns in the Patagonia Mountains. To safeguard them in the event of another communications failure, the drone has now been hardwired to fly itself to designated wilderness areas should the rack lock up again.

The emergency mission is marked out with a red line on the computer screen in front of the pilot in the ground control station. There is a separate mission for each sector the aircraft operates in. The lost drone will fly directly to the designated area and circle around until it runs out of fuel and drops to the ground.

Aside from professionalizing the systems for flying the drone, placing the mission in the hands of highly competent fliers is also important for securing the program's viability with the Federal Aviation Authority. In the eyes of FAA regulators, losing one drone could be regarded as a misfortune—to paraphrase Oscar Wilde—though losing two would look like carelessness.

"If I were the FAA and you had two crashes, I might raise my eyebrows," Rouviere said. "So we are constantly trying to improve the program."

Flight safety aside, there have also been other improvements in the program. Two years of flying the Predator B on the border have also produced a steep learning curve for the operators, who have spent so much time gathered around the screens at Fort Huachuca, planning flights and watching the streaming images from its belly night after night.

Some of its sorties are prompted by intelligence reports, but much of the action is cued by sensors going off. The drone crews have become skilled at directing the drone to watch over known staging areas on the south side of the border in Mexico, looking in the crosshairs of the thermal optics for the black figures as they prepare to cross.

Unwittingly, the different groups under surveillance semaphore to the unblinking eye of the drone and the party of analysts watching on the broad plasma screens in the dark control room, telling them who they are and what they are doing, and allowing them to decide how best to intercept and arrest them once they have crossed.

As I sit in a trailer next to the GCS, Rouviere plays one sequence shot by the drone. The B-roll—as operational footage passed on to the media is known—shows a large group of figures milling around a few yards short of the international line in Mexico, their warm bodies picked out in black against the cool white of the surrounding brush. Suddenly, one figure breaks from the group and crosses a few hundred yards into the United States alone.

"This guy is a scout, and it tells us that the group are probably drug traffickers," Rouviere says, watching the screen closely. Moments later, the milling crowd of figures swiftly arranges itself into a line and files across the border behind him. It is clearly visible in profile that they are all carrying backpacks, and not just the daypacks used by illegal immigrants, but large, bulky loads.

The group are walking purposefully in single file like soldiers on the march. The real tell, though, comes when they reach a road. The ground crew watch as they walk across in single file, each man carefully stepping in the previous one's footprints. Once they are all across, the last one to cross brushes out the foot sign with a mesquite branch. "That's the real giveaway right there," Rouviere says.

When the UAS crew dispatch Border Patrol agents to respond to the group, they know to expect drug mules. They know from experience that members of the group are likely to be armed—carrying anything from a pocketknife to an assault rifle intended to fight off the drug-stealing bandits known as *bajadores*—and will go in better prepared for any trouble.

As well as becoming experts in identifying the groups as they come across, the drone crews are also learning how to use the aircraft to its maximum advantage as a spy plane. That means allowing it to see without being seen, and to do that, it has to beat the vigorous countersurveillance of the Mexican drug and human traffickers, many of whom are equipped with binoculars, two-way radios, and even their own sets of night vision equipment.

Initially, the command duty officers were placing the drone directly north of the border line from busy staging areas in Mexico, until one evening they learned a valuable lesson. The sensor operators spotted a group of people gathering on the south side of the line shortly after dark, and waited for them to cross north into Arizona. They continued to watch, and to their bewilderment, two hours after sunset the group was still sitting there.

Rouviere explains what had happened: "There's some reason why they are not coming across. So we call on the radio, no, there's no agents around there. There's no reason why these guys should not be crossing the border. Well you know what it is? It's us. It's our lights, they see them," he added, speaking of the wingtip navigation lights on the UAS that are required by FAA regulations.

"If you are coming across the border, you are looking north. If you see some lights circling there, isn't that going to bother you? I say, 'Hey, let's go orbit over here for a while.' We do that, guess what?" Rouviere said. "The group gets up and moves. We say 'Aha! They must be reacting to our aircraft,' that's the only logical explanation."

Learning from the experience, the UAS operators now deliberately place the aircraft in the smugglers' blind spots. The deft move heightens the drone's passive role, lulling the illegal border crossers into a false sense of security, and allowing the aircraft to carry on watching the criminal dumb show as it unfolds for the cameras. That in itself carries a whole new set of benefits.

The powerful Raytheon optics not only allow the agents to follow the commission of a crime—groups hauling bales of marijuana either in backpacks or in stolen vehicles, or ushering through a group of aliens on foot as they head north to load-outs en route to Tucson and Phoenix—but allows them to record it as evidence.

After the group is arrested, the streaming video is then passed to prosecutors, giving them incontrovertible evidence of the crime in its entirety, sometimes from the moment of staging on the south side to crossing the border and the moment of arrest.

Rouviere, a fast talker who warms to his theme in conversation, describes one sequence several minutes long that was recorded by the drone as it flew high over the borderlands. It showed armed smugglers driving stolen vehicles stacked with pot across the line from northern Sonora. "You watch them coming across the line and you never lose visual contact up to the actual interdiction. Not only did these guys have narcotics, but they also had firearms and stolen vehicles. For us, that's a slam dunk, that's as good as it gets. It never went to court, because the prosecutors said, 'Beat this.' . . . Every one of them ended up pleading out. . . . When you have that kind of evidence, you have no choice," he says.

For CBP air operations director Martin Vaughan, the successes at spotting, directing interdiction, and providing incontrovertible evidence that enables the courts to jail smugglers are all part of a larger picture. The drone program helps create a tough environment of deterrence.

"There needs to be a consequence, and that's the real key to how effective we are. Ideally we want to get in such a position that anybody that's violating the law we are able to apprehend and then have enough evidence to prosecute that case. That's where the deterrent part comes in," Vaughan explains as he takes a break from a series of meetings at the Tucson air branch. "At some point in time, a smuggler, regardless of what he's smuggling, is going to have to make a decision: Does the benefit outweigh the consequence or not? Our job is to make the consequence so severe, so frequent, and such a possibility that that consequence far outweighs the benefit and financial gain." So far, at least, the program appears to be contributing to that goal.

Now that they feel that they have the right aircraft and the right systems in place for flying it safely and effectively, the next challenge for CBP is to be able to increase the number of drones in the air and extend their operational range.

The program is as yet quite new, and taking its first tentative steps. The CBP air wing in Tucson now has, at the time of writing, four drones. Another crew, which trained in Tucson, recently went to Grand Forks, North Dakota, to begin patrolling with a drone along the Canadian border. Another version is shortly expected to begin marine operations off the coast of Florida.

"We are the first satellite; we are building a core, developing an instructor cadre, the management processes, and the operating procedures. We are going to be a template assisting the other locations as they stand up," Vaughn explains. "One little caveat is that the dynamics in the northern border are not the same. . . . It's a whole different world up there. The northern border varies in terms of terrain and foliage. There are some places where there are seventy-five-foot pine trees. There is a whole different learning curve. Then when you get to the Great Lakes, there's a lot of water they have to deal with. There needs to be an expansion of sea search capabilities for the unmanned aircraft."

It is clear that the UAS crews will be tasked with very different operations there. I ask Vaughan what lessons the crucible on the southwest border has for the drone program as it is rolled out in other areas. He pauses for a moment. "Spending a year in Tucson is like dog years—it's like seven years anywhere else. What you really gain is a rapid learning experience," he says.

The rollout of the drone program is expected to be ramped up over the next two to five years, as the agency aims to get a total of eighteen of the stealth aircraft. They plan to deploy them right around the perimeter of the United States, under an ambitious Department of Homeland Security initiative to ratchet up security on the Mexico border, as well as along the Pacific, Gulf, and Atlantic coasts, and the huge, largely open frontier with Canada.

While cautioning that much could yet happen to change those plans, operators say six of the drones could be earmarked for the Canadian border, six for the Pacific and Atlantic seaboards, and six for the southwest border with Mexico.

Sources in the program think it likely that four of the drones would be based in Arizona, with two more for California and Texas. If technical and bureaucratic hurdles that currently limit the way they are flown are overcome, one possibility would be to have them up in the air around the clock, flying missions on both land borders and on the Pacific and Atlantic coasts. "It has a potential for a big future, [and] the goal is to use it borderwide," says Gasho. "It is kind of an overkill for us to be operating this just around here [in southeast Arizona]. This will go widespread throughout the United States."

The first obstacle to making that change from flying only local missions is in extending the operational range of the drones by changing the communications systems currently used to fly them. Right now, in the early stages of the program, UAS operations are limited to line-of-sight-control—literally keeping them within line of sight with the ground control station—giving them an effective range of about 125 miles from Fort Huachuca. This can currently be extended by taking a mobile ground control station mounted in the back of a Hummer, out into, say, the west desert.

After flying the drone to the limit of its range, the pilot can hand off control to the mobile GCS out in the wilderness, thereby effectively doubling the drone's operational range. Nevertheless, it still only covers just a little over a tenth of the whole two-thousand-mile border, and remains severely limited. That looks likely to change in coming years, with a switch to satellite communications, which already exist and are in use by the military.

Under the satellite system, the ground control station and crew at the three sites along the southwest border would coax the drones off the ground, much like a plate-spinning act at the Chinese State Circus. Then they would hand over control through the KU band—a microwave frequency pioneered by TV networks to receive feed from reporters and affiliates via satellite from remote locations—to pilots at the CBP's Air Marine Operations Center at Riverside, California.

"In the future, we'll take the UAS off and hand off to Riverside and they will fly it," said Rouviere, standing among a group of technicians and engineers on the apron outside the hangar used to house the drone. "The only thing we will do here is launch and recovery."

At present, the drone is also restricted by FAA regulations in terms of how high and where it can fly. Under the current rules, it is kept below 19,000 feet. If, as is hoped, the FAA relaxes its airspace rules for the aircraft, then they would be allowed to reach their maximum ceiling of around 50,000 feet—a whole mountain range above the ceiling for commercial jets.

It is far from clear that it would be a useful surveillance tool at its operational ceiling, although bumping up the altitude would bring several benefits. Gaining more height would naturally increase the stealth factor—even straining through binoculars it would be difficult to actually see the aircraft, and not even a jittery jackrabbit or prairie dog could hear it—and it would also give it a much greater fuel efficiency.

While the drone is unlikely to fly surveillance missions at its ceiling height, flying up toward 50,000 feet might be helpful for getting it places. It would allow the aircraft to climb above weather systems to give it a smoother ride and, again, greater fuel efficiency when it is sent on its way to an area to spot. This might prove a useful function up on the

Canadian border, which is, all told, more than twice the length of the southwest border.

With the turboprop engine burning lean at more than one and a half times the height of Everest, the drone could be kept up in the air for longer, enabling it to fly much greater distances, for periods of more than thirty hours at a stretch. At the middle-ranging altitudes where CBP plans to use it for surveillance, it would be able to stay aloft for twenty-two hours.

"Just imagine," one engineering contractor told me as we stood in weak winter sunshine on the apron of the runway at the base. "The pilot and sensor operator would come in to work in the morning, get the drone up in the air and fly it for eight to ten hours, then hand it off to another crew and go home to bed. When they came onto the base the next morning, they'd land the UAS."

To adjust to the possibility of flying surveillance missions at a higher altitude, the optical ball under the aircraft has also recently been upgraded. The new system is substantially larger than the current ball, and carries a more powerful set of cameras that allows it to record crisp day and night images from the upper end of its useful surveillance range. The images are so clear that it is almost like watching a black-and-white television set, operators say.

If it became possible to maintain several drones, each with longer operating hours, one possibility is that each sector of the border could one day have a drone in the air around the clock, monitoring activity day and night, with its specialist teams of pilot, sensor operator, and CBP command duty officer. The extended time and range of the operations would likely make them much more efficient at detecting and classifying intruders.

After several visits to the program over a three-year period, I am impressed by what I see there. While there are legitimate questions to be asked about how cost-effective this system really is, it does bring something unique to border security, and it is flown by highly competent and experienced crews. Quite how far it will go remains to be seen, but it works, and the crews are learning constantly.

"As far as the UAS system goes, we are still in the test and evaluation phase, and that's going to go on for a little bit longer, especially as we open up other branches," Rouviere said. "We continue to improve on the plan. As we learn more, as we experience more, we try to fine-tune the operation."

I felt, talking to Rouviere and other border police out in the desert, that I was getting a sense of some of the highly innovative ways that the line is actually secured from traffic headed north.

But what, I wondered, was to stop smugglers from going under it?

EIGHT

Going Underground

Housed in a gleaming white building, Mecalux looks more like a high-tech manufacturing plant than a distribution warehouse. But the firm based in the Border Business Park in Otay Mesa, California, imports industrial shelving from an assembly plant in Tijuana, Mexico. The unit's apron has a constant stream of flatbed trucks coming in from the border crossing nearby to be briskly unloaded by forklifts turning tight pirouettes in the busy parking lot.

As at dozens of other logistics companies scattered across the tree- and shrub-lined business park, the warehousemen take the merchandise into the loading bays and load it back up onto trucks hauling the products up the nearby Interstate 5 to clients in the greater Los Angeles area.

With rents for industrial space running at around $35,000 a month, the logistics business depends on receiving high volumes of goods from Mexican *maquiladoras* and turning them around fast. And they are good at what they do. Neighbors clustered in the park include UPS Supply Chain Solutions and NYK Logistics, as well as the stateside distribution operations of consumer electronics giants Hitachi, Bose, and Pioneer.

Working every day amid a flurry of activity, Mecalux warehouseman Luis Barraza immediately sensed there was something wrong with their new neighbor in the park, V & F Distributors LLC. The logistics firm at the large warehouse opposite had only one small pickup truck parked on the broad asphalt apron out back. Furthermore, the firm almost always had the doors of its dozen loading bays rolled tightly shut to the world outside.

"It didn't feel like they were operating at all, as they didn't have any business either coming in or going out," Barraza said as he looked across the service road and empty parking lot in front of the neighboring depot. "There was just that little white pickup truck parked on gate ten. Sometimes it would be there for a couple of days and then it would be gone for a couple of days. Whenever they opened a gate you could see right across to the other street as the warehouse was completely empty. We used to mess around all the time, joking that they were laundering money, but then the day we came in and all the police were there, we were in shock!"

The truth about the neighbors at V & F Distributors LLC was in fact much darker than Barraza and the others guys joshing around on the Mecalux apron had ever guessed. The barnlike warehouse measured 48,000 square feet, with an adjoining space of 4,000 square feet of offices set over two floors. Yet the only person on site was a Mexican watchman, forty-four-year-old Carlos Cardenas Calvillo. He made his base in the director's suite on the second floor, which has a commanding view of Siempre Viva Road out front, and, way in the distance, offers a glimpse of the tail fins of jets taxiing at Tijuana International Airport.

At night he would unfurl a bedroll on the gray carpet and watch Spanish-language shows on a small fourteen-inch color television. The reception was good despite the coat-hanger aerial, and all told, the arrangement was fairly comfortable. The movement in the corner office on the first story barely would have disturbed him. When the floor hatch, disguised with four large cream-colored ceramic tiles, was pushed up from below and rolled silently across the floor on rubber-tired casters toward the women's restroom next door, the only noise would have been that of stealthy unloading as packet after packet was tossed up out of the darkened opening and stacked in a laborious process, which often took hours.

The tunnel was the longest, deepest, and among the most sophisticated ever to run under the U.S.-Mexico border. Found in the last week of January 2006, it spanned a distance equivalent to eight football fields. While spectacular, the find was hardly unique. Since the September 11 attacks, more than forty tunnels have been unearthed running under the United States' borders, all but one of them ducking under the frontier from Mexico to cities in California and Arizona. That other tunnel began in Canada and emerged in Washington state, and, like most of the others, was used to smuggle drugs.

The surge in tunneling activity, coming in an age of jangled nerves over terrorist attacks, is a headache for the U.S. Department of Homeland Security. Concerned that the clandestine passageways might be used to smuggle terrorists and weapons of mass destruction into the United States, the department recently set up a crack federal task force (little known outside law enforcement circles) to combat the phenomenon in California, where twenty-one of the tunnels bored north from Mexico emerged. This was the group's first major success. Remarkably, the task force was on to the tunnelers before they had even come up stateside.

Since their group was set up in 2004, members of the San Diego Tunnel Task Force had been meeting weekly in a federal building a mile or so from the V & F Distributors depot, close to the border crossing in Otay Mesa. The Operations Alliance headquarters is the only unmarked building in a quiet side road filled with successful, high-turnover businesses with corporate logos and signs and neatly landscaped parking lots. For visitors attending meetings there, the sophisticated security cameras act as a discreet shingle, quietly flagging the sensitive operations coordinated from inside.

The group drew on input from field agents seconded from the Border Patrol, Customs and Border Protection, Immigration and Customs Enforcement, and the Drug Enforcement Administration. All of the

A Mexican federal agent stands guard in the tunnel
shortly after it was discovered. (Nancee Lewis,
The San Diego Union-Tribune/ZUMA)

agencies represented around the long wooden table in a windowless
conference room worked for the DHS or Justice Department, but had
never before sat down to pool their resources and work on this single
problem. Busting the tunnelers restlessly probing the U.S. border to
haul in narcotics and undocumented immigrants required new syner-
gies, and finding them, they believed, would depend on intelligence
provided by each agency.

Two of the agencies involved are uniformed, although the agents
wore civilian clothes and drove unmarked vehicles to attend the meetings. The Border Patrol agents at the table brought a close-up knowledge

of the front line in San Diego County, a dusty strip ceaselessly patrolled by their own in sport-utility vehicles, on quad bikes, and even on horseback. They had more experience than anyone at finding "gopher holes"—short, shallow passageways with little or no reinforcement that allowed just enough room for immigrants to wriggle north to California on their knees and elbows.

Equipped with backhoes and bulldozers, the agents get to bust them open and fill them in with dirt and, in urban areas, green cement that stands out from the asphalt. The agents working the border line get to know every inch of the strip, the faces of the coyotes, or traffickers, who watch and probe the border. They would also be passing back and forth over any tunnel running under the border in the area, and past the houses, shops, and businesses that would inevitably disguise the entrance and exit points in both the United States and Mexico. They would become the eyes and ears of the investigation along the border line.

The detectives around the table were the plainclothes operators from ICE and the DEA, many of them seasoned agents with years of experience snaring drug smugglers and immigrant trafficking gangs. Both of the organizations had agents working undercover on either side of the border. Their work involves developing intelligence networks, and some of the best informers they have are small-time criminals arrested on drug offenses.

Small-time mules nabbed with dope crossing the border or in the tough streets of San Diego's crime-ridden Barrio Logan district could be offered reduced jail time in return for giving up their bosses, the higherups in a trafficking operation with international reach. The agents, many of whom were young and bilingual, also got out on the border line and talked to homeowners and shopkeepers, who sometimes saw things that they couldn't even know were relevant to the investigation. Perhaps noisy trucks hauling dirt out of a depot bugged them, or maybe they saw an outflow of water. While it looked to them like a fractured water main, to a DEA or ICE agent it could indicate a marine salvage pump laboring in the darkness deep underground to keep a tunnel dry.

Just a few months after they had started meeting in the Otay Mesa war room, the Tunnel Task Force's web of observers, contacts, and informants started to jangle. Their threads of intelligence were beginning to snare chatter on both sides of the border indicating that someone in Tijuana had started digging. By early 2005 the sources told them that the tunnel was no gopher hole, but a big underground passageway, most likely built to smuggle drugs.

"At that stage, we still didn't have any specific information that would get us any further. It went from being information about generalities of a big tunnel to 'We think it's in this area, Otay Mesa, out by Tijuana airport,'" said Frank Marwood, ICE's senior special agent in charge in San Diego. "Then about two to three months prior to the discovery, we got enough specific information that we as law enforcement in the United States could independently start doing some surveillance activity."

It was now time to reach out beyond the Tunnel Task Force and their respective Homeland Security and Justice Department overlords to a special military unit within the Defense Department. Originally called Joint Task Force Six, the combined services team was founded in 1989 specifically to provide engineering, communications, and intel support to federal police going after drug traffickers on the Mexico border.

With the War on Terror in the wake of 9/11, the group's mission was expanded to cover the gray area between homeland defense and homeland security known as "the seam," and the group's name changed to Joint Task Force North (JTFN). For several years the unit had been developing cutting-edge geoscience technologies, including next-generation ground radar, magnetometers, and seismic detectors to search for "discreet voids" left by man-made tunnels.

Their work has attracted serious Defense Department attention as it also has key military applications in the war in Afghanistan, where the search for Osama bin Laden has focused on caves at Tora Bora on the Pakistan border. Aided by the California National Guard and Border Patrol, they went to work peering deep into the clay subsoil in the border strip north of Tijuana International Airport, while the Tunnel Task

Force team ramped up surveillance operations through their respective agencies.

Working up intel is a part of all ICE and DEA agents' routine. But the operation now in hand involved a full-scale deployment on the U.S. side of the border. Digging a tunnel is costly, time consuming, and involves an array of logistical problems in terms of removing dirt and water. All previous experience hunting tunnels suggested that the passageway would come up through a shaft in either the first or second line of warehouses in the business park. DEA and ICE special response teams with video equipment, night vision goggles, and directional microphones took up positions on the flat warehouse roofs overlooking targeted depots, monitoring workers and contractors as they came and went.

Other agents packed into unmarked vans or walked the business park on foot, looking for anything unusual or suspicious. This kind of surveillance operation commonly uses two distinct teams. The first operates up front and would not usually be noticed by average workers going about their everyday business, but may arouse the suspicion of individuals knowingly breaking the law and conducting their own countersurveillance sweep. That is where the second team comes in. Their job is not to watch, but to establish a presence near the target, and their arrival usually goes unnoticed. Should the first team's cover be blown, the second is in there, and operating almost invisibly.

But before the surveillance and JTFN operations could make any headway, the final piece of the puzzle fell into place, not in the Border Business Park, but south in Tijuana.

Tunnel Task Force intel had pinpointed a corrugated-iron-clad warehouse set a few yards back from a busy six-lane highway about half a mile east of Tijuana International Airport as the starting point for the tunnel. The depot was tucked behind a truck junkyard and a firm offering yellow dump trucks, earth movers, and backhoes for rent, and its white rooftop was just visible from over the border. The final push would now have to come on the south side through the Mexican authorities.

U.S. federal law enforcement officials describe their relationship with their Mexican counterparts as, at best, "arm's length." Underpaid and working in an environment of graft, time and again their federal police operations have been compromised by the cartels. In a bid to break free of the past, the Mexican government founded the AFI, a new federal unit like the FBI, although a videotape that surfaced around the time of the tunnel dig apparently showed several of its agents moonlighting as enforcers for the ascendant Sinaloa cartel. In one gruesome shot, a man who appears to be an AFI agent shoots a bound Gulf cartel captive in the head with a .45 caliber pistol in a brutal act that raised doubts about the integrity of the new force. Several agents were reportedly arrested in connection with the filmed execution.

Despite their reservations, the task force had no option but to tip the Mexican authorities off and rely on them to initiate the takedown. The *federales* rolled into action, sending a squad of more than thirty Federal Preventative Police and a contingent of soldiers to throw a cordon around the warehouse. Clad in gray paramilitary uniforms and flak jackets, they were led by a twenty-two-year army veteran dubbed El Capi (short for *el capitán*) and the PFP commander, whom everyone called *el comandante*.

The Mexican crew had pistols strapped into thigh holsters, and toted high-powered assault rifles, a level of armament that was entirely appropriate to the task in hand. When the federal units move on a drug bust, they go in hard, as they know full well what they are up against. The cartel security details for the Arellano Félix Organization in Tijuana have AR-15 and AK-47 assault rifles, which they usually fire on full automatic. Any encounter in the warehouse would likely be a close-up war with hundreds of high-velocity rounds fired in a space barely large enough to hold a cockfight.

Since the tunnel spanned the border, the takedown would involve a U.S. federal agent. In among the *federales* was an ICE agent seconded to the U.S. consulate in Tijuana. Bearded and with long hair, he looked more like a drummer from an East L.A. rock band than a cop, which only made him more effective working undercover on the south side. He would move in with the Mexicans. If they found a tunnel and pushed through it, control would pass to him before they emerged on the north side. They were ready to go, although there was a holdup. No one could move until a search warrant came in from the authorities in Tijuana.

The delay was maddening. Ahead, behind sliding barn doors that lay shut to them, could be the tunnel that they had worked for more than a year to find. Now they would have to wait patiently outside until the right form could be signed and stamped by the *licenciado,* as graduate department heads and line managers in Mexico are known. Late in the afternoon of January 25 it came through.

The PFP hit the depot fast and fanned out, shouting, "*¡Policía! ¡Muéstrense!*" ("Police! Show yourselves!") Breathing hard, they trained their rifles around the depot. In the first few moments, all they could make out was two white trucks and a wall of sawn and stacked lumber, although the building itself was deserted.

Then they saw it.

Attached to one of the building's upright steel beams was a pulley system poised tantalizingly above a concrete hatchway set into the floor. It led to a six-by-twelve-foot cinder block–lined shaft, reinforced on each corner and plunging to a depth equivalent to an eight-story building. Peering over the lip was a vertiginous experience. The only way down was on a red steel stepladder embedded into the wall.

As some of the PFP agents provided cover, a group filed one by one into the abyss. They gripped tight to the uprights, trying not to lose their footing on rungs worn to a steely sheen by frequent use. Touching down on a concrete plinth at the bottom of the shaft, they saw an opening rising up in an arch. It was tall enough to stand up in. They didn't need the flashlights that they had brought with them to explore it, as the passageway was fitted out with electric lights ranged along the wall. Looking down the tunnel neatly hewn from the clay, they saw it had a concrete floor and powered ventilation and drainage systems packed into two-inch plastic piping stretching on ahead of them. The opening beckoned.

With rifles locked and loaded, the group moved into the tunnel. Ahead lay an eerie voyage, a trip that would take them careening off into the darkness like a theme park ride. The Mexicans took the lead, with the unarmed ICE agent following behind.

The way ahead was partially blocked by dozens of bulky cardboard boxes, some stacked three deep in the tunnel while others were stuffed into wheelbarrows parked along the wall. They gave off a strong, pungent reek that all drug cops immediately recognize: marijuana.

Each box contained two to three bales of Mexican-grown grass, tightly wound in plastic tape. The group edged past the boxes, following the passageway as it sloped down to a low point filled with thigh-deep water, then climbed up and leveled off, opening up a view of the route ahead that made some gasp.

The passageway was not a short run ducking up to a borderline depot as they had thought, but reached out ahead of them in a long, straight run. It was so long, in fact, that the neatly finished walls and strip of lights converged into a vanishing point far in the distance.

"We had been to a lot of tunnels that the Border Patrol had come across, and those tunnels are crude—you pretty much crawl on your hands and knees, there's no lighting for some of them—but this was different," recalled the first DEA agent to pass through it. "The fact that you could walk upright comfortably was, well, fantastic is the only word for it . . . and it wasn't until you turned around that you realized you had been walking for about ten minutes."

The agents followed the path north on its straight run past a string of lightbulbs hanging at regular intervals, which acted like spacers to help them mark the distance walked. The passageway itself, with its walls and ceiling scarred with pickax marks, had the cool feel of a wine cave. It was littered with traces of its builders, who had left half a dozen wheelbarrows as well as carrier bags and clothing hanging from pegs in the walls.

At last they started to climb as the sweeping passageway veered off and up through the compacted clay. Following the trail, the agents saw the smooth floor give way to rough concrete risers worked into the floor for traction, as the roof lowered above them. A few steps farther on they saw broken plastic ground sheeting above their heads, then the concrete tablet of the foundation. They were coming up under a building. Ahead of them the shaft drew up short, beneath . . . what? Then they saw it: a neat, square opening above them.

The opening had been sealed with a steel plate a yard square. On the underside it had a swivel-mounted rubber wheel in each corner. When the smugglers raised it from below with a heave, it would glide silently across the tiled floor.

The *capi* and the *comandante* held the group quietly in the opening, waiting for the ICE agent to make it up the last few yards. After slipping under the border to California, it was now his jurisdiction. Raising themselves up and out of the tunnel, they saw they were in the corner office of a large warehouse, empty but for two forklift trucks and some flat packed boxes.

The ICE agent opened the door of the warehouse and stepped out blinking into daylight. He was so far back from the border that at first he could see no cops, and no pointers to locate the exit in the industrial park. Reaching for his cell phone, he called the team leader.

"I'm out on the north side. Where are you guys at?"

Law enforcement officers arrested the warehouse guard, Cardenas Calvillo, who was charged with conspiracy to import and distribute narcotics in the United States. A legal resident, but with no work permit, he was jailed without any application for bail as he was deemed to be a flight risk.

The warehouse had been rented to a distribution company, V & F Distributors LLC, on a five-year lease for $2 million back in August. The company had incorporated in California two months earlier. With no guarantors in the United States, the lease holders were required to pay three months' rent up front and a further four months' rent as deposit, an amount totaling $244,000.

Two principals were listed for the company, one with an address in San Diego, the other south in Tijuana. A reporter following up on the trail found that the San Diego address given by one principal was in fact that of a downtown car dealership where staff had never heard of him. The owner of the dealership had occasionally received mail addressed to the individual, but, puzzled, had sent it back to the post office.*

As the criminal investigation ramped up north of the border, the Tunnel Task Force was already at work trying to determine how the tunnel had been made, how long it had been open, and what on earth had gone through it. To do so, a few days later they brought a team of mining engineers from the coalfields of Kentucky. Decked out in hard hats, the men started by measuring the tunnel, and determined that it was 2,400 feet in length from the silolike shaft in Tijuana to the trapdoor in the warehouse floor.

The sandstonelike clay had been worked out by hand using pickaxes and electrical jackhammers used by professional and hobby builders alike to strip out concrete and plaster in refurbishment jobs. The consultants calculated that it took the Mexican builders up to two years to chip out the tunnel, although they could not be certain. "The reason they can't pinpoint that more fully is that they don't know how many people they had constructing it, or whether or not they were working twenty-four/seven," Marwood later told me. "The experts think they didn't [work around the clock], and that it took between one and two years."

The scale of the operation required to push the tunnel for half a mile through the clay and into the United States soon became clear. A rough calculation by civil engineers involved in the search pegged the amount of dirt taken out of the tunnel at 2,300 cubic yards. Since five or six cubic yards will fill a hard-sprung dump truck, the investigators calculate that it would have taken at the very least four hundred truckloads to shift all the debris, which was all relayed out to the surface by hand.

"It was a huge human endeavor, because there was no mechanical lift. I think they were just pulling the dirt up that eighty-foot shaft and out of there by hand," said one DEA agent with a background in civil engineering who worked on the case.

The stream of trucks calling to take away the dirt would likely have

---

*Leslie Berestein, "Drug Tunnel's on Hot-Potato Property," *San Diego Union-Tribune,* January 28, 2006.

attracted attention if the tunnel had been dug from California, where waste removal requires permits. But in Mexico, where regulations, if they exist, are often poorly enforced, it would have been easier to somehow spirit the huge quantity of dirt away. Furthermore, agents say, with a busy six-lane highway running outside the Mexican depot, and with trucks pulling into the junkyard above ground, it would have been much easier to pull off on the south side.

The scale of the undertaking aside, investigators were soon convinced that the tunnel had been built with the help of professional mining engineers. Apart from its neat finish, the passageway had been very carefully thought out from the spot it broke ground to the exit point north of the border, with the idea of structural integrity and concealment always in mind.

Investigators found that the entrance on the Mexican side had been deliberately recessed two feet into the dirt floor in the warehouse, and capped with four steel-reinforced concrete slabs. It had been built like that so that it could be backfilled and covered up with dirt after use and then tamped down to leave it well hidden. Had the cartel done that on the day the PFP squad burst through the door, the tunnel beneath their feet might never have been found.

Then there was the tunnel itself. The compacted clay subsoil is prone to drying, cracking, and settling. Dropping down to eighty-five feet, the Mexican builders reached a depth less prone to contraction, and at a sufficient distance below ground to minimize the shockwaves from traffic rumbling along the heavily potholed highway above, and the tremors from the sometimes heavy landings of more than 120 commercial jets a day at Tijuana International Airport nearby. The depth also took the tunnel way beneath the utilities trenches dug in the clay of the Border Business Park, where contractors grade new buildings' foundations down to twenty feet before backfilling with more than a yard of sand.

The Kentucky consultants worked patiently, casting an experienced eye along the underground gallery. They noted the gentle gradient the builders had given to the tunnel, which sloped down to its lowest point on the Mexican side of the border. The slope allowed groundwater to drain into the darkened dip, which, they say, functioned as a water trap. The tunnel operators then used pumps to suck up the pooling ground-water and relay it up and out of the shaft. Ingeniously, it was then fed into a large five-hundred-gallon domestic cistern hidden in the back of the sturdy box van parked in the warehouse. The stealthy tanker truck could be driven away and the water discreetly dumped in storm drains elsewhere in Tijuana, so as not to arouse suspicion.

The effectiveness of the hidden drainage system became immediately apparent in the hours after the discovery, when the water level in the deepest part of the tunnel crept steadily to chest height, creating the risk of electrocution should the string of bulbs lighting the underground gallery take a dunking. To make sure that the area remained safe for investigators, U.S. Navy salvage divers trained to pump out flooded compartments in ships foundering at sea were called in on day four to help investigators keep the underground passageway open.

Early newspaper reports noted that the passageway overran its desti-nation and backtracked, creating an impression of the tunnelers as bumbling amateurs who had, in fact, gotten lost underground. But the real reason for the detour was puzzled out by the Tunnel Task Force as the investigation drew on, and sheds interesting light on the way in which the diggers worked in cooperation with the cartel bosses and moneymen. Agents believe that the digging crew received only general instructions about the area to head for in the Border Business Park while the cartel negotiators worked to secure an exit point in the area.

"It seems much more plausible to us now that the tunnelers thought that they had to go to a different location. Then this site became avail-able, and so they just stopped, came back this way, and tunneled straight up to this site, which just shows how accurate they were. . . . It's a feat," Marwood said. To hit right on that mark after boring through hundreds of yards of clay also required quite extraordinary navigational skills.

"Tools such as magnetic compasses and GPS handheld satellite navi-gation systems don't work underground," said one agent involved in the case. "Guiding the tunnel by dead reckoning was also out as it requires getting someone to take an accurate measurement above ground and start from a known starting point, a luxury that they didn't have."

Working in the dark, way underground, investigators say, the digging crew had state-of-the-art surveying equipment to keep the tunnel correctly oriented in three dimensions. This would likely have included professional laser levels: tripod-mounted tools that look something like a small telescope and throw a sharp, piercing red beam ahead of them into the darkness. The tool provides measurements with tolerances as tight as one quarter of an inch over a hundred feet, and would have enabled the builders to keep the passageway straighter than a pool cue as they tracked it north. Using this in conjunction with a surveying pole, they would have ensured that the slope rose at the determined angle as they brought the gallery up, inch by inch, toward its exit point amid the unsuspecting bustle of the business park, where the logistics firms haul merchandise round the clock for next-day delivery throughout the west.

All evidence in the tunnel suggested that the cartel had been using it from the moment they opened the exit. Neatly finished for most of its length, the tunnel's final stretch was crude, rough hewn, and improvised, with ripped-up cardboard boxes replacing the neat concrete floor in some stretches, while the walls and roof became more like a burrow than a passageway. Investigators found a large quantity of wooden props and cut lumber in the warehouse on the Mexican side of the border, which they believe the builders were planning to use to shore up the last stretch of the tunnel at a later date. "They had built the tunnel and were using it prior to them being through constructing it. The tunnel wasn't safe. All of that lumber was there to come back through and shore up the tunnel so it would not collapse. As soon as they could open it, that's when they started using it," Marwood said, adding that he believed it had been open for about two months before it was discovered.

As they pieced together the riddle of its construction, the Tunnel Task Force also tried to determine just what the cartel had been running through it in the time that it had been open. With their homeland security role uppermost, their first priority was to sweep the shaft, tunnel, and warehouses on either end for radiation. Their major concern was that it had been used to smuggle materials that could be used to make a so-called dirty bomb, an easy-to-assemble doomsday contraption that gives more sleepless nights to counterterrorism professionals than anything else. While never yet used in a terror attack, it would likely consist of nuclear materials detonated with conventional explosives such as dynamite or C4. Experts say the blast would scatter low-level nuclear contamination over an area of perhaps a few city blocks. Though residual radiation levels from any such attack are unlikely to prove fatal to many people, it would sow terror nationwide.

The simplest way of obtaining the nuclear materials needed would be to strip down an X-ray machine, a piece of equipment containing a radioactive core that is in hospitals, dentists' offices, and veterinary clinics everywhere. Even though all X-ray machines in the United States have to be registered with the Bureau of Radiation Control, which can then keep track of them, the stringency of their oversight has in the past been questioned. Mexican controls are unknown.

In an effort to screen for nuclear contraband, all CBP inspectors are equipped with key-fob-sized radiation detectors. They have them permanently activated when they process vehicles and pedestrians crossing through ports of entry. The detectors are calibrated to pick up even low levels of trace radiation and are so sensitive that agents sometimes receive an alert only to find it had been triggered by a driver or pedestrian who had recently received radiation therapy for cancer. Another common false positive at the ports is triggered by kitty litter, a mix of gravel that contains trace background radiation.

As soon as the tunnel was secured, agents equipped with radiation detectors swept it, but came up blank. Whatever it had been used for, it had not served as a back channel to smuggle an improvised nuclear weapon.

A parallel concern within the DHS is that tunnels of this type could be used to smuggle undocumented immigrants, and possibly terrorists, north to the United States. The fear also generates a lot of chatter on Internet blogs, where list subscribers often see a natural kinship between olive-skinned Mexican drug runners and Arab militants, who, they feel, look pretty much the same and are both engaged in outlaw activities detrimental to U.S. interests. But law enforcement authorities discount an alliance in general, on the grounds that drug traffickers are ruthless pragmatists seeking to make a profit. They would know that aiding terrorists would draw way too much heat on their activities.

Furthermore, a criminal endeavor such as a drug tunnel requires total discretion to be able to function. Its existence would remain on a strict need-to-know basis within cartel command structures, and the possibility of opening it up to fee-paying outsiders would be nil, investigators say.

"You would never bring an economic alien through a big tunnel like the one that was found here," one law enforcement agent working the case said. "They know that down the road, if that person ever gets arrested, the first thing that's going to come out of his mouth is 'Get me legal status and I'll tell you how I came into the United States.'"

The tunnel was likely used for a range of smuggling activities tied to the cross-border drug trade from Mexico, worth by some estimates $30 billion a year. With respect to northbound traffic, the Tunnel Task Force believes that it was used as a conduit for all the drugs that they regularly see at the ports of entry in Southern California: namely marijuana, cocaine, heroin, and methamphetamine.

While only marijuana was found in the tunnel—more than two tons of it with a street value of around $10 million—they say that in strict business terms, it made much more sense for the traffickers to use the tunnel to run the other higher-value narcotics north. Pound for pound, cocaine, heroin, and meth can reap up to ten times more than marijuana in profit, and consequently represent harder-to-bear losses in terms of interdiction at ports of entry. "With a tunnel, whatever you send down it you'll get out the other side; you're not going to lose a percentage of it to interdiction," said one DEA agent. "If you hide it in a car, it could get caught at the border. If you give it to a backpacker jumping the fence, he could get caught. But if I give you a pound of drugs and you stick it in that tunnel, then a pound of drugs is going to come out in the U.S."

At the point of consumption in homes, in clubs, and on street corners nationwide, narcotics are generally taken in fairly small quantities. Cocaine is cut up into little lines on a pocket mirror or a toilet seat, while marijuana is scattered frugally in a joint. Moving up the line to the level of dealers, stashes of cocaine, heroin, and meth may fill a bag around the size of a five-pound bag of sugar, or, with marijuana, perhaps a container as large as a duffel bag filled with loose-packed buds and leaves. In short, the quantities are readily portable, and the question of the physical effort required to transport them never really arises.

But the drug trade in California is high volume and high weight. In one recent year, federal agencies in the state seized two hundred tons of the four drugs that likely went through the tunnel, and that total would only be a fraction of what actually made it through to the market. The picture that emerges from the investigation, then, is one of a tunnel operating around the clock, with traffickers engaged in hard physical labor in the darkened passageway to haul bulky, multiton loads of all kinds of narcotics north to the Otay Mesa warehouse, most likely using a fleet of rusty wheelbarrows found in the tunnel to do so.

It would have involved a massive human effort, something like a busy construction site swinging up into full operation. The two tons of marijuana found dumped in the tunnel mouth was broken down into three hundred bales, two or three of which would fit into a standard barrow. Just to shift it across the border would have taken a dozen men ten round-trip journeys through the tunnel, each leg taking ten to fifteen minutes. It is easy to imagine them moving the loads with the squeak of the barrows echoing down the tunnel, their arms burning with the effort of pushing them up the last sixty-foot slope to the tunnel mouth.

Pushing the hefty door out of the way would have been the least of the effort, as they passed bale after bale of dope, and multiple two-pound packets of cocaine, out to the cavernous loading bay. The smaller, high-value loads of methamphetamine and "black tar" heroin would have been the easiest, gathered up into packs weighing at the most ten pounds.

While drugs get smoked, snorted, and shot up throughout the San

Diego area as elsewhere in the United States, in terms of the overall trade it is not so much an end point as a transit hub. Just two minutes from I-905, the Border Business Park would have served as an ideal place to start distributing drugs, just as it does for the logistics businesses dispatching truckloads of flat-screen televisions and speakers throughout the United States. Any truck leaving the park is on I-5 north to Los Angeles in twenty minutes.

Furthermore, while rural roads in the states bordering Mexico are dotted with Border Patrol checkpoints, the sprawling urban area accessed from the park is subject to little more monitoring by law enforcement than any average U.S. city or highway network. While it is not clear how the gang distributed the drugs—whether in U-Haul vans or in private trucks and cars—evidence from former investigations suggests that they almost certainly flowed out of the park to all places north and east, including Los Angeles, Chicago, and perhaps even New York.

It also seems unlikely that the flow was all one way. Analysts in Mexico say the tunnel was almost certainly used as a conduit to smuggle contraband south of the border. First and foremost, this consisted of cash profits from the multibillion-dollar drug trade. Success in cracking down on money laundering in recent years has considerably frustrated the cartels. In the heyday of the 1980s and 1990s, U.S.-based drug distribution networks could very simply repatriate billions of dollars in profits by, in many cases, wiring them back to Mexican or South American suppliers in bank transfers, or laundering them through banks like the now defunct BCCI.

Alternately, they could launder the funds north of the border by buying real estate, cars, and even caprices such as Thoroughbred horses with cash, building up a hefty stateside asset base. But a severe blow was dealt to them in 2000, when a federal law made reporting cash purchases or transactions over ten thousand dollars a mandatory requirement. The paper trail immediately created all kinds of problems for gangs flush with hot money that had no legitimate provenance. In response they developed various schemes to try and get around the restrictions.

One method was "smurfing," which involved making multiple deposits and transfers using amounts a few dollars shy of the limit to beat detection. Others included buying hefty life insurance policies and then redeeming them at a loss, in a bid to retrieve a reduced return in "clean" money, or racking up credit on store and bank cards that could be redeemed abroad. But specialist ICE, DEA, and FBI units targeting money laundering swiftly got wise to their ruses, leaving the cartels with billions of dollars in hard currency that they could neither spend nor transfer. The solution for them was simple and bold: They would take it back to Mexico in cash. While they run a slender chance of interception at customs checkpoints as they drive cash over the border in cars and trucks, the tunnel would have cut that risk to nil.

Cartel currency smuggling operations in San Diego are tracked by a special ICE unit that endeavors to nab the cash couriers before they hit the border line. Their interceptions show that drug cash tends to be in lower-denomination bills gathered from thousands of street deals across California. The cartel moneymen often use high-speed portable cash counters to tally and batch up the bills. Authorities say that one million in twenty-dollar bills translates to six stacks of bills three feet high, weighing more than a hundred pounds total. The money is often packed into plastic-wrapped bales for transport, and crammed into every conceivable compartment in a car or truck. These include door, dash, and roof panels as well as floor and even tire compartments. Occasionally the ICE team will also come across cleverly engineered stashes for cash heading south from Los Angeles, including one hydraulic dash compartment that was opened by a combination of keystrokes on the car stereo.

To be taken through the tunnel, the cash would likely have been stuffed into bags and have been wheeled south under the border in the same barrows used to bring the narcotics north. Once on the other side it would have been hauled up and out of the shaft in a gurney found at the warehouse, before being repacked for disposal in Mexico. With looser currency-reporting requirements there, it is easier to launder cash.

One recent scam used in Tijuana, to the chagrin of the DEA, involved running hot money through local currency exchange houses flanking the city's Avenida Revolución tourist strip. The laundered funds were then sent back north to San Diego, where they could be enjoyed by the gang capos and accountants, living their dreams in swank condos and beach houses in the upscale neighborhoods like Coronado and La Jolla. Other schemes include hauling the cash further south into Mexico and laundering it through the construction industry in booming cities like Guadalajara or in coastal holiday resorts such as Cancún and Acapulco.

While towns and cities on the north side of the Mexico border are by and large peaceful—El Paso consistently comes in the top three places in national safety polls—Mexican border cities are increasingly convulsed by brutal drug gang violence that killed more than 4,000 people in 2008. To fuel this drug war, the other contraband routinely smuggled south by the Mexican gangs is firearms, a fact documented by a sweep of seizures throughout the past year of assault rifles, pistols, and ammunition at ports of entry across the length of the border and at Mexican customs roadblocks further inland. The U.S. Bureau of Alcohol, Tobacco, Firearms and Explosives describes the flow as an "iron river of guns," and agents work closely with Mexican authorities to curb the trade.

Police say that weapons used in crime in Tijuana most likely come from over the border in California and Arizona, for the simple reason that the city is cut off in the remote reaches of the vast Sonora Desert. The nearest neighbor is Hermosillo, the capital of Sonora state, around four hundred miles to the southeast, across highways marked by military checkpoints. Dubbed *retenes,* these inspection points are manned by Mexican troops—the least corrupted of the country's graft-wracked authorities—who carry out thorough searches for drugs and illegally held guns.

The weapons are used by brutal cartel enforcers who are little more than vicious amateurs. With no pretense at marksmanship or knowledge of the finer arts of warfare, they mostly kill in one of two ways. In the first, the victims are generally picked up by an armed snatch squad. Taken to a safe house, they are beaten, tortured, and finally driven out to a lonely out-of-town spot and executed with a shot to the back of the head. The *tiro de gracia,* as the death shot is known, is fired at point-blank range, in most cases with a 9mm or .40 caliber pistol.

The other method involves hit squads armed with assault rifles, which often target victims when they are in their cars with their safety belt buckled up, making a routine journey either to or from their homes. The executioners, often death squad members who dress for the occasion in black paramilitary fatigues and flak jackets, usually unload a full clip of ammunition in the attack, pinning the victim and anyone traveling with him in their seats, riddling them with bullets.

The weapons most commonly used are identified by sometimes hundreds of spent brass cartridges that litter Mexican crime scenes. They are invariably of one of two calibers. The smaller .223 caliber ammunition used by AR-15 assault rifles leaves a neat, almost punctilious signature. The bullets punch through vehicle windshields without shattering them and leave a trail of small, orderly holes in the chassis as if it had been punched by tungsten knitting needles.

The other is the heavier-duty .762 round fired by the Kalashnikov assault rifle, dubbed the *cuerno de chivo,* "goat horn," in Mexican organized crime, for its curved ammunition clip. The full-metal-jacketed rounds are wider and heavier than those of the AR-15, and smash windshields, rip up the bodywork, and routinely pass right through car engines. The impact slows the bullets down but doesn't stop their onward flight. When they spit out through the dashboard they are no longer supersonic, but are tumbling fast, and the resulting crime scene is very hard to look at.

The cartels will generally kill for two reasons: The target is either a rival or has betrayed their operation. In the wake of the tunnel find, ICE issued a public statement warning that anyone involved in the passageway's construction was now in mortal danger, and gave a hotline number for them to come forward and seek protection. A handful of people subsequently did so.

To see what might have happened to them had they stayed around, one only has to look at a round of bloodletting unleashed in Ciudad

Not all contraband heads north. Bureau of Alcohol, Tobacco, Firearms and Explosives senior special agent Tom Mangan (left) and special agent Peter Forcelli (right) seized Kalashnikov assault rifles bought to order in Arizona to arm the Mexican cartels. The bullets in the foreground are belt-fed rounds for a heavy .50 caliber machine gun. (Jeff Topping)

Juárez after tips led police to a stash of more than seven tons of marijuana and cocaine two years earlier. The first victims to appear in the city's streets were shot dead, then the killings twisted. One corpse was torched with gasoline on a makeshift funeral pyre of wooden pallets left in the street. Then police found the body of the *soplón,* or snitch. After the man was beaten and strangled, his index finger had been sliced off and placed in his mouth. The gesture was as eloquent as it was terrifying. It simply read "sssshhhhhh!"

Several months after the tunnel find, the investigators still had no one other than the watchman under arrest, although they had identified several people of interest. Intelligence from the investigation had identified the Arellano Félix Organization as the group likely behind its construction. The cartel, once all-powerful in Tijuana, had been losing a bloody war with the Sinaloa cartel for control of the *plaza* in the city in recent months.

Steadily in decline since the death of enforcer Ramón Arellano Félix in February 2002 and the arrest of his capo brother Benjamín a month later, the passageway may well have been the group's last hurrah in a brutal and sinister criminal career stretching back to the 1970s. However it is far from likely to be the last big tunnel found by increasingly specialized border police, for the simple reason of the tunnels' enormous value to traffickers.

While estimates suggest that the tunnel found at Otay Mesa may have cost several million dollars to build, in the broader economy of drug smuggling it is *chicle*—chewing gum money. Ten million dollars could be recouped by the sale of about three hundred pounds of cocaine on the streets of San Diego. That amount could be pushed through the tunnel in a couple of wheelbarrows in less than fifteen minutes.

Given that the passageway was likely up and running for at least two months before it was discovered, it could potentially have recouped its full construction costs many, many times over before it was discovered. Seen in that light, the risk-to-return ratio, even over a very short period, is clearly quite favorable for such a grand drug tunnel, and its loss becomes merely part of the cost of doing business for the ever-pragmatic cartels.

To date, border police have only found drug tunnels in towns and cities in the western stretch of the border, where the international line is dry and has a geology that is favorable to mining. But given the advantageous relation between cost and return, police don't rule out the possibility of one day finding a large tunnel, perhaps with lights, ventilation, and even a transport system, running under the Rio Grande between cities in northeast Mexico and south Texas.

Nuevo Laredo, for instance, faces its Texan twin, Laredo, over a narrow ribbon of water less than a hundred yards wide, which in some areas is built up right down to the rush-flanked waterline. The same is true of Piedras Negras and Eagle Pass. While the prospect of building a tunnel between them sounds like a fantasy at first take, far stranger plans have been brought to fruition in the topsy-turvy world of the cash-rich cartels, where police reports sometimes read like magical realist fiction.

At the beginning of the millennium, police in Colombia broke into a warehouse in Facatativá, a mist-wreathed town of market gardens on the outskirts of the Andean capital, Bogotá, following a tip-off. There, inside the darkened space in the chill several thousand feet above sea level, was a partially built submarine, made of steel plate machined to high tolerances from a set of Russian blueprints also found in the building. More than one hundred feet long, it had an engine room ready to fit out, and the capacity to carry a cargo of up to two hundred tons of cocaine in its hold.

Perhaps not surprisingly, Leo Arreguin, the DEA chief in the country at the time, said he had never seen anything like it in his thirty-two-year career. It got even weirder. At least one newspaper reported that there was little doubt that the sub would have been equipped to fire live torpedoes if the cartel engineers had ever managed to get it built and down out of the mountains from its landlocked eyrie to the coast. By comparison, a drug tunnel under the river would surely not be unthinkable.

"Could they build a tunnel under the Rio Grande?" Marwood mused, weighing the question carefully. "It's really just an engineering question. If the money is right for them, they can do whatever is possible. But what they should know is this: They now have every resource of the federal government looking for them, and we're getting better and better at what we do."

Researching this one drug tunnel, I had heard the police who had found it say how such tunnels are regarded by smugglers as one of the most effective ways of ensuring that contraband gets from one side of the line to the other, with minimal risk of interdiction.

There is, however, another: a corrupt gatekeeper. While one group of federal police in San Diego hunts for the tunnels burrowing under the line, there's another working around the clock to ferret out the cops on the take.

NINE

Corruption

The border inspector in the far traffic lane is stopping each car coming up from east Tijuana, diligently checking ID documents and running some of them through a computer system. But his burly colleague alongside in the nearside lane looks up the lines of traffic, waving the cars straight through the port in a technique known as flushing, which is sometimes used to clear backed-up traffic in rush hour. Only thing is, it's before dawn and traffic is light. What's going on? Is he tired? Is he burned out? Or is there something else? It is the something else that the video camera has been set up to determine.

Trained discreetly out of a window in an office at the Otay Mesa port of entry, southeast of San Diego, it records every move that Customs and Border Protection inspector Mike Gilliland makes during his twenty-minute rotations through the traffic lanes on the graveyard shift. The surveillance is part of an undercover investigation by a federal anticorruption team that is trying to gather conclusive evidence to prove that he is working with a Tijuana human smuggling ring, funneling hundreds of illegal immigrants into Southern California in exchange for thousands and thousands of dollars in cash.

The Border Corruption Task Force is led by the FBI, and comprises the ICE Office of Professional Responsibility and the Department of Homeland Security's Office of Inspector General, as well as Customs and Border Protection's Internal Affairs and the Internal Revenue Service. It focuses only on credible allegations of border-related graft.

It seemed to investigators, at least at first glance, a long shot. A former Marine with sixteen years at the port, Gilliland knew his job backward, and above all, his colleagues at the port felt safe around him. He was over six feet tall, heavily built, and was always the first to dive in if another inspector was struggling to detain someone. To cap it all, he was also well liked by commuters from Mexico, who remembered he always had a ready smile for them as he reached out to sweep their passports or border crossing cards. "He was loved down there at the port. If you wanted a poster boy for Customs and Border Protection, he was your guy. . . . He was a picture-perfect inspector," said Herb Kaufer, the chief of ICE's Office of Professional Responsibility in San Diego, of the tall, fair-haired inspector under investigation.

The investigation into the former Marine began in June 2004 after a tip was passed to the FBI by an informant about a corrupt inspector at the port. Someone on the line at Otay Mesa, the tips gathered among the underworld in Tijuana insisted, was waving hundreds of illegal immigrants through the traffic lanes for a human smuggling ring.

Gilliland should have been above suspicion, but for one nagging detail: The only pointer that the investigators had was a nickname that the group had for the inspector. Underworld tags in Tijuana usually involve some kind of physical description, such as El Gordo, the Fat Guy. This one was no different. The inspector was known as El Guero, the Blond Guy.

There was no way around it. Of all the inspectors at the close-knit port of entry, the tag brought to mind one above all others: Gilliland, the tall, striking, former Marine with the fair complexion, who got on with and was liked by everyone.

Proving that a border cop is corrupt is no easy matter. With their positions inside the loop in law enforcement, they have a clear idea of how an investigation might proceed against them, and almost invariably take some kind of countersurveillance measures.

Having exhausted other investigative efforts, the FBI put a tap on the phones of two known coyotes, Aurora Torres Lopez and Marina Pérez de García, to see what leads their chatter might turn up. That, too, was no easy task as the two Mexican women, both in their late thirties, changed phones constantly to frustrate a wiretap.

Like many natives of the Tijuana and San Diego corridor, both women had lives that spanned the border, and Torres had a home in one of the rolling subdivisions of Chula Vista. Most commuters who travel frequently through Otay Mesa from east Tijuana go to work, shop, study, or visit friends and relatives. Torres and Pérez also smuggled people.

The human smuggling trade invariably involves a network of conspirators, often linked by family ties. In this particular network, investigators discovered a cousin who would handle some of the driving, and a daughter who would occasionally be called on to handle payoffs. Pérez, they learned, even had her own nickname: La Chata. Like El Guero, it is a physical description, a tag used south of the line to refer to people with a little button nose.

Most human smugglers will either target the ports with a variety of scams to conceal illegal immigrants, or *pollos,* cramming them into spaces in cars or trucks, or slipping them through the ports on stolen documents. But the ongoing surveillance of Torres and La Chata revealed that the two women were touting something resembling a business-class service for migrants. It was a pricier ticket north, between $3,500 and $4,000 for the short hop from Tijuana to San Diego, but it was more comfortable, with *pollos* sitting up in the back of a vehicle. And, most important, it was *una cosa segura*—"a sure thing."

The premium ticket was not something that most Mexican illegal immigrants heading up north to work as chambermaids or do yard work would necessarily need. It would be extremely useful, though, to felons who couldn't afford to be caught walking through the port or out in the desert, where as a matter of procedure border police of all stripes run all detainees' prints through the IAFIS system, which in seconds picks out those with a prior criminal history.

Investigators listening in to the wiretaps found that Torres spoke regularly with prospective clients and other smugglers in the busy urban corridor, and chatted a great deal with family and friends on both sides of the border. They also found that she occasionally called Gilliland, who had a broad social network of his own. The former Marine had a son from a previous marriage who had followed him into the Marine Corps and was frequently in touch. He was also at the heart of a broad extended family from a subsequent marriage, where the youngsters called him Uncle Mike and often sought him out for advice. Gilliland also went to a church in National City, close to Interstate 5, where he was known and liked by the Hispanic pastor. It was a full life with a lot of intersections.

While Gilliland's infrequent conversations with Torres often touched on family life, they also involved some rather stilted exchanges about going out that struck investigators as suspicious.

"Are you going to invite me to the movies tonight? It's going to be four tickets," Torres said in one somewhat strained call monitored from a windowless wiretap room at the FBI's offices in San Diego.

"Right at twelve. If I can't make it, I'll send you a nine-one-one," Gilliland replied.

The investigators knew Gilliland worked the graveyard shift at the port, between midnight and 8 A.M., when the port takes on its own, rather strange nocturnal life. The drab approach to the inspection booths is lit up by stadium lights, giving it the somewhat desolate feel of a railroad stockyard. It is, also in a curious touch, a time when the pedestrian hall is closed, and pedestrians and cyclists are funneled through the traffic lanes, almost like rush hour in old Beijing.

Gilliland's shift would be broken down into two four-hour blocks, one working in the secondary inspection area, the other working at the line of blue primary inspection booths. There he would be rotated through the lanes in twenty-minute cycles, punctuated with rest breaks. Listening to his conversations with Torres, investigators soon figured out that Gilliland was alluding in code to his shift patterns. They soon established that Torres was asking if he was working that night. The "tickets" referred to the number of alien-packed vehicles she planned to run through his lane at the port. Some subsequent calls substituted a restaurant theme for the cinema, referring to the load cars as "plates."

It wasn't just logistics that were firmed up in the calls, but also the money that the well-regarded agent would be getting for turning his government inspection lane into a clandestine tollbooth. His cut was $1,500 off the top, not for every vehicle waved through his lane, but for every undocumented immigrant riding in them, and it soon added up.

On a good night at the port, with three load cars through his lane with perhaps seven to ten illegal immigrants in each vehicle, Gilliland could expect to make anywhere between $31,500 and $45,000. A tidy sum, equivalent to what a local policeman or sheriff's deputy might make in a year, and around half what he, as a federal policeman, might expect to make out on the line in his blue CBP uniform.

Gilliland got paid in cash, usually stuffed in white convenience store grocery bags, and the drops' arrangements were also couched in code. One time Torres told her daughter to call him and tell him to "come to the house to check the roof." Sure enough, he drove around to her home in suburban Chula Vista, watched by a surveillance team. He walked in empty-handed, but came out holding a plastic bag, apparently filled with cash.

Another time the payment was made by La Chata's daughter. They chose a smart place for a money drop: the parking lot of the Burger King restaurant in San Ysidro, a public place with a lot of cars rolling in and out, and where everyone is on the move.

As the investigation ramped up, the wiretaps helped agents develop the next step in building a case against Gilliland, which was observing the inspector interact with the smugglers while he was on the line.

From the wiretaps, investigators knew when the coyotes would attempt to cross a load car packed with illegal immigrants, and arranged to train surveillance cameras on Gilliland's booth at the darkened port of entry, recording every move he made when he was on the graveyard shift.

Herb Kaufer's office had one investigator assigned to work on the Border Corruption Task Force case. A no-nonsense New Yorker who looks a little like the actor David Strathairn, Kaufer has more than a decade of experience ferreting out corrupt federal agents. For him and other experienced investigators, it's a matter of looking coolly at the evidence turned up by an investigation to see whether there is a case to answer. "The challenge is to prove they're corrupt and not just lazy, or stupid," Kaufer explains.

It was early summer in San Diego. The evenings were growing longer. Shortly before midnight, when he started his shift, Gilliland spoke with Pérez. This time their varied code had a culinary theme. He had spoken to the manager, he said, and they could "eat together at four o'clock."

Cued by the call, Border Corruption Task Force agents had a video camera trained on his booth at the well-lit port. They knew the time to expect the load vehicle. Sure enough, shortly before five in the morning a gray Lincoln Navigator rolled through his lane with a number of passengers in the back.

The task force's investigations are invariably highly discreet, as agents involved don't want to show their hand until they have enough evidence to bring charges that will stand up in court. Nevertheless, they needed to see what was in the load car. To that end, San Diego Police Department officers, working in tandem with the FBI, pulled the car over on a traffic violation.

La Chata's cousin Rosalba Raygoza was at the wheel when she saw the blue light in the rearview mirror. The cop pulled her over for speeding on the 905, the short stretch of freeway that begins at the Paseo Internacional at the port and then heads westbound to link up with Interstate 5 heading up to Los Angeles. It was fortunate the Navigator's suspension was tough, as she had quite a load: nine undocumented aliens in the back.

News of the arrest got back to Gilliland. At 8:01, just one minute after his shift ended, he called La Chata. The police had "busted one of her cars," she said, although he already knew. He had been listening to the police radio, and was anxious. Aliens traveling westbound on the 905 could only have come through Otay Mesa; that's where the highway starts. Could it somehow be linked back to him?

"She's not going to say anything, right?" he asked of Raygoza, who was now under arrest.

"No."

"She doesn't know anything?"

It was tense. A few days passed and, with them, Gilliland's anxiety that the arrest would be traced back to him at the port diminished. Undeterred by the close call, he called Torres and coached her to make sure that her drivers didn't make the same mistakes as those made by La Chata. From now on, he said, laying down the law, she should only use "cars without any problems with the registration plates."

Gilliland thought they had got it straight. What he didn't know was that the task force now had enough evidence to arrest him, although they had been biding their time so as to gather sufficient evidence to nab the smugglers and their accomplices. The following day, June 6, the sky would fall in.

Gilliland was on lane 8. Shortly after four in the morning, agents watched as Torres herself pulled up to the booth at the wheel of a black GMC Yukon. Moments after she had driven the Yukon through the port, she pulled over and stepped out, while another driver took her place. Investigators watched as she trotted across the highway all dressed in white, and hopped into another car and drove back south to Mexico. It was a busy night. She had crossed one load, now she had more work to do.

With Torres back in Tijuana, the Yukon drove on up the interstate. It had almost made it to San Diego by the time Border Patrol agents and task force investigators pulled it over. They were stunned. The hefty sport-utility vehicle was packed like a shuttle bus. Inside were eleven illegal immigrants from Mexico, including a toddler and a baby.

Just eleven minutes after she crossed south, Torres was back behind the wheel of another load car. She slipped through the port with another five *pollos* tucked in the back. Police tailed the car to a drop house in suburban San Diego—ironically just a few blocks from the FBI's offices—where accomplice Patricia Santamaria was waiting. It was her job to drive the *pollos* on the last leg of their journey up to Los Angeles, three hours away.

Task force agents arrested Torres shortly after sunup. Thinking fast, she made a rushed phone call. Most people facing charges under arrest would think to call an attorney. She called an accomplice with the group. "Take my kids out of the house and have them get the safe. . . . Take the safe out, all the money that's in there."

She was right to be concerned about the money. It was a lot of cash. Piles and piles of it. When the FBI later tallied it up it came to $458,000. Pérez, meanwhile, had $60,000 at her home. Between the two women, the cash was equivalent to fees paid by more than 160 illegal immigrants, or, put another way, four tourist buses filled with fee-paying illegal immigrants. That, of course, was just the cash they had at home, although how much they had already laundered in a scam reaching back at least two years is anyone's guess.

While a team of agents prepared to nab Torres, Pérez, and their crew, another group had already moved in to arrest Gilliland. He had been having a very busy shift at the port. Agents had watched as he waved car after car packed with aliens through his lane that evening.

For Kaufer, who later watched the surveillance tapes of Gillland's final shift, it was his body language that was the most striking, finally nailing doubts about whether he was burned out, lazy, or on the take. "It's June, and it's night, and it's cool down there at the port, but he's sweating, he's nervous, he's rocking on his feet, and he says 'Go! Go! Go! Everybody go,' and he's not even looking at them," Kaufer said, his expression somewhere between disbelief and contempt. "At one point one vehicle must have been out of lane, as he's directing them to his lane. . . . That lane is rocking. . . . It's something to see. It was obscene," he added.

Gilliland's hour had come. He had rotated off the vehicle lanes and was chatting in the break room with his colleagues. An FBI agent leading the investigation for the task force called out to him, and asked him to step into the "fishbowl," the command room at the port filled with monitors drawing video feeds in from across the traffic and pedestrian lanes.

Inside were three men that no corrupt inspector ever wants to see: Kaufer from ICE's Office of Professional Responsibility; Andy Black, the FBI's Border Corruption Task Force chief; and James Black, agent in charge of the Department of Homeland Security's Office of Inspector General. They also had several heavily built agents for backup, and they were tense.

Gilliland was a veteran built like a linebacker, with a reputation for going in hard. Not only that, he was packing a service pistol, and about to be placed under the greatest stress of his life. They could give him no quarter. As soon as he stepped through the door they pounced, got the pistol, and handcuffed him, all the while reading him his rights. Gilliland was stunned.

The blood drained from his face. He staggered backward and slumped into a chair. It reminded one agent present of *Sanford and Son,* the popular 1970s sitcom, when L.A. junkyard owner Fred Sanford would clutch his chest and totter back on his feet faking a heart attack to get out of a tight spot. "It was like, 'This is the big one! Ya hear that, Elizabeth? I'm coming to join ya, honey!'"

Disarmed, cuffed, and under arrest, Gilliland was ready to be moved out. The investigators chose to lead him across the traffic lines at the port. He walked head bowed, his hands held behind his back, past the inspection booths, and in full view of secondary.

None of Gilliland's colleagues had any idea that the popular agent was corrupt, and his final walk carried a chilling message about consequences: If you take a crooked dollar, then you will be caught, and you will make that same of walk of shame in front of your coworkers. As he walked, there wasn't a head that didn't turn in his direction from the eight lanes of traffic.

A search of Gilliland's house in Chula Vista found $3,700 in cash in the bathroom and another $2,000 in cash in a truck parked outside.

More troubling, they also found more than 25 million Iraqi dinars, at that time worth around $18,000. Where had they come from? Had his son, a Marine, brought them back from Iraq, or had they come from ushering Iraqis over the border? (Investigators later found they had been bought from a currency trader in California as an investment.)

Gilliland was charged with allowing hundreds of illegal aliens into the United States over a two-year period, and with receiving between $70,000 and $120,000 in cash for doing so—an estimate considerably on the low side as far as investigators were concerned. There was also the more puzzling matter of why a decorated Marine who had served sixteen years at the port had done it.

No one wanted to believe it, not his colleagues or anyone in the community. Misael Zaragoza, Gilliland's pastor from the fake mission-style church in National City, wrote to the court with a glowing testimonial. Members of his extended family also wrote in with kind words for the principled man they called Uncle Mike, a sententious figure who would pull up a chair and offer solemn advice. "One of the most important lessons he has instilled in me is that a man is only as good as his word," one young member of his wife's family wrote to the court, recalling Uncle Mike's advice. "Without that, he is nothing."

Why Gilliland threw away his reputation as a Marine and his long years at the port remained a puzzle, with various pieces. In comments made through his attorney in a sentencing memorandum, Gilliland said he let aliens through his lane because of his frustration at witnessing "the injustice and harsh, abusive treatment of Mexicans at the border." He said he reported mistreatment to his supervisors, although investigators later found that he had lodged no formal complaint, and remained skeptical. "If you're such a humanitarian, well, why do you have to get paid for it?" Kaufer said. "If you're all coming here for a better life, then just come on in. The gate's open. Why do you have to get fifteen hundred dollars a head for it? It's nonsensical."

Other evidence marshaled by investigators also sought to demolish the notion that Gilliland was some kind of an idealist championing Mexicans, or, alternatively, had gotten ground down by the job, as his lawyer would later argue. Instead, it painted him as a cool-thinking pragmatist who used his long years on the line to plan and carry out his crimes. They revealed that Gilliland had found a way of obtaining his lane assignments shortly before he went on the line. Sometimes he did this by calling ahead to the port of entry—in violation of established policy—then passing the details to the smugglers to ease their lucrative arrangement along.

He also found a way to cover his tracks by disabling his automated license plate reading system for the traffic lanes he rotated through. This meant that when he admitted load vehicles for the traffickers, he could then sever one key link tying them directly to his lane.

"Did he really care about the Mexicans on the border?" Kaufer asked rhetorically. "I don't think he gave a rat's ass about them."

The investigation into Gilliland was placed in the hands of federal prosecutors, who would now take the lead in bringing the case to court with the investigators' continuing involvement. The corruption task force's job, though, was far from over. In fact, a short drive across town they had another agent under watch at San Ysidro, and the trap was about to be sprung.

Special agent Andy Black oversees the FBI's Border Corruption Task Force from an office building close to one of the busy freeways that crisscross metro San Diego, the eighth-largest city in the United States, and the most prosperous on the entire southwest border.

The parallel investigation led by his team was unconnected to that of Gilliland. It began with a call to ICE from an informant who had heard gossip that an inspector at the San Ysidro port of entry was helping a coyote with whom he was having an affair.

The investigation focused on CBP inspector Richard Elizalda, another decorated former Marine who had, like many servicemen before him, moved to a second career in law enforcement. By now well into his fifties, he was short in stature and heavily built, with a creased, careworn face that seemed to record every blow from a sad and troubled life.

As a child he was abandoned by his parents, and had been sent to four foster homes in four years before being taken in and raised by a half sister. He had joined the Marine Corps as soon as he was old enough, and served in Vietnam, Korea, and Japan. He married twice. Neither marriage worked, and now he was staring at middle age, alone.

One of the things that struck colleagues was his air of sadness. He didn't socialize much with the other agents at the sprawling twenty-four-lane port, and sometimes he would take his breaks in his car in the staff parking lot. The only bright spot to his day, it seemed, was looking out for the attractive single mother who crossed through his lane from Tijuana.

Raquel Arin, a Mexican-born naturalized U.S. citizen, was in her late thirties. She crossed frequently through San Ysidro, like thousands of commuters who have ties on either side of the line, only in her case, many of the journeys north to California were strictly business. She made her living smuggling people through the port Elizalda guarded.

One time as she passed through his lane, he asked for her telephone number and she gave it to him. They became friends, and then lovers. Before long, he became involved in the smuggling network, and, at least initially, showed a talent for his new double life as a cop turned criminal.

Elizalda bought Nextel phones, the models favored by Tijuana smugglers, which he would dump every few months to frustrate a possible wiretap. He gave them to Arin and Carmen Alvarado, another smuggler. The two women worked independently, but were aware of one another's existence. Alvarado was initially responsible for bundling the *pollos* into groups south of the line and organizing the load cars and drivers to shuttle them north through the port.

As the trade prospered, Alvarado enlisted the support of her daughter to drive, and her role became more managerial, handling the cash transactions and laundering the proceeds.

At the start of his shift at the port of entry, Elizalda would text his lane allocation to the coyotes in a code that he had made up that told Arin and Alvarado when and through which lane to cross their load cars packed with illegal immigrants. "You looked good in your yellow top and blue jeans," ran one message. Flirtatious and apparently sexual, it was in fact a cipher he had devised based on colors, with different shade combinations identifying each of the twenty-four lanes at the port.

When they are working with a corrupt agent, some smuggling organizations flag load cars, perhaps with a folded newspaper on the dash, or, as in one case in El Paso a few years back, a distinctive Olympic medallion left swinging from the vehicle's rearview mirror. Elizalda, though, wanted to know who to look out for and to be able to wave known drivers swiftly through his lane and out into the concrete gullet of the I-5.

The investigation, like the one focused on Gilliland, was led by the FBI. As with that case, investigators wanted to get a glimpse of what Elizalda was waving through his lane. To provide a peek, an antiterrorism contraband enforcement team chose one load car that had passed his inspection booth to be targeted for secondary inspection. There they found that the car, driven by one of Arin and Alvarado's drivers, Kenneth Web, was packed with illegal immigrants.

The team had pulled off the stop in such a naturalistic way, though, that Elizalda didn't suspect he was under surveillance. Transcripts of conversations with Arin showed they discussed the arrest the following day. He was soothing. He told her that the stop was "nothing but bad luck."

For smugglers, having a corrupt inspector is almost like having a drug tunnel. The risks for interdiction are greatly reduced, ensuring that whatever they line up in the inspector's lane will get through the port and into the United States. In fact it is such a gift for smugglers that they get all the use they possibly can out of it, to run all the aliens and contraband through that they can.

Another vehicle that had come through Elizalda's lane was found to be carrying not just illegal immigrants—there were four of them—but more than two hundred pounds of marijuana stuffed casually into the trunk. The smugglers, it seemed, were piggybacking drug loads through the inspector's lane, to get every last cent in value from it.

Like Gilliland, Elizalda was being paid handsomely for his aid to the smugglers. His motivation for doing so seemed to go beyond money, and became clearer in how he spent the thousands of dollars in cash proceeds. Much of it went toward expensive gifts for Arin, the attractive younger woman whom he had fallen for.

The baubles included a sterling silver necklace and bracelet with a heart-shaped clasp, a heart and solitaire pendant, and a coiled snake charm, and they didn't just come from any shop. They came from Tiffany & Co., that most romantic of jewelers.

Then there was the plastic surgery. Elizalda was out of shape and considerably more than a decade older than Arin. She suggested he might want to make some changes to his appearance that would make him more appealing to her. He went ahead with it. There was clearly something blind and reckless about what he was doing, and it would become more so as time went by.

Elizalda gave his younger lover cash to buy a swank BMW X-5 sport-utility vehicle, taking her old car, a 2000 Lexus, in return. Astonishingly, the border inspector was now running around San Diego in a coyote's set of wheels. Aside from the gifts, the pair's meetings were also becoming reckless. On at least one occasion, they met in the staff parking lot at the port of entry. It was, or so it seemed, almost as if he wanted to get caught.

By early June 2006, FBI investigators had all the evidence that they needed to nab him. They planned to arrest him one morning as he arrived at the port for his shift. Acting somewhat erratically, he had started to get dressed for work, then called in sick. He then set off from his home in the Eastlake area in his truck, curiously dressed in a casual shirt and his work pants.

A few blocks down the road he was pulled over by the Chula Vista Police Department as half a dozen cars packed with FBI agents pulled up and swarmed around his truck with pistols drawn. Elizalda looked up, very matter-of-fact, an expression of infinite weariness on his face, an agent working the case recalled. He had no questions. In fact, he seemed relieved that his double life was over.

Arresting agents placed him in the back of a car for the trip across town to the FBI's offices at Aero Drive, a journey that takes about twenty minutes when the traffic is flowing smoothly. They were surprised to see Elizalda had shut his eyes and fallen asleep on the way.

The spectacular fall of CBP border inspector Mike Gilliland was shocking to many of the people who knew and worked with him. For loner Elizalda it was less so, as many of his colleagues suspected he was on the take, and cooperated with the task force investigators. But perhaps most shocking to those who didn't know either man was the fact that the two corruption cases occurred so close together. The two inspectors were arrested within two days of each other, Gilliland on June 6, 2006, and Elizalda on June 8.

Also striking was the fact that both cases involved human smuggling. In the past, the majority of graft investigations on the border had turned on agents and inspectors slipping dope in for the cartels. But now with increased profits due to tightened border security, the cases flagged the fact cash-flush coyotes were now increasingly in the market to seduce, bribe, or otherwise corrupt the gatekeepers, and the effects were shocking.

Between them, the trusted border guards had simultaneously compromised the integrity of the two ports of entry into San Diego, which is arguably one of the most sensitive areas of the western United States in terms of security. It has more than a dozen military facilities, hosting the United States Navy, Coast Guard, and Marine Corps, with tens of thousands of people in uniform.

Pretty much anyone carrying anything could have come through the two inspectors' lanes during the estimated two-year period that they ran their respective rackets. The evidence against them was overwhelming and both of the inspectors pleaded out.

Gilliland ended up before Judge John Houston at the U.S. District Court in downtown San Diego. What had begun years earlier as a flirtation with one of the coyotes passing through his traffic lane had enormous personal consequences, as his life, first as a Marine and then as a respected border inspector, unraveled in the courtroom. The judge sent the inspector to prison for five years and fined him $200,000 for waving hundreds of illegal immigrants through his lane for fat profits. He wept in court and struggled for coherence. "He wanted me to express to the court how sorry he was," his attorney Michael Pancer said on his behalf. "He's devastated by what he's done."*

A month later, Elizalda was sentenced to fifty-seven months in jail. The moment of reckoning was tough for him, too. While emotional, he found the words to apologize to both Judge Larry Burns and the American people. "I know I did something wrong. . . . I let my family down and I let the United States down—the people of the United States—and I'm sorry. I apologize for what I did, and I'm ready to pay my sentence."†

The cases of the two men—one who sold the badge for money, the other perhaps to fill some bottomless void he had carried around since childhood—are just one of an avalanche of border-related graft cases to have come to the fore in recent years.

Investigators have uncovered scores of public employees on the take for helping to move drugs, and, increasingly, illegal immigrants over the border from Mexico in a slew of investigations from California to the sultry Gulf Coast since the 9/11 attacks.

The sheer diversity of the various acts of corruption, the motivation of the agents, and the broad range of agencies involved is quite stunning. The cases have involved both federal and local police at work on the border, and have even included members of the military and National Guard. They add an extra sievelike dimension to a line that is often described as being porous, and their implications for border security are huge.

The following is far from a complete list of the cases that have come

*Kelly Thornton, "Ex Border Inspector Gets 5 Years in Prison, Fine," *San Diego Union-Tribune,* February 16, 2007.
†Kelly Thornton, "Smuggling Nets Border Inspector Prison Term," *San Diego Union-Tribune,* March 27, 2007.

to light in recent years, but something of a sampler, a synthesis to give an idea of the sheer range and breadth of the problem faced by internal affairs investigators, federal prosecutors, and the agencies themselves.

A recent case in San Diego involved a port inspector at San Ysidro named Michael Taylor. Taylor was remembered as a flamboyant figure who, aside from being a border inspector, fancied himself as an entrepreneur. He was sentenced in 2005 to serve almost four years for running illegal immigrants and almost a ton of marijuana through the port in a racket run using cell phones and pagers.

His wrongdoing was all the more worrying as it also implicated the assistant area port director. Daphiney Caganap was in charge of overseeing the intelligence unit and antismuggling operations at San Ysidro, a task that included graft investigations. Taylor took Caganap out to dinner and allegedly gave her $30,000 in cash, and a swank spa pool, to watch his back. When Taylor's high-spending lifestyle came under the spotlight, Caganap allegedly dropped a note in his locker warning him it was "time to take a vacation."

Caganap agreed to resign from her job in 2005—by then she had moved on to Michigan, where she oversaw Customs and Border Protection operations at the Detroit airport—and admitted lying to the FBI when she said she had not met with Taylor. Originally facing long years in federal jail, she was generally held to have been fortunate to cop a plea and only get probation on lesser charges. The problem was that not only was a border inspector corrupt, but the integrity of the official charged with weeding out corruption at the port was also in doubt.

It's not just the port inspectors and, in this instance, one middle-ranking CBP director who get snared in graft. The problem is far more widespread. Another case that came to court in Southern California in 2006 involved Border Patrol agents working the vast, empty spaces between the ports. Supervisory Border Patrol agents Mario Alvarez and Samuel McClaren were based in El Centro, a few miles to the east of the furious urban smuggling corridor between San Diego and Tijuana.

Both agents were former servicemen with more than a decade apiece in the Border Patrol. Liked and trusted around the station—colleagues there called McClaren "Sammy" and remember sharing jokes with him—they worked closely with Mexican authorities. The job involved rolling south of the border in their government-issued Chevy Tahoe to meet with officials from the Mexican attorney general's office on the south side.

Their role was to share intelligence on human trafficking networks under GIPP, the Guide Identification and Prosecution Program, which aimed to ensure that smugglers identified by the Border Patrol would be charged and tried for their crimes in Mexico. The only thing was, both the agents were on the take from one of the most prolific of them: the Perfino-Sánchez Alien Smuggling Organization, which hustled undocumented immigrants across the line. The range and extent of their services to the smugglers was breathtaking.

The two agents picked up Perfino members and crossed them to California in their truck in return for a $4,000 payment. They also showed the coyotes the precise location of Border Patrol sensors and cameras so that they could bring their loads in safely on the blind side. On one occasion they also took the group's *pollos* out of Border Patrol custody, and, instead of repatriating them to Mexico through the port of entry in Calexico as they were supposed to, they handed them over to the smugglers in the local Wal-Mart parking lot.

Alvarez, who served in the air force before joining the Border Patrol, gave some insights into how the scam snowballed after meetings with an informer during trips to Mexico. "It started very simply and grew to the point that there seemed to be no way to turn back," he said, according to court filings.* "At first the informant would buy drinks, then drinks and dinner, and before I knew it, I was doing something I never imagined myself doing—breaking the law."

While Alvarez and McClaren worked their scams at the line—or actively crossing back and forth over it for their criminal Mexican paymasters—other Border Patrol agents have shown their usefulness to

---

*Onell R. Soto, "Agents Aided Smugglers, Land in Prison," *San Diego Union-Tribune*, November 1, 2006.

smugglers far back from the border line. Texas is one of the great smuggling routes for cocaine and marijuana from Mexico. Smugglers push it through the ports of entry, haul it over the olive-colored waters of the Rio Grande by rope, and even drive over sandbags laid across the river in areas called *brechas* (breaches). But once over the river, the smugglers still have to push their contraband through checkpoints set along freeways and back roads before reaching major cities like San Antonio, Austin, and Houston, where border-related enforcement ends.

The checkpoints are a real headache for smugglers as they are, in effect, live ports of entry. Drivers can be asked to show photo ID, passports, or border crossing cards, *micas*. Vehicle plates themselves can be scanned, run through the Treasury system, and even checked against records at the ports of entry for further information to see if a driver's story about if and when he or she has crossed the border from Mexico check out. Even worse for the dope smugglers, the stops have dog teams. With fewer lanes over which their highly sensitive noses have to catch a telltale whiff of narcotics, the K-9 units can be even more effective.

A scam at the checkpoint in Hebbronville, a speck of a town about half an hour's drive inland from Laredo, was a case in point. There, senior dog handler Juan Alvarez and his brother José waved tons of Gulf cartel marijuana and multipound loads of cocaine through their inspection lanes in a carefully planned scheme that was a godsend for the cartel and netted them a staggering $1.5 million in proceeds. The pair splurged the money on trips to Las Vegas, a $20,000 cash deposit on a house, and expensive items like a Tag Heuer watch—high-rolling baubles that helped internal affairs investigators to build a case against them.

While a lot of corruption cases involve long-running scams that take considerable planning by agents, not to mention the cartels and coyotes, others have been more opportunistic. The crooked gatekeepers do not so much set up and work a lucrative scam at a port of entry or an inspection post, but create their own opportunities, seizing the day, as it were.

One case in point came in Arizona in late 2005 when Border Patrol agent Michael Gonzalez turned up at an unfolding crime scene in a rugged area of high desert. A state trooper pulled over a pickup truck packed with dope near Sonoita, a few miles northeast of Nogales. The driver and passenger fled into the desert with the trooper in hot pursuit on foot, leaving Gonzalez to watch over thirty bundles of pot left in the bed of the truck.

Thinking quickly, he backed his Border Patrol vehicle up to the truck and unloaded a hefty bale of the Mexican grass before carefully rearranging the remaining bales to make it seem as if nothing had been disturbed. He first put it in the front of his truck, but it must have looked a bit obvious or somehow out of place in a police vehicle, because he then stashed it in the trunk. Who would ever know, right?

Well, as anyone who has seen Court TV well knows, cop cars are fitted with video cameras that passively record crime scenes in all their startling candor. The cop drove off from the scene believing nothing was amiss. Only later when he reviewed the tape did he discover this extraordinary theft by a fellow officer. Gonzalez was subsequently arrested and jailed for seven and a half years, although the bale of pot was never recovered.

Corruption cases frequently involve CBP inspectors and Border Patrol agents, since they are the principal point of contact for Mexican drug and human smugglers. However, cases of graft have also been recorded among just about every kind of public employee imaginable working the length of the border, including local police in several of the twenty or so counties along the line. One involved the former sheriff of Cameron County, a sweltering district that flanks the Rio Grande where it spills into the Gulf of Mexico in southeast Texas.

Lying over the river from Matamoros, the hometown of the notorious Gulf cartel in the Mexican state of Tamaulipas, the low-lying border county is a busy two-way criminal conduit for drugs headed north to San Antonio, and cash profits heading back south to Mexico. Investigators found that the Stetson-wearing former sheriff Conrado Cantu ran the county like the cartel bosses ran their *plazas* on the south side, charging *derechos de piso,* or a cut, for contraband on the move through his territory.

The gregarious lawman—who was known for breaking into teary mariachi ballads at fiestas—used his buddy Geronimo "Gerry" Garcia as a go-between, wringing cash payments out of drug and cash runners that crisscrossed the county. Investigators finally caught up with him after he hit a cash run they set up as a sting, hauling $13,000 in supposed drug proceeds south from San Antonio. To their surprise, when Cantu's crew pulled the car over, they didn't just take a cut, they took all of it.

Cantu was arrested in Brownsville on a sweltering day in June 2005, when I was in the city. He was later sentenced to spend more than twenty-four years in federal prison for his extortion racket. Garcia was also sent down, gaining a fresh perspective on life behind bars, which was already familiar to him: At one time he reportedly ran the commissary at the Cameron County lockup under Cantu.

Besides the federal and local police on the border who have been found to be on the take, there are troops. A recent sting by the FBI in Arizona, dubbed Operation Lively Green, snared soldiers who used their uniforms, identification, and even official vehicles to drive what they believed was cocaine through Border Patrol and police checkpoints in Arizona and Nevada for a Mexican drug gang. The cartel never existed. The contacts were FBI agents, and the sting led to the conviction of thirty-five people.

In another case that occurred at the time of writing, police in Texas arrested three National Guardsmen for running illegal immigrants through Border Patrol checkpoints, like the one at Hebbronville, in return for cash. José Rodrigo Torres was arrested while in uniform, driving along Interstate 35 south of San Antonio with the immigrants in his van. Ironically, he and two National Guard accomplices arrested with him had been specially sent to the border under Operation Jump Start, President Bush's stopgap initiative begun a year earlier to seal the border.

It's not just the foot soldiers that get caught up in corruption. Sometimes it snares high-ranking officials. It shouldn't be more troubling—after all, an oath to uphold the law is an oath to uphold the law—but it seems like they really should know better. One case that came to light in 2006 shocked everyone, from cops to reporters. It involved a notorious

money launderer and drug cartel figure from Ciudad Juárez—home of
the notorious and hyperviolent Juárez cartel—who struck up a friend-
ship with the highest-ranking FBI official in El Paso, Special Agent in
Charge Hardrick Crawford.

Businessman José María Guardia operated the Juárez Racetrack. He
had been investigated by the Mexican attorney general's office for ties to
the cartels. U.S. authorities, meanwhile, believed his dog- and horseracing
stadium in the border city was used by traffickers to stage narcotics before shipping them over the border. Guardia had become an informant
for the FBI, but used the opening almost like a Cold War double agent
working both sides of the fence. While ostensibly aiding investigations,
he saw clear advantage from befriending Crawford, who ran the key
field office with 220 special agents and other employees, which dealt
with a lot of border-related crime.

Guardia sent Crawford on paid trips to Mexico City and Las Vegas,
and arranged a job with a $5,000-a-month salary for his wife at the
Juarez Racetrack. Guardia also paid for the couple's membership at the
exclusive Coronado Country Club in El Paso and even paid for lawn
maintenance at their home. He called in the favor when he was publicly
accused by a former Mexican attorney general of involvement in drug
trafficking, calling on Crawford to cross over the border to defend him
at a news conference in Juárez. Astonishingly, the FBI chief went.

Reading from a prepared statement that he had had translated into
Spanish by an FBI interpreter, Crawford said he was not aware that
Guardia was involved in any criminal activity, and described him as "a
good friend." He was asked by shocked reporters to clarify whether he
was speaking as FBI chief or as a private citizen. He replied that he was
appearing as Guardia's friend and as *jefe,* or boss, of the FBI. Within
days, the outraged U.S. ambassador to Mexico had Crawford's travel
authority revoked. Guardia, though, was delighted.

Not only did he compromise Crawford, he appeared to revel in it. Taking one reporter for a Juárez newspaper on a tour of his home, he boasted
that the FBI chief reported to him daily by telephone. He then proudly
showed off a framed photograph of himself with Crawford and two other

shady associates. "I tell people for a laugh, 'Look, here's Al Capone, Lucky Luciano, Eliot Ness, and [Meyer] Lansky.'" Far from being "untouchable," Crawford subsequently faced a grand jury indictment and was convicted of concealing information about his association with Guardia.

Watching cases unfold over the last few years, I have been struck by the variety and frequency of instances of graft. It seems that the number of cases is increasing in step with tightening security on the international line. Ironically, the buildup at the border is in turn a market maker for the professional smuggling economy, where fees for coyotes have risen by several hundred percent in recent years.

Second, the appearance of more walls, more sensors and other technologies between the ports of entry, and more X-ray machines and dog teams at the ports themselves, has made finding a corrupt guard more of an urgent priority for the many cash-flush smuggling networks in the towns and villages on the south side.

Graft is increasingly becoming the answer to tightened security for both people smugglers and drug traffickers, who take recruitment extremely seriously. One investigation by ICE in San Diego turned up a scrapbook kept by a human smuggling ring with photos of border inspectors and lists of their quirks and vulnerabilities. FBI agents in El Paso recall how the Juárez cartel, in its heyday in the late 1990s, had a unit dedicated to corrupting agents, which was known simply as Grupo R. The R stood for *reclutamiento,* "recruitment."

Aside from the dedicated efforts of smugglers to corrupt, there is also the issue of increased hiring among federal border police. In the post-9/11 world, CBP has beefed up hiring at ports of entry, and the Border Patrol is currently in the throes of increasing its size by half, hiring some six thousand new agents to work on the line. In a certain sense, it seems like a much-needed move to get operational control over the border. Yet at the same time it brings more and more cops down to the line, and creates more and more opportunities for the smugglers to approach and rub shoulders with the new hires.

It can start with a pretty girl with a heartbreaking smile at a border crossing looking to see which inspector might grin shyly back. It might be rubbing shoulders at a bar or a party on either side of the very permeable line, or buying a guard first drinks and then lunch, and seeing how far he is willing to take it. It will prove crucial to make sure that the agents hired have integrity and can act based on a clear sense of right and wrong.

In two conversations, one with Herb Kaufer, and another with Paul Charlton, a former U.S. attorney in Arizona who vigorously prosecuted border corruption cases in the border state, both pointed to the problems in Miami in the 1980s, when police were rapidly recruited to rein in the rampant trade in Colombian cocaine, at the time being shipped and flown into South Florida through the Caribbean.

One alarming consequence was the Miami River Cops investigation in which about one hundred officers were arrested, fired, suspended, or reprimanded for robbing cocaine dealers of cash and dope, and even plotting to murder a witness, a debacle that still stirs troubling memories for investigators.

"The more people on the border, you'd think the tighter it would be," Kaufer told me. "I look at it as, 'Wow! Border Patrol is going to fire up another six thousand employees in the next five years.' Well, if it's not done right, similar to Miami fifteen years ago when they just hired a whole bunch of people almost off the street, then five to ten years from now, we are going to see the backlash from that in terms of corruption cases."

For Charlton, who saw a steady rise in cases of crooked federal and local police as well as troops in the border state in the five years he was in the job in Arizona, starting in 2001, it is crucial to ensure that new hires are subjected to thorough background checks to weed out agents with any propensity for corruption, and then to encourage a strong culture of whistle-blowing within border police ranks.

"In order to prevent agent corruption, the first key is good vetting and background checks on individuals. The second part, after you have done your best in that regard, is to make sure that the ethic that surrounds individuals working in that environment is one that encourages the reporting of corruption. That may be one of the most difficult parts of law enforcement, it's a fraternity and sorority that protects its own, and for understandable reasons."

To take a swing back at graft, Charlton said, it was also important to beef up the resources allocated to internal affairs investigators, and then ensure that the penalties are brought into line for officials caught taking bribes. At present, Charlton said, there are great discrepancies for offenses related to drug and human smuggling, which may reinforce the attractiveness of taking money for turning a blind eye to alien smuggling on the border—a crime that is definitely on the rise.

"If I were to come across the line with five grams of pure methamphetamine—what you could get in five little packets of sugar—my sentence would be five years mandatory minimum, I wouldn't leave prison until I had spent my five years there," said Charlton, who has testified to the Senate about sentencing disparities. "Were I, on the other hand, to cross the line into the United States with five human beings in tow, my sentence would be a matter of months."

Then there is the larger picture. The real heart of the problem for Charlton is a concern about what might happen if a culture of corruption is allowed to take hold among police charged with securing the border. It isn't just that corruption breaches border security, it's actually more troubling: It threatens to denigrate faith in public office itself.

"My greatest concern is that the public will lose faith in law enforcement and our government. You only have to look at government south of the border to understand what that means," he said, in reference to Mexico's corrupt authorities, regarded with a mixture of apprehension, contempt, and despair by most Mexicans. "Once the public loses faith in its law enforcement, once they no longer trust that the individuals wearing uniforms are working to protect them but [see that] instead [they] are working for their own benefit, then there is a whole greater degree of lawlessness. That kind of disrespect actually attacks the fundamentals of our democracy."

TEN

Hizballah

I am standing in a long line of brightly dressed people that stretches back from the tall steel gate of one of Latin America's largest jails in the northern reaches of Mexico City. I catch a whiff of tortillas and spent gasoline—the Mexican capital's signature aroma.

Ahead of me men and women dressed in every imaginable shade of reds, blues, and yellows take up the first few hundred places in the line, shuffling steadily toward the guards, carrying bags stuffed with cakes, biscuits, tamales, cartons of orange juice and water.

They are there to visit prisoners corralled within the high walls of the Reclusorio Norte jail. I am standing in line with them as part of a quest to try and find out what substance there might be to many Americans' fears of terrorist infiltration over the border. The man I am hoping to meet was jailed for his part in a pipeline that funneled hundreds of Middle Easterners, and possibly even Hizballah militants, over the U.S.-Mexico border.

Everyone is dressed in garish garb in respect of the prison's dress code. The rule board above the gate explains that no visitor can wear white or beige, as those are the colors of prison livery for the thieves, kidnappers, murderers, and drug traffickers crammed into the overcrowded institution. Black is also forbidden, as that is the color of the guards and turnkeys at the notoriously corrupt lockup.

By 10 A.M. there are more than a thousand of us lining up. Everyone is using whatever ploys they can to streamline the wait. Most have checked forbidden items like cell phones, pocketknives, and car keys at a line of stalls and hole-in-the-wall restrooms across the street thronged with the city's unmistakable green and white taxicabs.

Some among them have even gotten rid of handbags and rucksacks altogether, to save standing in a second inspection line inside the hefty steel door to the jail's reception hall, where guards pick through each of the items in a bag, squeezing out toothpaste, probing the frosting-topped cakes with a skewer, and fingering the seams of coat linings for guns, cell phones, packets of drugs, and gently furled banknotes to ease life behind bars.

A middle-aged couple standing behind me tell me they have come to see their son, who has been locked up for armed robbery—though naturally they say he is innocent. The father can see that I am a first-time visitor and gives me whatever helpful advice he can. "Go and break down whatever banknotes you have to make sure you have a pocketful of change. You'll need a lot of coins once you are on the inside," he tells me in the singsong accented Spanish of the Mexican capital. "If you offer the guards a little something for a soft drink, it will help move things along," he tells me.

He and his wife say they will hold my place in the line while I trot off to the shops, lose my bag, and cash out my banknotes. I come back rattling a fistful of chunky ten-peso bits, with a dull gleam, pleased but more than a little nervous.

Locked up in the labyrinth of patios and dormitories is a Mexican-Lebanese described in a report by September 11 Commission staff as the only Mexican "human smuggler with suspected links to terrorists" arrested to date.*

---

*Pauline Arrillaga and Olga P. Rodriguez, "Smugglers Carry People with Links to Terror to the U.S.,"
 Associated Press, July 3, 2005.

Until his arrest in 2002, restaurateur Salim Boughader ran the popular Café La Libanesa in an upscale neighborhood of Tijuana, just a stone's throw from the U.S. consulate and a couple of miles from the steel border fence drawn like a rusted veil across the southwest border of California, the forbidden land to the north.

Boughader was a key link in a transcontinental human trafficking pipeline that had smuggled more than two hundred Middle Easterners from the war-ravaged streets of Lebanon to the land of Sea World.

A cause for further alarm: A number of the illegal immigrants moved by the ring may have been involved with, or at the very least had sympathies for, Hizballah, the militant Islamic group described by the FBI's counterterrorism chief as "one of the most capable terrorist organizations in the world."*

Hizballah, which means "Party of God" in Arabic, was founded in response to the 1982 Israeli invasion and occupation of Lebanon, a Connecticut-sized country on the eastern shores of the Mediterranean, fatefully lodged between regional antagonists Israel and Syria. Its leaders have a deep loathing for the United States, which they have called the "Great Satan," and for the United States' regional ally Israel, which they call the "Little Satan." Long before the founding of Al Qaeda and the 9/11 attacks, Hizballah militants had killed hundreds of Americans in bloody bomb blasts that reverberated around the world. They included the massive October 1983 truck bombing that partly demolished the U.S. Marine Corps barracks in Beirut and killed 241 servicemen. Then, thirteen years later, a huge gas truck bomb killed nineteen U.S. airmen at the Khobar Towers residential compound in Saudi Arabia.

Hizballah's ferocious attacks are not limited to the Middle East. They struck half a world away with attacks on the Israeli embassy and cultural center in Argentina in the early 1990s, which together killed more than one hundred people.

Clearly, for the U.S. authorities in the months and years following

*Statement of John Kavanagh, chief of International Terrorism Operations Section II, Counterterrorism Division FBI, to House Subcommittee on International Terrorism, September 28, 2006.

the 9/11 attacks, any possibility that a pipeline smuggling anyone even remotely connected to Hizballah into the United States was of the greatest concern. When federal investigators first learned of a smuggling operation bringing Middle Easterners—more specifically, Lebanese—into California, pursuing the case became a top priority as a national security threat, immigration police have told me.

Boughader was arrested by U.S. authorities as he crossed from Tijuana to San Diego in December 2002 to buy supplies for his restaurant, on a sixteen-count indictment of conspiracy to bring in, transport, and harbor illegal aliens from the Middle East. Also named in the charges were two Mexican coconspirators, Patricia Serrano-Valdez, who allegedly operated a drop house in National City, in the sprawling suburbs just north of the San Ysidro port of entry, and José Guillermo Álvarez-Dueñas, a Tijuana coyote.

In a separate operation carried out by Mexican authorities, the former Mexican consul in Beirut, Imelda Ortiz Abdala, was also arrested for her alleged involvement in a ring selling visas for travel to Mexico, and was detained along with seven other alleged coconspirators. (Ortiz Abdala was eventually freed and cleared by a Mexican judge.)

Jailed in the United States for a year, Boughader was then deported to Mexico, where he was immediately rearrested, and was subsequently convicted by a Mexican court of crimes relating to aggravated human trafficking and organized crime statutes and sentenced to fourteen years in jail.

His case is one of a kind on the border. It apparently brings together some of the key elements of a U.S. homeland security doomsday scenario in which a human trafficking network with a transcontinental reach funnels illegal immigrants from the Middle East—some with possible ties to a terror group—right to Mexico. Once in Mexico, they hook up with the organized criminal underworld in Tijuana, arguably the greatest talent pool for smugglers anywhere in the world, to spirit them into the United States.

While the southwest border is widely seen as vulnerable to terrorist infiltration, every account of Islamic militants probing the border that had come to my attention over the years failed to check out. A few calls and they proved to be anecdotal, overplayed, as evanescent as bubbles on a bar of soap.

This, though, was different. The case had details: names, places, indictments and charges on both sides of the line. Furthermore, it was regarded as sensitive by federal investigators I had raised it with. It was clearly worth pursuing.

I am committed to finding out all I can from Boughader, and seeing if I can find just one solid, concrete example of a terrorist brought over the border from Mexico.

After a couple of hours in line, I step at last through a small door in the steel gate and into the jail to visit Boughader. I set my name down on a list of visitors for Dormitorio 2, the prison wing where he is expecting me. I am then ushered by guards into a dark, wooden cubicle like the changing room of ancient public swimming baths. The two guards order me to take off my boots and my jacket, and turn out my pockets, spilling the coins to the side as they feel along the seams. A perfunctory search also yields my reporter's notebook and a pencil, which they tell me I can't take in with me. Stationery, I learn, is against prison regulations. I look from one to the other, trying to figure out who is in charge.

"I wonder," I ask the more commanding of the two. "Would you perhaps like a *refresco*?" He shrugs with an embarrassed smile that suggests he could be persuaded, clearly relieved that I have saved him the embarrassment of explaining how they do business in the jail.

I emerge into a barred walkway, where a heavyset guard in sunglasses and a black uniform holds the keys to the dormitories. I am waved through the last guard station, not into a visitors' room but into a sunlit prison yard. The gate clatters shut behind me.

The jail is the largest in Mexico City and holds more than twice the number of prisoners that it has space for. The men locked up there are among some of the most dangerous in Mexico, which is no small statement in a country where there is no shortage of brutal criminals.

A few months earlier the jail held Archibaldo Iván Guzmán, the son of Mexico's most-wanted man, drug kingpin Joaquín "El Chapo" Guzmán, currently waging Mexico's bloodiest-ever drug turf war, with an annual body count several times higher than that of all the coalition troops lost in one year in Iraq and Afghanistan combined.

The prison recently held members of Los Tiras, one of the most vicious and notorious kidnap gangs from the capital's grim Iztapalapa neighborhood, and several high-ranking lieutenants of the Gulf cartel, one of the warring gangs whose enforcers shoot, stab, and torture opponents to death with gusto from Acapulco to Matamoros, and post some of the most gruesome of their hits on YouTube. When I am left standing alone in the patio, I feel panic welling up within me.

Out of the corner of my eye I can't help noticing one man sharpening a shank with long rasping strokes on the razor-wire-topped wall. I feel my shoulders tense and my hands ball up into fists. I want to get this over with, so I turn to a prisoner and ask if he can direct me to Salim, the Lebanese. He nods, and points to a man in his middle thirties, of middle height and with powerful shoulders, standing at the top of a flight of steps, deep in conversation with another prisoner who appears to be chatting on a cell phone. I look up and Boughader raises a hand to greet me.

Among the white-clad prisoners, Boughader is particularly immaculate. He wears a tight white polo shirt tucked into well-pressed cream slacks, a black belt, and polished black shoes. I notice his neatly cropped hair is flecked with gray and carefully brushed over. Somehow the aura of the well-turned-out maître d' has followed him to the prison block.

With my slightly jangled nerves, I am immediately taken by how self-possessed he appears to be, his hands thrust casually into his pockets as he walks with a slow, rolling gait. He leads me back up a flight of steps and along a second-floor corridor to his barred cell, where we can sit down and talk. The cells are standard prison pens, with one innovation: The inmates have blocked out the bars that open the cells to the corridor with plywood for privacy, which many of them clearly need. As we walk by the open cell doors, I see that a number have either wives or girlfriends visiting them. There is also a cloud of smoke as someone is smoking grass in his cell.

To prepare for the visit, I have been reading up on Lebanon, in particular its turbulent history and complex multifaith society. It has suffered invasions, occupation, and wars with Israel, and constant meddling by Syria in its national affairs, including recent assassinations of emergent nationalist leaders seeking to shape their country and assert their sovereignty in regional affairs.

The fiercely proud Lebanese themselves, I learned, represent a complex mosaic of faiths scarcely seen since the fall of Granada in 1492. The country comprises Maronite, Melkite, and Chaldean Christian sects, among others. Representing Islam are the Shia, the "followers of Ali," most living in the south of Lebanon.

Then there are the Sufi mystics with their whirling and poetry, and the Druze, like Boughader and his family, who folded elements of Christian Gnosticism into their Muslim faith. Finally, there are Lebanese Jews, once a large group spread throughout the small country, now reduced to perhaps just a few hundred that remain in Beirut.

The conflicts with Israel and the bloody civil war that ripped the country apart in the 1970s and 1980s triggered a massive diaspora. Large groups of Lebanese scattered throughout Australia, the United States, and even Latin America, where prominent people of Lebanese descent include Colombian rocker Shakira, Mexican screen goddess Salma Hayek, and business tycoon Carlos Slim Helú, locked in a waltz with Bill Gates for the title of the world's richest man.

Then there is the history of Boughader's own family. He will tell me that he was born in the diaspora in Mexico, to parents who shared the hopes of many Lebanese of one day returning to their homeland. In fact, they did go back, when he was nine.

His father brought the family to his home in the villages of the central mountains, which have commanding views over the smashed-up streets of Beirut, and the international airport backed by the shimmering Mediterranean. In times of peace, it is a breathtaking spot, Lebanese say, surrounded by pine trees, and dusted with snow in winter.

The children went to local schools, but when the harsh civil war washed up the mountainside from the coastal strip, the family once again packed their bags, this time heading to Germany, where they spent several years before fetching up back in Mexico.

Boughader steps into the cell and gestures for me to follow, then closes the barred door behind us. The space inside is dark, lit by a single bare lightbulb. It has two bunkbeds. Alongside them, he has set out two plastic patio chairs next to a table topped with a neat green tablecloth that suggests a restaurant.

He invites me to sit down and uses a hot plate to prepare a strong cup of coffee laced with cardamom, serving it up in delicate espresso cups with an olive sprig logo. I take a sip and I am stunned. It is one of the best cups of coffee I have ever tasted.

"The people from the U.S. Consulate used to say my coffee was better than Starbucks," he says in English, his broad-set eyes twinkling in the light of the bare bulb, rattling off some of the different styles and types of coffee he would serve up in the café he ran with his sister in Tijuana's Hipódromo neighborhood.

The Café La Libanesa was set back from the street in a row of small shops. It was best known for the rich dark cardamom-laced Café Najjar coffee, imported from Beirut, and a range of Arabic pastries—mouthwatering mille-feuille confections whipped up from pistachios, pine nuts, and honey.

Aside from employees from the U.S. Consulate a few yards up the street, the clientele during the day was mostly the well-heeled Mexican families from the neighborhood, who would lunch on fresh hummus, falafel, and tabbouleh salads, tangy with mint and lemon juice. They liked the food, the pastries Boughader brought in fresh every day from his mother's bakery up the road, and the flat breads and other supplies he would buy during the weekly trips he made over the border to suppliers in San Diego specializing in Middle Eastern fare. At night the restaurant regulars would be replaced by a younger crowd who would come by to shoot pool on the tables he kept in the bar and sip cool beers.

Polite and well turned out in slacks and a shirt, sometimes a suit and tie, Boughader had the easy, welcoming manner that turns a nice eatery into a neighborhood success. "We opened every day at ten and kept going through midnight," he tells me in English, one of four languages he speaks. "At the weekend, if you wanted a table you had to call ahead and book, it was that busy."

A special welcome was reserved for visitors from Lebanon, who were drawn to the cedar tree emblem picked out in gold on the café window. The cedar is much more than just a tree for most Lebanese. The symbol of the age-old evergreen, with its broad spreading branches, has long associations and shared meanings uniting every ethnic and religious group in the country.

For diaspora Lebanese living in exile, it has become a beacon and a symbol, allowing Muslims, Christians, and Jews to transcend their differences, and to find common ground beyond the narrow, sectarian politics of the last few decades that have drawn them into conflict. "People would see the cedar tree outside and they would know to expect a welcome," Boughader says.

I look at Boughader, who is sitting on a smashed-up plastic patio chair, mended with an improvised wooden leg, in this prison cell. What was he involved in? I wonder. How did the smuggling pipeline, if that's what it was, get started? Who went through it?

"My only mistake was having a restaurant on the border in Tijuana, where two out of every three people are smugglers," he says, as we sit sipping the delicately perfumed demitasse of coffee. "It all started when a Lebanese guy came into the café one afternoon. He was upset because he had been denied a U.S. visa by the consulate." Downcast, the man looked for consolation in the café a short walk from the consulate. Had it been any other city in the world, it would likely have ended with a little commiseration, Boughader says.

But this was Tijuana, after all, and the café proprietor started talking to the man and explaining to him that he might make it across to Southern California by other means. If he couldn't go with the visa, maybe a coyote could help him. "I tried to help him. I told him he shouldn't try to cross through the mountains—to the east of the city—because it was dangerous and he could get robbed or killed. I told him he would be better off going into town, finding a smuggler, and getting across that way in a car," he says.

Hooked up with a local coyote, the man successfully crossed over the border to San Diego hidden in a vehicle, and then on to a new life within the United States, where there are large diaspora communities of Lebanese in the metro Detroit area and in New York. When he reached his new home stateside, word soon got out that he had slipped into the United States with the help of a sympathetic Lebanese restaurant proprietor in Tijuana.

According to Boughader's version, an informal people trafficking network arose almost organically, without guidance, direction, or encouragement from him. This version would later be dismissed as absurd by U.S. human smuggling experts I spoke with. They would tell me that smuggling exotic aliens to the United States from the Middle East, Asia, or Eastern Europe involves a large outlay. The transcontinental networks often begin with a "recruiter" in the country of origin, in this case Lebanon. That person will solicit individuals who want to travel, and draw them into the network, which has routes and other logistics all worked out in advance.

There are then further expenses for buying visas or other travel documents from corrupt consular officials—in this case out of the side door of the Mexican consulate in Beirut, for a fee of $3,000. Then there are air tickets, as well as additional funds for bribing immigration officials in Mexico, and providing hotels or safe houses, often not just in one transit country, but several. The network would have had nothing random about it.

In Boughader's truncated version, it was more like priming a pump. "The first ones across sent out my name and telephone number to their families in Lebanon, and told them how I had helped them get to the United States," he says.

By the start of the new millennium, a steady stream of Lebanese, many from Shia villages in the south of the country, would come trekking to Tijuana and beat a path to Boughader's door.

"Lebanon is a very small country. The communities are very close. Everybody knows everybody. All the Druze know each other," he said. "All the people I helped knew each other. They were a brother, or a cousin, or a friend of a friend."

Many would come from a village in the south of Lebanon, where most inhabitants are Shia, Boughader tells me. The area, which is close to the Israeli border, is a stronghold for Iranian-backed Hizballah militants, who have used the strip for years to fire barrages of short-range Katyusha rockets at civilian targets in northern Israel. Dubbed "Little Katies," the rockets are generally made of galvanized steel, and packed with TNT and ball bearings, blasting scalding metal across an area the size of a soccer field. The attacks have occurred for years, most recently in 2006 during the monthlong war with Israel provoked by the kidnapping of two Israeli Defense Force troops by Hizballah.

The number of people using the route was growing, Boughader recalls. Sometimes several people would show up on the same day. Often, to his chagrin, they would barely order anything, but just sit at a table as they planned their next move.

Boughader said he would receive them and feed them up. Some would stay in local hotels, others would stay at his home in the city. They would pay him for his hospitality, usually between one hundred and five hundred dollars, while he helped them sort out a way of crossing into San Diego.

The migrants would often show up with two or three telephone numbers for *polleros* that had been passed on by family sponsors living stateside, Boughader said. They almost invariably turned out to be cell phone numbers that didn't work, so he played the role of broker, helping his compatriots to make a new link with a coyote to help take them across to the United States.

Sometimes the smugglers would drop by his restaurant, and Boughader would act as translator, helping arrange the deal between the Spanish-speaking Mexican smugglers and their Arabic-speaking clients from Lebanon. "They'd say, 'Do me a favor,' and I did it just to help," he says, insisting that he had not initiated any of the contacts.

"I never knew who the smugglers were, just their nicknames. There was one guy who was called El Gordo, but more than that I didn't know," he says. "If you are not Mexican, they would kill you in a week. They are mafias. They have a job, and they don't like competition."

Prices were usually settled at between $2,000 and $3,000, Boughader says. (Other sources and reports would peg that cost higher, at between $3,500 and $4,500 for the final hop over the border.) He would advise the Lebanese *pollos* not to pay until they got across to the other side.

Helping Middle Easterners enter the United States illegally was something that would always be of particular concern to U.S. federal immigration police seeking to keep terrorists out. But when the passenger airliners struck the World Trade Center and the Pentagon on September 11, Boughader knew that his smuggling activities would inevitably come under even closer scrutiny from over the border.

Concerned at the consequences that his involvement might bring him, he tried to back away from the smuggling operation that had by then taken on a life of its own and grown beyond his control. But by that time it was too late, it had gotten out of hand.

"I had first two people, then three more talking in Arabic in my restaurant, and that started looking bad after 9/11. . . . My Mexican friends told me I was stupid to help them," he says.

The people he helped to cross over the border were not terrorists, he says, nor were they connected to terror groups, but were only interested in seeking a better life in the United States, many of them among the Lebanese community in Michigan.

"They went to work. Lebanese are hardworking, very good at business," he says, growing a little impatient, when I ask him if any of them were terrorists, or had links to Hizballah. "Do you know any Lebanese terrorists in the United States? For sure not! . . . Terrorists don't exist!"

U.S. federal police see it all very differently. They had been aware of Lebanese groups who had kept ties to Hizballah living in the United States for years. What they found in at least two investigations in Michigan was nothing short of alarming, and that trail would lead back to Mexico.

It was time for me to get on a flight to Detroit, where some of the illegal immigrants moved by Boughader's network ended up. I wanted to see for myself what evidence I could find that Boughader had moved a terrorist.

It is a cold, wet April evening when I land in Detroit. The journey from Phoenix took me over ten hours, as the American Airlines plane I was due to fly on was grounded. By the time I arrive, I am in a peevish mood as I take a cab to Dearborn, quarreling pointlessly with the cabdriver over a three-buck surcharge. I almost miss the transition from what feels like Middle America to the Middle East.

This suburb is to Arabs what Miami is to Latin Americans. The city, more particularly the stretch bounded by Michigan and Warren avenues in Dearborn, is known as the Arab capital of North America, and is a haven for people from across the Arab world.

The area is home to communities from Lebanon, Syria, Iraq, Iran, and Yemen, among other countries, and is dotted with schools providing a bilingual education in English and Arabic. There are television and radio stations broadcasting in Arabic, and several newspapers catering to an Arab-American readership.

The suburb also has the largest mosque in the United States, the Islamic Community Center, and several churches catering to the many Christian Arabs, including Chaldeans from Iraq and Christian Palestinians from Ramallah on the West Bank.

I roll by rows of convenience stores, pastry shops, and businesses, some with bright neon signs in Arabic and English, selling everything from water pipes and green almonds to eyeglasses, as I head for a dinner with the executive director of the local chapter of the Council on American-Islamic Relations.

Dawud Walid is a tall, serious African-American. He is dressed in a suit, and greets me with a handshake, welcoming me to the Al-Ajani restaurant in the strip. We sit down to a meal of kabobs, tabbouleh, and quail, drinking fruit smoothies and, later, a few cups of aromatic Lebanese coffee as we chat.

Over the meal, Walid explains the complex mosaic that makes up the Middle Eastern and Islamic communities in metro Detroit. Besides distinct groups of Middle Easterners, it also comprises Muslims from Senegal, Guinea, and Somalia in Africa, as well as African-American Muslims like Walid himself. Their interactions are complex, as are their ties to their homelands, if indeed they have one.

"For the people here, all politics are local," he says, giving as an example the local reaction to the hanging of deposed Iraqi strongman Saddam Hussein more than a year earlier. As the news broke that cold December night in 2006, Iraqi Sunnis and Shias clashed on the streets of Dearborn, just a few hundred yards from the restaurant where we are having dinner.

I am struck by how some Arab immigrants are clearly still living in the Old World, and are swayed by its tensions. I ask Walid whether he thinks that the U.S. security services monitor the wider community for possible ties to terror groups, and I am surprised by the frankness of his answer. "If they didn't, they wouldn't be doing their job," he tells me.

To try and give me a better sense of the Lebanese community, and how its members relate to the old country, Walid put me in touch with a Shia imam from south Lebanon, Baqir Berry, whom I arrange to meet at the Islamic Institute of Knowledge in Dearborn the following day.

The institute comprises a mosque and a charter school for girls. The youngsters are piling out of the school as I arrive, dressed in traditional headscarves, chattering and laughing as they wait to be collected by their mothers, who are also wearing hajib.

The imam greets me warmly and leads me into his office, where he summons coffee and iced water. Berry looks to be in his forties, with dark hair, a ready smile, and an open, engaging manner. I tell him that my knowledge of Lebanon's turbulent recent history, especially the events surrounding the birth of Hizballah, is scant. He nods. It is something that he has lived through, and he shares a couple of personal recollections of two pivotal events.

His memory of the 1982 Israeli invasion of Lebanon—to weaken or turf out the Palestine Liberation Organization based there—is of seeing a badly burned boy refugee from Palestine with his skin hanging off him in strips in the streets of Beirut. In the second memory, a year or so later, he recalls a pressure wave striking his family's home and sucking the air right out of it—it was the blast from the huge Hizballah truck bomb ripping apart the Marine Corps barracks.

These traumas are in the past. The Lebanese settled in Michigan, he tells me, are by and large outward-looking, progressive, and eager to integrate into life in the United States, sharing key traits such as entrepreneurship and a tolerance with respect to cultural differences. Nevertheless, there is sympathy in his community for Hizballah, which many Lebanese see as having liberated the south of their country from Israeli occupation in the early 1980s, and as a source of support and services for refugees and displaced families from the conflicts.

"People look at the humanitarian side," Berry said. "They may support Hizballah in their hearts, but they are cautious and want to follow the law in the United States. They know where to draw the line."

That line was clearly drawn with the 9/11 attacks. However, both before and after that pivotal event, there have been cases, some of them egregious, when Lebanese have supported the radical extremist group. Investigations by federal authorities have, at one time or another, uncovered Lebanese individuals and even networks that have been deeply involved in a range of activities supporting radical causes back in the Old World. The extent of that involvement became clear in a case that broke in North Carolina several years before the September 11 attacks, back in 1995.

An alert off-duty sheriff's deputy working at a tobacco wholesaler in Statesville, North Carolina, became suspicious when he spotted a group of Middle Eastern men with $30,000 to $40,000 in cash stuffed into a Wal-Mart bag attempting to buy cartons of cigarettes.

Members of the group would come into JR Tobacco most days when the deputy, Bob Fromme, was working at the store, buying as many as 4,500 cartons of cigarettes at a time with bundles of cash. Running the plates of the vehicles, Fromme began to piece together a picture of what they were doing.

The group, a number of whom were Lebanese illegal immigrants, were part of a ring buying thousands of cartons of cigarettes in North Carolina, where taxes were just a nickel a pack, and then driving them to Michigan, where duty was levied at seventy-five cents a pack. Investigators found that the group had as many as half a dozen drivers working full time, cramming cases of Marlboros, Newports, and Kools, among other popular brands, into cars, vans, U-Hauls, and even semitrailers for the twelve-hour road trip to Michigan. Once in the metro Detroit area, they would deliver them to garages, restaurants, and convenience stores in the Middle Eastern community, realizing cash profits of up to $40,000 on an average day from three van loads crammed with cigarettes.

The ringleader of the group, Mohamad Youssef Hammoud, funneled the profits generated by the scam back to Hizballah in Lebanon. Investigators also found that Hammoud had an eye-popping shopping list of paramilitary gear he sought to obtain for militants in the old country. The list, detailed by the investigation, included night vision goggles, cameras, scopes, surveying equipment, global positioning systems, mine and metal detection equipment, video equipment, advanced aircraft analysis and design software, laptop computers, and stun guns. Other gear bought with the proceeds of racketeering in the United States included radios, radars, ultrasonic dog repellents, laser range finders, and equipment for mining, drilling, and blasting.

Fromme, who initiated the case and followed it through to conviction in 2002, has as clear a sense of what Hammoud was like as anyone involved in the case. "He was very quiet and soft-spoken. If you looked at him you would think he was shy, timid, and unassertive," Fromme told me in a telephone conversation. "But in reality he was a trained killer." Hammoud, investigators discovered, had undergone extensive training as a Hizballah fighter in Lebanon, and had entered the United States on a fake visa obtained in Venezuela.

After he was arrested, his readiness to use violence would come out in a letter to his accomplices, in which he set out a plan for them to spring him from prison. In it Hammoud explained how he planned to fake a kidney stone attack. As he was moved to the hospital, he wanted his accomplices to ambush the vehicle taking him there, shoot the guards, and, in one chilling detail, murder the U.S. attorney Ken Bell, who had brought the charges against him. "The letter read, and I am quoting it directly: 'Put two into the left eye of that arrogant bastard U.S. attorney,'" Fromme told me. The "two" referred to the number of bullets they were to use in the hit.

The letter was intercepted by police and Hammoud was subsequently convicted by the court and jailed for a total of 155 years, although his brother, who was also arrested and tried, is now free, presumably in Lebanon. Five other people originally indicted in the case along with Hammoud are currently on the lam, Fromme said.

The case was troubling for federal police, as it involved Lebanese militants based in the United States brazenly working on the wrong side of the law to raise funds and buy equipment for Hizballah, a paramilitary group that had killed hundreds of U.S. servicemen in devastating bomb attacks.

The investigation involving Hammoud was not the only one carried out by police that uncovered Lebanese Hizballah activists at work in the United States. Another detailed activities of a man who sought to raise funds for Hizballah even after the 9/11 attacks had led many in the stateside Lebanese community to reexamine their support for the group. The case, subsequently prosecuted in Michigan, involved a Shiite illegal immigrant living in Dearborn who was convicted in 2005 of providing material support to a terrorist organization, once again Hizballah.

Mahmoud Youssef Kourani was arrested after holding a public meeting at his home in Dearborn during Ramadan in 2002 at which a guest speaker from Lebanon solicited funds for Hizballah. Tens of thousands of dollars he raised in the Detroit area were destined for Hizballah's Orphans of Martyrs program, which supports the families of militants killed carrying out Hizballah terrorist operations, including suicide bombings and rocket attacks.

According to a federal grand jury indictment, Kourani had received specialized training in "radical Shiite fundamentalism, weaponry, spy craft, and counterintelligence" in Lebanon and elsewhere in the Middle East.*

The fact that these activities were being carried out in the United States was alarming enough. But the kicker from this investigation was how Kourani had entered the United States and made his way to Dearborn.

A Senate judiciary subcommittee heard testimony that Kourani paid a three-thousand-dollar bribe to a Mexican consular official in Beirut to obtain a Mexican visa. After traveling to Mexico, almost certainly by air via Europe, he crossed surreptitiously over the U.S. border in the trunk of a car in February 2001.

It was a stunning and tantalizing detail. Did Boughader, I wonder, smuggle Kourani into the United States? As the case is of some considerable sensitivity, I could find no one among my contacts in law enforcement who was prepared to comment in detail on it. Boughader, meanwhile, told me in jail that he can't remember the names of any of the people he helped slip into California. Nevertheless, there is considerable circumstantial evidence that suggests he may have helped move him. The Hizballah supporter was slipped north using the same techniques used by Tijuana coyotes, in the trunk of a car, at a time that Boughader's smuggling pipeline from Lebanon was in full swing in the city.

Boughader told me that many of the Lebanese who passed through his café in Tijuana heading for a new life in either New York or Michigan were Shia from villages in southern Lebanon, the same area that Kourani came from. Illegal immigrants traveling to the United States from that troubled strip of southern Lebanon would be coming from an area where Hizballah has a strong presence, and where militants are active in carrying out attacks on Israel, including firing salvos of Little Katies at settlements.

Whether that would make them militants themselves, and whether

---

*U.S. Senate Judiciary Subcommittee on Immigration, Border Security, and Citizenship and U.S. Senate Judiciary Subcommittee on Terrorism, Technology, and Homeland Security, *Border Security and Enforcement: The 9/11 Commission Staff Report on Training for Border Inspectors, Document Integrity, and Defects in the U.S. Visa Program,* March 20, 2005. http://judiciary.senate.gov/testimony.cfm?id=1414&wit_id=4067.

Kourani was among them, is only, at least in these pages, speculation. It is clear enough, though, that for U.S. authorities it was fertile ground for concern.

I try and put myself in the shoes of the immigration police and the investigators of the Joint Terrorism Task Force that set out to investigate cases like these. Viewed through the hard lens of law enforcement, there can be no distinction between a would-be suicide bomber and someone who wants to provide help for social projects supported by Hizballah in southern Lebanon. Their bottom line is safeguarding the U.S. homeland, period.

While the porous southwest border seems to be the greatest area of concern for many Americans worried about homeland security, there are also a number of other soft spots that might provide an alternative way for any militant to press through and carry out whatever activity it might be, whether fund-raising for a group such as Hizballah, or shopping for them, or actually planning to carry out an attack within the U.S. homeland.

The only terrorist to have been caught crossing the U.S. land borders to carry out an attack was the so-called Millennium Bomber, Ahmed Ressam of Algeria. Ressam, a petty thief who had trained at an Islamic camp in Afghanistan, actually crossed by ferry from Vancouver Island, arriving in Washington state with nitroglycerin and timers, en route to try and bomb LAX on December 31, 1999. The attempt was foiled by alert inspectors at Port Angeles, but nevertheless flagged the Canadian frontier as another vulnerability in U.S. homeland security.

Then there is the case of Youssef Hammoud, which also has lessons. The Hizballah supporter bought a fake visa to enter the United States, although it was subsequently discovered. He had entered seeking political asylum, ironically citing persecution from Hizballah.

The 9/11 attackers themselves all entered the United States legally, most of them from Saudi Arabia, a close ally in the Middle East. The processes for granting asylum, awarding visas, and allowing students to come and study in the United States also clearly present vulnerabilities of their own.

Finally, there are lessons from the suicide bomb attacks on the transportation system in Britain, my home country, in July 2005, which are really tough to assimilate if secure borders are taken to be the greatest priority for a nation vulnerable to attack by Islamic extremists. The subway and bus blasts that killed fifty-two people—the worst attack on London in terms of loss of life since the Blitz in the Second World War, incidentally—were carried out not by immigrants, legal or otherwise, but by young men born and bred in Yorkshire, in the very heart of England. The family of one even had a fish-and-chip shop in Leeds.

How on earth, I wonder, do you begin to address that? The answer can clearly not be found in better border or travel document security. Beginning to understand, let alone find a remedy for it, would involve a much wider discussion about national identity and about social marginalization within a nation, moving into areas of foreign policy. It's a fascinating and very necessary debate, but one that lies far beyond the reach of this book.

ELEVEN

The Minutemen

The trucker in the Stetson and plaid shirt is packing a .44 Magnum in a holster shaded by the overhang of his belly. But the elementary school teacher at his side has trumped him. He has a Smith & Wesson .50 caliber revolver a foot long. The glinting hand cannon is dangling from his neck and shoulder in a tooled leather holster like a papoose, and with its heavy brass shells it weighs as much as a newborn baby. "It's so heavy it hurts my back," quips Anthony Ford, dressed in a white T-shirt and sunglasses. "You could shoot a polar bear with it," says another man, and they laugh.

I am standing among a group of Minutemen mustering at a ranch in the Altar Valley, the sparsely populated corridor leading up from the Mexican border in southern Arizona. It's a hot day at the end of March, so bright my eyes are scrunched at the sunlight. The dusty parking lot is filling up with pickup trucks and RVs, as the group of veterans, teachers, engineers, and picture framers from around the country gather at the start of a monthlong stakeout, dubbed, somewhat portentously, Operation Stand Your Ground.

Some of them have driven hundreds of miles to take part, and two of them have even turned up in their own antique aircraft, left at a strip nearby. They are here to spot for crossers that have slipped past the Border Patrol and National Guard watching the rusted barbed-wire fence several days' walk to the south. Setting up tents, rolling out awnings and coconut mats outside their mobile homes, the group of a few score volunteers is getting ready for the first of the weekend shifts, scouring the mesquite for intruders from the comfort of a candy-striped lawn chair.

"Our government isn't doing their job," engineer Roger Plank says, explaining why he has given up a weekend to sit out in the "hot zone" southwest of Tucson with members of the Minuteman Civil Defense Corps. "When I go to the airport they take away my toothpaste, but yet anyone can walk across our border with who knows what. . . . So there's something definitely wrong there," he adds with a shrug.

The Ku Klux Klan had pioneered civilian border patrols thirty years earlier, when Grand Wizard David Duke and California Grand Dragon Tom Metzger roared up to the San Ysidro port of entry in a car, in a scene reminiscent of *The Dukes of Hazzard*. It had a white sticker stretched over the door panel announcing the Klan Border Watch, which aimed to keep Mexican hordes from crossing into the southwestern states. The flashbulbs popped, but the movement fizzled.

There were isolated ranchers over the years who rounded up migrants in the borderlands, some at gunpoint, although the civilian border patrol movement proper sprang up in the wake of the September 11 attacks. The Minutemen—a name contested by several volunteer groups—set out to patrol the line. Supporters give up the occasional weekend or a few days of vacation and join in the patrols, which serve the dual role of what they see as helping out the Border Patrol and protesting what they say is the government's inability to secure the border.

The movement had begun five years before my visit to the muster with a splashy headline in a weekly paper in Arizona's Cochise County, on part of the most heavily crossed stretch of the entire border. "Enough Is Enough! A Public Call to Arms! Citizens Border Patrol Militia Now

Minuteman Civil Defense Corps volunteer Wes Pecsok scans a trail used by many illegal immigrants. (Jeff Topping)

Forming!" thundered the banner headline on the *Tombstone Tumble-weed* newspaper in the fall of 2002. "Concerned citizens turn off the t.v. Join together to protect your country in a time of war!"

The announcement might have struck a discordant note anywhere but Tombstone. But the former silver-mining town on the high plains had been blasted into Wild West lore in 1881 with a staccato burst of gunfire at the O.K. Corral, and it now had a certain reputation to keep up. Former sheriff Virgil Earp, his hastily deputized brother Wyatt, and consumptive gambler Doc Holliday had laid down the gold standard for frontier justice with blazing six-guns when they blasted the cattle-rustling McLaurys and Clantons into nearby Boot Hill Graveyard—a lonely plot with sweeping views over the barren Dragoon Mountains.

The town now lives by that past. Gnarly cowpokes in dusters tout tickets for gunfight shows reenacting that thirty-second gun battle at two o'clock sharp every day, and stagecoach drivers tack up their horses and don microphones and headsets to drive visitors along a tawdry strip of adobe and wooden-fronted stores selling pistols, cowboy gear, Indian jewelry, and ice cream.

Like many in the town, gravelly-voiced newspaper publisher Chris Simcox was a recent transplant. Slightly built, boyish looking, and in his early forties, the former private school teacher had packed his bags and left Los Angeles in a funk in the days after the 9/11 attacks, just over a year earlier.

Imagining a dark mushroom cloud curling over the city from an imminent terrorist attack, he had wound up his teaching business, bought guns, and headed out east to Arizona, leaving two broken marriages behind him. With ideas forming about protecting the homeland, he ended up in Tombstone, where he worked in a gunslinger show before he bought the *Tumbleweed.*

The sixteen-page paper billed itself as the "news in the town that was too tough to die," and it used a tall seriphed typeface as Old West as a honky-tonk piano in a miners' saloon. Striking a revivalist note, Simcox challenged residents to attend a recruitment drive for a new militia at the newspaper's office on the appropriately named Toughnut Street the following Saturday.

Like many Americans after the fall of the Twin Towers, Simcox was deeply alarmed by the porous southern border. Calling the group Civil Homeland Defense, he pictured volunteers patrolling the borderlands in southern Cochise County to stanch the flow of undocumented "invaders" into the United States, more than 400,000 of whom had been arrested crossing north through the Tucson sector of the line alone since the 9/11 attacks.

"No weapons are necessary at this time. . . . We will gather info on training; we will organize and plan responsibly in order to peacefully turn the invaders away from our selected stretch of border," Simcox wrote in a rambling call to action. The "committee of vigilantes" would reclaim the rugged borderlands a few miles south of Tombstone "bit by bit, mile by mile," he said, adopting a rousing, constitutionalist tone, pledging that "we the people can solve the problem the feds will not deal with." Unlike the federal border police, the new border militia would be "free from the constraints of jurisdiction," and "less controlled by the laws that create the paralysis in our government agencies that are sworn to protect us!"

Raising a civilian militia to help secure the border in the post-9/11 world was not an idea unique to Simcox. As he put together his posse in Tombstone, out west in suburban Orange County in Southern California a retired tax accountant was on the verge of a revelation of his own.

Jim Gilchrist was a Vietnam veteran who served in the U.S. Marine Corps and received the Purple Heart. He returned to the United States and trained as a certified public accountant specializing in tax, after a dalliance with journalism in the 1970s. He later became an admirer of Ronald Reagan, and drifted toward more conservative values, with clear leanings toward the GOP and the Constitution Party, with occasional support for a "principled rogue Democrat," he would later say. Then, in his midfifties, his eclectic range of interests included "studying home-building" and political activism, and an ever more pressing preoccupation with illegal immigration and border security.

By the fall of 2004, his ideas on immigration and homeland security were taking shape for what he called his "project." He envisioned some kind of direct civil action, although he still didn't know what to call his movement. He was sitting in a Starbucks in Aliso Viejo when it finally struck him: He would call it the Minuteman Project. After all, it had a certain ring to it.

The name came from an American Revolution–era militia that was made up of loyal New England patriots who volunteered to fend off marauding British redcoats on the turbulent cusp of independence in 1775. The group of Massachusetts fishermen, farmers, traders, and artisans—which included silversmith and legendary "midnight rider" Paul Revere—got their name from their claim that they could be ready to fight for their nascent country at a minute's notice.

But that wasn't all. The patriotic cachet of the Minuteman name had gained a more lethal twist in the last century after one of the United States' key intercontinental ballistic missile systems was named for the group. Lurking in underground silos across the American West, these

Minutemen were aimed at the former Soviet Union, keeping the peace in the Cold War with the threat of a massive retaliatory nuclear strike. The giddy mixture of patriotism and bellicosity rode before the incipient movement like a bow wave before a tanker.

Gilchrist had heard Simcox on talk radio. Sensing that they had a similar vision, he picked up the phone and called him in Arizona. Soon the retired accountant and the former teacher got together, hammering out a plan for how they might bring citizen patrols to the role of border security, under the banner of the Minuteman Project.

Recruitment for Civil Homeland Defense had been limited to residents of Cochise County. But the idea that began to take shape was more ambitious and far-reaching in its scope. The Minuteman call went beyond the rugged Arizona border county to the heartlands of the United States, urging patriotic citizens nationwide to step up and help secure the international line.

Within six weeks the group had a star-spangled Web site—courtesy of Gilchrist's brother in Rhode Island—complete with the logo of a Minuteman in Georgian garb on his way to rout the British. Soon the telephone started to ring and ring. Simcox and Gilchrist began fielding calls and e-mails from volunteers from as far afield as California and Maine who were looking to find out more about the patrols, and wondering how they might take part. Calls also began coming from the media, including FOX News, which had Gilchrist on the *Hannity and Colmes* show for the first time. "I felt like a deer in headlights," he later told me. "I wasn't used to it."

Simcox had envisaged a group freed from some of the restraints placed on law enforcement for his border patrol militia. But the new Minuteman Project that he and Gilchrist developed had a softer tone. There was now no talk of vigilantes or vigilantism. For Gilchrist, as he would later tell me, it was more of a "call to voices" than a call to arms. It was about using First Amendment rights of free speech and free assembly to make a political point. "It wasn't about going down there with jugs of moonshine and shotguns. . . . That wasn't what we wanted, it was to be peaceful, we thought, 'Let's force the debate,'" he said.

Before the first volunteers arrived for muster in the storied streets of Tombstone, the Minuteman Project had adopted a standard operating procedure, or SOP, which was quite clear on how they should treat any border crossers they happened to encounter. Unlike earlier Cochise County vigilantes—ranchers who had beaten, hog-tied and even blasted migrants with buckshot to mete out their own backwoods remedy for illegal immigration—the Minutemen would operate within the letter of the law.

Volunteers could carry sidearms for their own protection (although Gilchrist chose not to), but they were told they could not effect arrests, and were advised against having any kind of direct contact with migrants. They could only report the number and direction of a group to the Border Patrol so that agents could detain them.

The first patrols began along the seven-strand barbed-wire fence along the border road between Douglas and Naco, Arizona, in April 2005. A couple of hundred volunteers, some sporting T-shirts declaring them to be "Undocumented Border Patrol Agents," camped out in lawn chairs under fluttering Stars and Stripes flags, training binoculars south over the wastes to Mexico. At the end of three weeks they claimed to have reported 336 intruders to authorities.

The Border Patrol came out against the action, saying that they did not welcome untrained civilians out on the border, where they might set off ground sensors, make their agents' tasks more difficult, and even injure themselves. One federal agent later told me he felt uncomfortable seeing some volunteers in Border Patrol caps, ostensibly passing themselves off as a police outfit to migrants who knew no different. Nevertheless, and despite the fact that cracks had appeared in their own relationship, Simcox and Gilchrist claimed the patrol as a success.

Citing personal differences, they split, with Gilchrist retaining the Minuteman Project name, and Simcox forming his own group, which he called the Minuteman Civil Defense Corps. Sparks from their falling-out caught in the underbrush, and soon there were several other groups, including the Friends of the Border Patrol, set up by Andy

Ramirez in California, and the California Minutemen, a kind of lumpen mob assembled by a former Minuteman Project volunteer from Ocean-side named Jim Chase.

Revealing the breadth of the movement in all its unregulated glory, Chase, a retired postal worker, called for volunteers to bring "baseball bats, stun guns, and machetes" to a summer stakeout near Campo, California. Recruitment was open to "all those who do not want their family murdered by Al Qaeda, illegal migrants . . . alien barbarians [and] Ninja-dressed drug smugglers."

I had followed the Minutemen, in their variety of forms, from the beginning. It was clear that they had become a conduit for many Americans' frustration at their government's apparent inability to se-cure the porous Mexico border. Leaving aside what they said, I had decided to go out with Simcox and the Minuteman Civil Defense Corps to see what it is that they actually do. The group has been out on the border longer than anyone, and claims the greatest number of volun-teers, nearly nine thousand in all. Since I first reported on them, they have also received hundreds of thousands of dollars in donations, bought a lot of equipment, and gained considerable experience from several operations on the line, and I wanted to see what they actually do for border security.

To that end, I am standing outside a white trailer to enroll for the muster, along with a few score of mostly middle-aged men and women in jeans, sweats, or army surplus military fatigues. I had called ahead and arranged the visit with Simcox, who greets me in the yard. He is dressed in jeans, a black T-shirt, and prescription sunglasses, and looks young for his years. He tells me I will have to go through the same back-ground check as all volunteers, which is designed to screen out felons and racists. (There is, though, no national database for racists.) The vol-unteers get field ID cards, identifying them by name and their state of origin, while I get a temporary media pass.

A friendly woman volunteer processes me in the trailer, and then waves me on through to a training workshop. It has already begun in a shady mess tent set up next door, and I slip inside and snap open the lawn chair I bought at Wal-Mart on the drive down from Phoenix. I notice it still has its $9.98 price tag and a MADE IN CHINA sticker, a reminder that goods and money know few borders under globalization, though the flow of migrant labor is increasingly tightly regulated, first by governments, and now even this group of civilian activists. I look around me at my new companions.

Instructor Barry Arcala is wearing military fatigues and is addressing a group of volunteers gathered in a semicircle. He explains what we should bring out on the stakeout, and what we should and shouldn't do while out on the line. A Marine Corps veteran, he looks and talks like a drill sergeant, and I notice he has a pistol holstered on his belt and a whistle on a lanyard around his neck, like an NCO about to send troops over the top at Gallipoli.

"You will take long-sleeved shirts, clean socks, hats, windbreaker, sturdy boots. When you step on a cactus, or in a ground squirrel hole, you'll know it. . . . Gloves, sunblock, insect repellent, and water! Water! Water! All the water you can think of," he says, galloping through the SOP as I glance around at the other volunteers. Out of the corner of my eye I see two latecomers arrive, an elderly couple with a navy blue stroller. In the child's seat they have a tiny dog sitting in a wicker basket. I wonder how the dog will hold up on the line.

"You need a chair," Arcala thunders. "There ain't no place to sit out there, except on the ground. That's hard and dirty and there's scorpions and all kinds of creatures crawling around down there. The big ones will scare the hell out of you, but the little tiny ones are the most dangerous. Don't get stung by one." I look around and see that most of the volunteers are listening carefully, and some are taking notes. Many of them are not from the Southwest, and the desert is about as familiar to them as the surface of Mars.

Volunteers are allocated to a couple of dozen lookout posts spread out on one of two strips of about ten miles each—dubbed the Bravo and Caballo Loco lines. They stretch out across the parched Altar Valley toward the Baboquivari Mountains that stand over the plain like crumbling ramparts. I have been assigned to the four-till-midnight shift, which I will spend with Simcox out on the Bravo Line, somewhere beneath the Kitt Peak Observatory.

"Bring any food you want to bring, and a flashlight, batteries . . . binoculars, night vision if you've got it," Arcala says, rattling through a list including personal first-aid kits, warm clothes, and of course a sense of humor, which he tells us we are definitely going to need. Finally he gets to the firearms that around half the group wear on their hips, like latter-day Doc Hollidays.

"Carry this for self-protection only, but you had better damn well know the law," Arcala says, tapping his holstered semiautomatic pistol. While it's legal to carry a gun openly in Arizona, I learn that you can't take it out of its holster and flourish it, as that is considered brandishing. It can get you arrested or, worse still, shot by the cops.

I still don't really get it with the guns. Quite what is the point of bringing along a heavy-caliber pistol you could shoot a polar bear with? There are no polar bears here, and if you pull out the weapon and train it on a Mexican, you can go to jail for it.

On reflection, though, carrying weapons is somehow central to what the group is doing, and in a variety of ways. Looking around me, I see that several of the older men are in military fatigues, recalling for them some time spent in the armed services. Being out here is somehow like being in the army, without being in the army; shades of glory and memories of service in a life now routine.

It's also something to do with the shiny fascination of guns, and their role in the foundational myths of the United States. In the earliest years first muskets and later revolvers were needed to take and then defend territory, in a role that somehow reverberates in the current immigration and border security debate centered on safeguarding the homeland.

Then there's the right to bear arms enshrined in the Second Amendment to the U.S. Constitution, which also shadows what the group is doing in a broader political sense. The amendment declares a well-regulated militia as "being necessary to the security of a free State," and prohibits Congress from infringement of "the right of the people to keep and bear arms." Under the founding fathers' vision, if people don't like the government, they can keep heading west and form a new one.

While "the right to bear arms" sounds arcane, you only have to visit a gun show to realize that it is very much a part of the lives of a lot of people, many of whom can recite the Second Amendment by heart. When glancing around at the group, it is obvious there is still something of those aims and that purpose that follows the volunteers. However dated it might seem to me, it has deep historical precedents, and a lived relevance for a lot of the people sitting around at the ranch.

Arcala gets on to the procedure itself, the meat of what we will actually be doing when we get out onto the two lines: "Minutemen observe, report, record, and direct Border Patrol or other appropriate emergency or law enforcement agencies to suspected illegal aliens or illegal activities. . . . You do not verbally contact, physically gesture to, or have any form of communications with suspected illegal aliens," he explains, reiterating the position that the volunteers going out on the watch have no arrest powers, and should have no direct contact with any migrants or intruders.

If we see any intruders we are to make a call in to the communications center, who will report them to the Border Patrol in the local Tucson sector. Agents will then be dispatched to come and make the arrest, rolling out along the trail in their own paddy wagons—Ford pickup trucks with small lockups bolted in the beds.

Arcala explains another procedure that they have developed since they started out two years earlier, and it was one that I was completely unaware of. Volunteers are given powerful rubber flashlights with huge reflectors when they set out for their posts. When they see or hear a group coming up the trail at night, they don't just call it in to the Border Patrol, they also light it up with the flashlights casting a 15-million-candlepower beam—rock concert bright.

"You're out in the dark, you are going to hear these folks coming toward you. You're going to hear them way before you see them. When they get close enough, take those big, powerful flashlights we have and light them up," he says.

Arcala explains that the procedure has a dual function. First, it allows the volunteers to provide an accurate head count of the number in a group. It also seeks to startle the footsore intruders and throw them out of a rhythm they have built up over several days marching north, in the hope that they will just give themselves up. "A lot of these people walking up here . . . now, keep in mind they have been walking for two or three days, thirty-eight miles from that fence. A lot of times by the time they get up to this point, they are tired, dehydrated, and sick, and if you spot them, they'll just sit down. They are waiting for a ride. You light them up, and they just sit down."

Arcala looks around the arc of quizzical faces. The technique requires a certain amount of practice, he explains. They will have to choose the right moment to flick on the switch and bathe the trail in a blaze of light given out by the powerful lamps, which are the size of a small toolbox.

"If you hit it too far out, they are a hundred yards out, they are going to scatter. We want to get a head count to be able to report them to the Border Patrol, so you wait until they get in close," he says.

"How close is close?" asks one man in the group.

"About from here to the port-a-john," Arcala says, pointing to the phone-booth-sized toilet about ten yards from the improvised farmyard classroom. It is clearly going to be a close encounter, something that I had not really counted on.

Arcala also explains that in this busy corridor—where Border Patrol agents nab several hundred people every night—they may well come across drug mules. Cops and local residents know they hack up through the valley at night, hauling bales of pot as they make their way up to a load-out. They travel on foot, on horseback, on even on bicycles—I imagine a kind of ramshackle Tour de France peloton with luggage, pedaling like crazy in the dark.

"There's another situation out here, and it's very rare and I doubt if any of you will see it, but sometimes people come up through here carrying a gun. They are the smugglers, and we have seen it. If you see somebody with a gun, you call that in to coms, you say 'I've got a Code

Black.' You don't light them up, you don't give your post away, you hunker down by your car. If you feel yourself threatened you leave."

One unshaven and grizzled-looking man shares with the group an experience he had in a heavily trafficked area close into the flanks of the darkened mountains by Kitt Peak Observatory. Sitting out on the trail for the night, he saw a group of backpackers carrying dope, and escorted by gunmen with rifles. "There will usually be somebody in front carrying a long-arm [assault rifle], right behind him is going to be a pack of half a dozen guys carrying drugs on bicycles or in backpacks, and right behind him is going to be another guy with a long-arm. . . . The only reason I've run into them is because I'm out there in their territory, by the mountains," he says.

A discussion breaks out in the group on what's the best thing to do if an armed smuggler threatens them. Is it best to leave, or draw your weapon for self-protection? The grizzled-looking guy (who steadfastly refused to give his name to me afterward) is adamant that it is best to err on the side of caution. The best option is to get out of the area as quietly as possible, and to leave your gun at home. "I'm not going to tell you not to carry a weapon, but it can get you into more trouble if you pull that weapon," he says.

The training session comes to an end, and I have an hour or so before I set out on the first shift of the night with Simcox. It has been interesting, and has challenged a couple of assumptions. First, both the instructor and some of the members of the group have a good grasp of what is going on in the valley in terms of trafficking—an understanding that I only have from hanging about with cops of all stripes and talking to people on the south side in my work as a reporter.

Second, despite all the guns on show here, there is a prevailing sense of realism that tempers their outlook. They seem to have a firm hold on the fact that they are civilians, that they are out there to spot and not to get involved in any kind of confrontation with any of the people they might meet picking their way north along the darkened trails.

I am also surprised by the expectation the line supervisors have that they are going to encounter people coming up through the valley. On the first stakeout that I reported on in April 2005, men and women trained their field glasses over a largely empty landscape, with little to report or do—at least that was my clear impression after several days spent around them.

Here, though, the line leaders are expecting to encounter groups trekking up through the valley throughout the night, and they are planning to engage them—lighting them up with powerful flashlights. It is actually quite bold, and I am looking forward to it.

At five o'clock it's time to head out. I follow Simcox as he rolls out of the parking lot heading west on the Bravo Line in a silver Jeep. We drive by the adobe ranch house with children playing on a swing in a yard ringed by an ocotillo fence, and out past the holding pens for cattle. We roll on over a strip of irrigated pasture out toward the Baboquivari Mountains looming several thousand feet above the valley floor.

Gazing up the dirt road, I can clearly make out the large dome of the giant reflecting telescope on the Kitt Peak Observatory, standing proud like a lone tooth in an ocher jawbone. It lies on sacred land of the Tohono O'odham nation, and was built after several tribal elders were won over by a trip to an observatory in Tucson as guests of a group of research astronomers. The elders dubbed their hosts "the long-eyes," and gave them permission to be there as long as their research had no military application and the site remained nonprofit.

We follow the trail over and around cattle grids, passing groups of volunteers setting up at posts spaced to secure a line of sight over the ten-mile reach of the line. I see two volunteers settling into their lawn chairs in the bed of a pickup, giving them a raised-up view over the cactus, greasewood, and mesquite trees to the south. Another group we pass has set up a short way from the road on a low ridgeline where they can get a better view.

At the end of the line, we park by a cattle grid. Roger Plank is out there with another volunteer, and a truck full of new kit. The area is thick with thorny mesquite, creosote brush, and tricky chollas, with their cluster-bomb-like barbs. We are parked at a point where the ranch road, which runs east to west, bisects a broad cattle trail running up from the south.

The loose-packed sand is crisscrossed by dozens of foot tracks, an engaging human drama scribbled in the dirt with tennis shoes, boots, and even sandals. Staring at the ground, I can make out the tracks of men, women, and children meandering across the ranch road and weaving north through the mesquite.

"You can see by the size of the trail it's well worn, it's been used for years," says Simcox as I walk over to join him at the remote high desert crossroads. "For some reason the coyotes love this trail. We don't find too much west of here, this is pretty much the main trail."

Whoever has come up the trail in a two- to three-day trek is by now weary. They have at least another day ahead of them in order to reach a commonly used load-out point by a saddle-shaped hill up on Highway 86 that runs from the Tohono O'odham nation into Tucson. For the migrants, it's the point where they can finally stop walking and flop into a load car for the final ride into the city.

The place where we are setting up for the night lies way behind the rusted metal fence just north of El Sásabe, Sonora, which is watched by Border Patrol and National Guard units. Whoever makes it up the trail to where we are standing would have a fairly good chance of making it through to Phoenix or Tucson, where they would just melt into the city crowds.

The sun is dipping below the mountains and darkness is beginning to steal over the valley, chasing out the last of the golden light. I am very eager to see who will come up the trail later, and also to see what the Minutemen will do.

Just to the north of the spot where Simcox and I will be sitting, Roger Plank is busily trying to camouflage a hulking Dodge Ram pickup truck. He and Paul Farmer, a retired backhoe driver from California, are wrestling to pull a desert camouflage tarpaulin over the hood and roof of the truck in the last golden light of that afternoon and set up for a night of spotting. "There's a full moon tonight, and unless we hide it, they'll see it [when they are] coming up that trail," Plank says.

It is interesting to watch them work, as I see they are using the same materials and techniques that the Sonoran dope smugglers use to hide load cars from Border Patrol and ICE helicopters in the same stretch of desert. It is one more example of the close-up sparring I have seen between smugglers, cops, and now civilian patrols, facing off across the borderlands. They are all circling the same areas with the same kind of kit, bought at army surplus stores.

With Simcox's help, the two men anchor the tarp with bungee cords, working at it until all but the tailgate is covered. I take a few steps back in the gathering twilight to look. The truck's bulk has been gently massaged into the parched landscape, and the glinting windshield and chrome fenders have been tucked out of sight. Cheap stealth. It's a job well done, and Plank goes to the tailgate and starts putting together the surveillance gear.

When I first came across the Minutemen in 2005, many had binoculars for spotting, although little else. But two years and hundreds of thousands of dollars in donations later, they now have a lot of very new kit. This includes third-generation night vision equipment—which scoops up ambient light, magnifies it thousands of times, and throws the crisp image up against a phosphorescent green screen—and very expensive forward-looking infrared (FLIR) thermal imaging cameras. It's the same kit that Bortac has.

Simcox tells me the group has ten of the cameras (each of them costs about ten grand) divided up between groups on the four southwest border states and their chapter in Washington state on the border with Canada. The cameras discern forms, but also give pockets of heat and cold a different tonality. The sharp contrast makes it easier to spot for movement than the conventional night vision optics, where images, while clear, are flattened by the green tonal hues of the scope's visible range.

Plank, an engineer by day, has been busy in his spare time knocking up a telescopic pole for the FLIR camera using a welder and steel tubing in a friend's workshop. The post, anchored with steel guy ropes, will raise the FLIR camera twenty-four feet above the desert, like the camera poles the Border Patrol have in cities like Laredo and El Paso. The black-and-white images will then be relayed to a monitor set up in the back of Plank's leviathan of a truck.

"The idea is to give us better use out of the thermal imagery. In the past, it has only been handheld and at ground level," he explains. "As you can see out here, you can probably see about a hundred yards. That particular device can go out to six hundred to eight hundred yards when it is properly focused, but first you have to get above all this stuff," he says, his hand sweeping around at the brush ringing the post. "We will be able to see a long ways. We will be able to see them coming down the trail and report to the other groups long before they get here."

The crew struggle to get the pole up while I check out the communications equipment that the volunteers have, linking up the posts on Bravo and Caballo Loco lines through the command center, which is set up in part of the trailer back at the ranch and is staffed constantly.

Each of the posts has a brick radio—a solid lump of electronics, shaped as it sounds—linked through towers and repeaters to the communications center, which has a retro feel to it like the radio room on an outback farm in the 1950s. It has an aged, freestanding broadcast mike on the desk, and I find myself looking around for telltale Bakelite fixtures.

Each group of volunteers on the line also has a "peanut"—a small walkie-talkie for short-range use. The idea is that volunteers remain in contact at all times with others on the post and at nearby lookouts, and it also gives them a degree of redundancy if the principal system goes down.

For ease of identification over the ether, each person has a call sign, much like cops and the military. (With chutzpah or swagger, depending on your point of view, Simcox's tag is "Too Tough.") When they sight border crossers, they call in the number of people in the group, their current location, and the direction they are headed. The information is then logged by control and passed on to Border Patrol.

"If we see a group coming, we call in, say, 'This is post twenty-five.' They'll call in and give our post number and GPS coordinates to Border

Patrol, who also have them," Simcox says, explaining the procedure. "The dispatcher will just look in his book and he knows exactly where that is—then an agent will drive out and pick them up," he adds.

Aside from reporting people heading north, the communications system is designed to keep volunteers safe. If they step on a scorpion or get bitten by a rattlesnake they can call for help. Also, if they see armed groups hauling bales of pot north they can call in a Code Black.

The system is a step up from their first patrols, when connectivity along the line was spotty, and many people were calling in whatever they spotted with cell phones. As I mull over the changes in the dying embers of the day, a small light aircraft swoops overhead at rooftop height. It's the Minuteman Air Force, or half of it.

The pilot, a picture framer from California named Dave, flies a 1946 Aeronca along the trails, spotting for border crossers at the rest stops en route to the load-outs in a low, slow flight just short of stalling speed. He is pretty much the last piece in the operation.

The shadows lengthen, the sun slides behind the sacred range of the Baboquivari Mountains, and we are set up. As night falls over the strip of desert, there are around fifty volunteers covering a twenty-mile corridor north of the border, waiting to see who and what slips through the grasp of the Border Patrol and National Guard down on the line.

It's now quite dark. The moon has risen from the east over Tucson. As I sit in my lawn chair with Simcox, I wonder whether it's a good night for stargazing with the long-eyes at the Kitt Peak Observatory, or if there is too much ambient light. The moon is so bright I see that I cast a deep shadow on the blue-gray desert floor. Not only will it be easy to see people walking up the trail in this light, it will also be easy for them to see me.

Simcox is obviously thinking the same thing. He whispers to me to pull my chair into the moon shadow cast by his Jeep. I wonder what I must look like, sitting out there on the trailhead, white, silent, and motionless in my lawn chair, like a lost soul, a ghost from a tailgate party.

I look up for Plank and Farmer, and I can't see anything but mesquite shadows. They are about one hundred yards away behind Plank's truck, sweeping the horizon with the FLIR, and looking for movement up to half a mile down the trail. Anyone they see will appear as dancing white dots against a black background, as the sensitive optics pick up on the heat signature of their faces heading toward the sensor.

We keep in touch in whispers relayed by radio. Both they and Simcox have their heavy flashlights at the ready. They will flick them on and floodlight any border crossers, holding them transfixed in the path of two beams more powerful than aircraft landing lights—that at least is the theory. I am still skeptical that we will actually see anyone.

Trying to sit still in my chair is proving difficult, and in an unexpected way. To my complete surprise, the temperature has dropped more than thirty degrees in just three or four hours. I am wearing a sweatshirt with a hood and a corduroy jacket and I am shivering to stay warm. I have clearly misjudged the conditions, and while I can jump back into my truck and throw on the heater, whoever is out on the trail can't. If I were a migrant, my misstep may very well have been fatal.

Simcox's radio has been crackling with traffic since we sat down. The first report was of a group of seventeen border crossers spotted on the Caballo Loco line; then came a second with another group of around twenty migrants walking up on a post further west from our position on the Bravo Line. The desert seems to be full of people making their way north toward the load-out tonight, but why not here? I wonder.

Then, suddenly, the radio hisses and pops into life. It's Plank. He's been panning the camera in a 270-degree sweep across the flat desert valley to the south, and he has a hit a few hundred yards down the trail. White faces dancing against a black background, like the disembodied visages in a haunting and playful Black Light Theatre company production in Prague.

"Too Tough, this is Two Five. We have a group coming up on you. Copy."

I lean into Simcox and start to ask him a question, but he raises his finger to his lips and tells me, "Shhhhhh!" He is listening intently, straining to hear them.

I am quite still for a moment in the chair, looking out over the moonlit desert floor at the looming backbone of the mountain range. I listen hard, and then I make it out . . . the sound of soft chatter drifting up the trail. I can make out the rising and falling intonation in a kind of hissed stage whisper, but I cannot hear what the voices are saying. And then I catch it, male voices talking in Spanish, and they are closing in on us, getting louder. They walk closer and closer, and now I can hear their tread over the coarse sand, squeaking like footfalls on tight-packed snow.

"Light 'em up, Two Five!"

Two beams flick on, bathing the cactuses and mesquite in a blaze of light. The scene is framed by the arcing vault of the desert night sky, reaching over it like a star-studded proscenium arch. But where are the players? I wonder.

Simcox sets off at a trot into a maze of brush and I follow, jogging behind him, threading in and out of the cholla cactuses and greasewood trees in the moonlight. For all the light, I can't make out anybody in the eerie, leaping shadows cast by the moonlight and flashlights.

"Where did they go?" That's Simcox. "Did they see the trucks?"

"I'm on them. They are to the west of you . . . you're right on top of them," Plank says, talking us in to a group he can see picked out in white on the screen.

I am following Simcox, who is already several yards ahead on the trail, and my sense of orientation is off. I can no longer see the Jeep, I have no sense of where the Dodge Ram is parked. I only see the dancing beam of Simcox's flashlight.

Suddenly I feel a stab of pain in my leg. I have blundered into a cholla. A fist-sized ball of spines has broken off and pinned my pants to my leg. I look up, and Simcox, who is surprisingly sure-footed, is pulling ahead again, and I trot on.

"¡Hola, amigos! Buenas noches," he calls out.

Still I see nothing. Simcox slows to a walk, then stops, shining his flashlight on the ground. I see only shadow. Then movement. A man dressed in dark pants and black sweats peels himself up off the desert floor. A few feet away, two more men clamber wearily to their feet.

I am reeling. There are three young men standing before us, blinking in the light. For a minute, no one says anything. Now what? I wonder. It's a strange, newly minted moment that seems to fall between the cracks in terms of jurisdiction and who should be doing what.

The three youngsters make no attempt to run. They are effectively surrendering to Simcox, who has no powers of arrest, and has done nothing but shine a flashlight on them. As for me, I am a British national, and have absolutely no jurisdiction over anything or anyone in the United States. I realize that I hadn't really expected to come across anyone in the desert, and I have been caught totally off my guard.

"¿*Necesitas agua?* [Do you need water?]" Simcox asks, and the spell is broken.

"*Sí, un poquito* [Yes, a little]," replies one of the young men, straightening himself up and looking at the pair of us. He wears a dark woollen cap and gloves, and his face is scratched up, probably from stumbling into the thorny brush on his long journey to this lonely spot. I remember my leg. The pincushion is still anchored on its tiny barbs.

"Are you hungry?" Simcox asks, and they nod.

I have seen a lot of migrants in Border Patrol custody over the years, and hundreds more at migrant shelters south of the line from Tijuana to Reynosa, resting up after attempting the journey—either on foot or in a tire inner tube over the Rio Grande—and getting sent back. But I realize I have never before encountered anyone in the very act of crossing the border, without being kept at arm's length by arresting officers. I am fascinated and I want to know all about them.

"Where are you guys from?" I ask, speaking to them in Spanish.

"Mexico."

"What part?"

"Michoacán."

"What's your name?"

"Jorge García."

I tell him that we are not cops, but civilian volunteers, Los Minute-men. He nods nervously. The group features in a comic book published by Mexico's National Human Rights Commission, identifying the hazards of the crossing, alongside corrupt Mexican cops, pistol-toting bandits, and the withering heat that sucks the life right out of the un-prepared.

A civilian group appears in one panel. It's night. Two Stetson-wearing "vigilantes" blaze away at migrants with rifles as the text warns, *"te hos-tiguen, te detengan, o te maltraten"*—"they will harass you, arrest you, or mistreat you."

I tell García that none of that is going to happen. His shoulders relax, and his story comes spilling out. The group are from a *ranchito* about forty minutes from Apatzingán, a town notorious for drug cartel vio-lence. He is twenty-five, a farm hand, married with a wife and son and a second child on the way. He tells me he had been picking lemons until about ten days ago, when the season ended, and his hundred-peso-a-day income dried up.

A neighbor lent him a few thousand pesos for the trip, and he set out with his twenty-one-year-old little brother Miguel and their friend José Luis in search of a job in *los fields* in California. They took the bus through Altar to El Sásabe, where they spent a couple of days trying to hook up with a coyote.

Finally they found two young guides who demanded one hundred dollars up front, and a further thousand once they got to the other side. They set off in a group with a couple of dozen men and women from all over Mexico, some from Guanajuato, others from Sinaloa and Micho-acán, at the start of a four-day odyssey. Before they even reached the line it all started to go wrong.

"We hadn't even got to the fence when they robbed us. The bandits. They had a pistol. They told us, 'If you want to live, give us your money!' so we did," García says, munching on dry crackers Simcox has given them along with a bottle of water, which he swigs.

They crossed the border and had been walking as a group for more than a day when the Border Patrol helicopter flew over. They scattered, running for cover in the brush, and never saw their guides or the rest of the group again. Trekking on alone, they had multiple encounters with law enforcement that they managed to avoid. Jorge rattles off sightings of Border Patrol agents on quad bikes and on horseback, as well as in the helicopter.

The details sound entirely authentic, as the agents use all those forms of transport in the area. It's also interesting to me to hear that they have had these near run-ins without actually being nabbed themselves. It seems that hiding out, blending into the dark in black clothing, still works for at least this group of youngsters, in the age of FLIRs, motion detectors, and other high-tech gadgets.

One of the largest difficulties they had was running out of food and water on the trail, as the coyotes lied to them, telling them the (unspecified) city they were heading for was no more than a two-day walk. The group also had no adequate means of keeping warm on the journey north.

"We slept in the wild, huddled up," García says. "We have been drinking out of cattle troughs for two days, and we haven't eaten."

Their feet burning from blisters, they carried on north, keeping the mountains to their left and the city lights of Tucson to the northeast. As the cold began to bite at the start of their fourth night in the desert, they found gloves and woolly hats abandoned along the trail, just a couple of hours before they ran into us.

"It has been so cold. We walk at night to keep warm, and sleep a couple of hours in the day," he tells me.

We have all begun to relax a little bit, and I start to notice the dynamic in play. The boys are from a humble ranch background, and are clearly used to responding to authority. Because I am the big *gabacho* (the word Mexicans use for a gringo) and speak Spanish, I have become, in the fluid dynamic of this situation, the *patrón*, or boss. They look to me to explain what's going on and, though it's not spoken, to tell them what to do.

I explain that they are not under arrest. I tell them that if they want to go on their way, we cannot hinder them. To my surprise, it is as Arcala had predicted. They shake their heads and say they are ready to give up.

"We're tired, we've had enough," the brothers tell me. I tell them that Simcox has radioed the Border Patrol and that an agent will be there to pick them up in the next hour or so. Jorge nods and looks at the twinkling lights of Tucson in the distance.

"Is it far?"

"Tucson? It's about thirty miles," I tell them.

He looks wistful for a moment. "Perhaps we'll get to see it, if only in passing."

The radio crackles on again, and it's Plank with more news. A group of about twenty to thirty migrants is heading up the same trail, walking wide of us in an arc, probably jittery at the flashlights. Simcox sets off again in their direction, and I follow, leaving the group of lads from Michoacán sitting down on the trail, munching crackers and waiting to be arrested.

Within a minute I have lost sight of the trucks and I am totally disoriented, while I follow Simcox on the trail, as he calls out "*¡Buenas noches, amigos!*" The call is greeted with silence as before, and once again I see no one. It is becoming clear to me how easy it is to disappear in the deep moon shadows, especially if you are dressed in black.

The group evades us, slipping on north up the trail, probably closing in on the load-out and a ride into the city. Within an hour or so, the temperature has dropped to close to freezing. The battery has died on the FLIR, and by about one in the morning it is time to pack up. Simcox and Plank start pulling up the anchor cables, tugging the camouflage off the truck, and preparing to head into the camp for the night.

As Simcox works I quiz him about what we have seen and experienced over the last few hours: the multiple sightings, the surrender of the undocumented migrants, and the constant traffic over the radios from other posts along both lines, reporting multiple sightings throughout the evening. Is it always like this? I wonder.

"We've been covering a twenty-mile section. In just five hours we are well over a hundred sightings and I don't know how many apprehensions, but it's dozens and dozens," Simcox says. "Border Patrol is out trying to support us, but it's obviously a very busy night and a lot of people have made it through the front line of Border Patrol and National Guard and have made it this far north. What else can you say? The government says crossings are down? I don't think so."

Then he launches into his schtick, which has become familiar now in the national debate about secure borders: "The border is not secure by any means. Do you know how many of these guys could be potential terrorists or criminals? For every one that we can locate and let Border Patrol apprehend, that's one less potential problem in our country."

Shivering hard, I turn to Plank, and ask him for his take on the evening. A Tucson resident and long-term volunteer, he shares Simcox's view that the border police are not able to keep up with the sheer volume of people streaming up across the border, day in and day out and around the clock.

"They are coming across literally in waves. Tonight we have seen groups of twenty and we've seen groups of three, and everything in between, and this is probably a small fraction. There's more coming across," he says, adding that the influx is spread out across the 180 miles that make up the Tucson sector of the Border Patrol.

"It's not just here in the Altar Valley, there's Green Valley to the east, and the Tohono O'odham reservation over the mountains here. They are just coming across in waves through all these valleys. There are people just shooting across, and their odds of making it are unfortunately too good."

With all their gear packed away, we rattle down the track in a convoy, dodging lolloping jackrabbits every few yards as they bound off down the trail ahead. I have the heat up full in my truck, and I battle to keep my eyes open. I park in the yard, wriggle into my sleeping bag fully dressed, and fall asleep with my feet jammed up against the windshield. I wake up shivering at dawn, turn on the engine for a blast of warm air, and steal another hour's sleep. I am exhausted.

When I wake up again, I drive the few miles up to Three Points and stop at the gas station. I pick up a large, steaming cup of coffee, and sit out front on a concrete bench to ease myself into the new day. It's cool and bright and clear.

I had briefly checked in with the Minuteman command post on my way out the gate, and picked up the night's tally for the first day of the watch. I learn that the volunteers have spotted more than 290 border crossers along the two lines, and I really don't think that can be far wrong. It gives me something to think about.

The night out in the Altar Valley has shown me firsthand that a lot of people get through, due to the immensity of the desert and to the sheer pressure of numbers the length of the line. It is a mass human migration that goes on year round and around the clock, across a huge area. The migrants who make the trip are also motivated, resourceful, and resilient. Jorge and his group had been abandoned by their guides, but they trudged on regardless. When they were challenged on the trail, they scattered. I have found out firsthand how easy it is for them to remain hidden—with the simple step of dressing in black. You likely won't find them unless you trip over them or have a FLIR. It is, in fact, quite spectacular to have seen the secret life of the border close up.

The Minuteman Civil Defense Corps also struck me as having a good working knowledge of the area they operate in. The volunteers had a sense of the dangers of the desert, and how to work in it and move through it safely, which is more than I can say for myself. I was quite unprepared for the cold. I had also learned the hard way the truth of the adage that pretty much everything will either "stick, sting, or bite you" out in the desert.

It struck me that the volunteers, drawing on the experience of their line leaders, also have an accurate grasp of the people they are likely to meet out on the line, and how they are likely to behave. Many of the migrants, as they foresaw, will be tired, and often too exhausted to continue on their trek once they have been challenged. As to the drug mules, the volunteers seem to understand that they are likely to be armed and dangerous, and should be left well alone.

Their spotting gear, from binoculars to the pole-mounted FLIR, is also much more high-tech and workable than I had imagined before I set out with the group. They used it effectively, relying on a good, workable communications system to get reports and the location of their sightings back to the Border Patrol, the federal police empowered to make immigration arrests. In short, they worked quite well in their self-designated role as extra pairs of eyes and ears for the Border Patrol on one of the busiest stretches of the border.

Furthermore, their proactive intervention technique, to stop border crossers by using high-powered flashlights, is also an unexpected and practical innovation. It actually works out on the line. I have seen three youngsters brought up short and snapped out of their march by a sudden blaze of light. Scores, and possibly hundreds more people—either harmless would-be landscapers or potential suicide bombers, depending on how tweaked your fear dials are—might otherwise have gotten through.

Out on the trail the night before, I asked Simcox what he felt the group had achieved. He makes it quite clear that spotting is just part of what they do. Their real success, as he sees it, has been in stirring up the political debate. Whereas before, the border was pretty much off the political agenda, it has now become a real issue addressed by both Republican and Democrat contenders in the election, and is a cornerstone of all the candidates' immigration policies.

"Our goal was to be a lightning rod that would attract people's attention down here. What we did was to get America to pay attention, and they then applied pressure on the government. Five years ago nobody paid attention to this problem, except the people who lived on the border. Now every candidate in this country hears about illegal immigration and crime and the threat to national security," he says.

Some of what he says is grandiosity, some of it is wishful thinking. Some of it is also pretty much on the money.

TWELVE

The Future of
Border Policing

John (not his real name) cuts quite a figure in the bar in the old gold-mining town. He is wearing a battered black Stetson hat, reflective pilot's Ray-Bans, and a blue cowboy shirt with mother-of-pearl buttons, and he is missing his right arm.

Someone in the bar tells me it was blown off a while back when he came into the saloon with a shotgun hidden under his duster. The gun went off accidentally, taking the arm with it.

The La Gitana Cantina in Arivaca, a few miles from the border in southern Arizona, is one of the most unusual in the Southwest, a watering hole for the residents, who include Vietnam veterans, artists, teachers, felons, American Indians, and at least one former stuntman and gun juggler.

The ceiling, bar, and walls are marked by holes left by bullets fired off by customers down the years. The pool table was also used as an informal dentist's chair by one regular, who would pull out teeth with pliers as patients lay stretched out on the green baize. He is now barred for rowdiness.

On a darker note, the hardwood floor beneath the table was for a time stained with blood after one regular cut the throat of another drinker in a knife fight. Then there's the mesquite wood bar itself. The amber-colored countertop has the ashes of three regulars embedded in it, tucked with care between the cracks in the wood and sealed in with varnish.

An entire wall of the bar, backing onto the patio, is given over to remembrance of the dead. "That's Cowboy Gene, that's Wally, that's Gerry, that's Johnny, that's Ben, that's Leroy," John says, pointing to the aging photographs of the men and women who would prop up the bar, swill a cool beer or a shot, and raise merry hell together.

Quite a number of them committed suicide over the years, I would learn, or drank themselves to death, unable to shake the demons that drove them to seek solace here. Unless of course fate had reserved some other surprise for them. "Little Pauly there, he quit drinking. But a year later, almost to the day, he stepped off the curb and got run over by a Budweiser truck," John says.

Getting a tour around the bar is an uncommon courtesy in a town where the residents are renowned for their fiercely independent streak, an orneriness, or perhaps even a cussedness. They live by their own set of rules and are suspicious of outsiders.

Sitting out on the patio in the cool sunshine of a January afternoon, one regular, Shirley, tells me an anecdote to help me understand that retiring side shared by many.

"This is how clannish the town is," she says. "I was sitting in the passenger seat in this truck, and some people from Illinois pulled up beside us and said, 'Hey, do you know so and so?' I said, 'No, I ain't never seen him in my darn life,' and I was sitting there right next to him!" Shirley laughs. "That's the way it should be. We don't want anyone violating our privacy."

For that reason, it seemed perhaps one of the most provocative places in the United States for the Department of Homeland Security to use as a proving ground for a state-of-the-art surveillance system to secure the border.

The stretch of the line south of the town was picked in 2006 to be part of an area in which the government would try out a network of video and infrared surveillance cameras and ground radars, all knitted together by a common operating picture, or COP.

The project was part of a huge squeeze by the government to close off the wide open spaces of the border, while at the same time gaining better control over visitors entering the United States, whether by air, land, or sea, through border crossings, ports, or airports.

Since I began covering the border five years ago, the issue of illegal immigration and homeland security has been gathering momentum, with groups like the Minutemen capturing a popular mood, demanding that the government must do more—something, anything—to secure the border.

In November 2005, President George W. Bush responded to this pressure. The government came up with the Secure Border Initiative, or SBI, a multiyear, multibillion-dollar juggernaut of a project that sought to send more border police to the line, while adding more infrastructure and technologies.

The technology component of the plan, the so-called SBInet, set out to create what Secretary Chertoff called a "virtual fence," which would enable the government to develop smart, effective, nonintrusive ways to secure the border.

It is a controversial work in progress that raises questions about the limits of technology, as well as civil libertarian issues for border residents. It is accompanied by other technological innovations at the ports that have implications for all international travelers to the United States, legal and otherwise.

"We will use a mix of technology and Border Patrol and infrastructure to create what is, in effect, a barrier to entry," Chertoff said, giving an idea of the scope of the project at its launch in 2005. "We're talking about stuff like unmanned aerial vehicles, satellite imagery, sensors, cameras that are computer-programmed to be able to operate based on algorithms that identify certain kinds of movements that the camera targets on. All of these systems, if integrated together, allow us to create a force multiplier for Border Patrol, taking the Border Patrol assets we have and [making] them more effective to intercept and apprehend those people who are crossing the border illegally." Chertoff added: "It's going to be a smart fence, not a stupid fence—a twenty-first-century fence, not a nineteenth-century fence."

The technological buildup at the border was prefaced by a push under the SBI that sent thousands of National Guard troops to the border as a stopgap measure, building hundreds of miles of steel fences and staffing command centers under Operation Jump Start. Meanwhile, the Border Patrol set about recruiting another six thousand agents, effectively increasing their size by half, to get to grips with the problem of securing the border.

Then came the technological component. After a lengthy process of deliberation, the government awarded a contract to aeronautical and defense giant Boeing to develop and integrate the different technologies that would comprise the SBInet itself. It would begin with a system to detect and identify intruders along a twenty-eight-mile stretch of the line in the much-trafficked Altar Valley, and, if successful, be extended across much of the United States borders.

Project 28, or simply P-28, as it became known, covered a rugged area reaching across the Altar Valley. The area included some extremely challenging terrain reaching from close by the hamlet of Sasabe in southern Arizona to the rugged mountains and canyon lands south of Arivaca.

Red and white towers, which were almost a hundred feet tall, began popping up across the valley, like high-tech totem poles, along with facilities used by contractors, and an increased National Guard presence. Residents would tell me they had little idea of what was going on.

The concept was for radar on the towers to detect movement and direct high-resolution day and night vision cameras to take a closer look. The images would then be streamed to command posts where supervisors could determine whether they were looking at, say, a man out walking his dog or a group of drug smugglers. Data would then be relayed over a high-speed wireless network to laptops in Border Patrol vehicles, showing agents what they were to apprehend and where it was.

The residents in the vicinity of the tower, some of them living in Arivaca, others living off-grid on isolated ranches, would point out that the tower's view of the Mexico border, around a dozen miles to the south, was blocked by a looming range of mountains, raising the question of who was being watched.

"I'm sitting down on Ruby Road, looking at the tower. I'm thinking, everything else is over here on the other side, and there ain't no damn way the tower can see over there. It's looking at Arivaca, and we're not migrating anyplace," Mike, a former stuntman and gun juggler, told me as we chatted on the patio at La Gitana.

Another local resident, Nancy, was also riled by it: "I heard that its intention was to watch Mexico, but there it is pointing right at me. It can't see over that mountain to Mexico. It is Big Brother, it is. I don't know what their true purpose is."

The residents of Arivaca sparred with the Border Patrol and DHS at a raucous public hearing in Arivaca's community center in May 2007 while the contractors pushed on with the project, seeking to get a better view of the plentiful illegal traffic crossing up through the area, and pass that on to the Border Patrol.

While the new virtual fence was welcomed by some ranchers fed up with having their cattle fences cut through time and again, night after night, by illegal border crossers, the introduction of the new technological push had clearly wrong-footed the majority of local residents.

Aside from the civil libertarian issues that it raised for concerned local people, it soon became apparent that the virtual fence was running into technical problems in the government's haste to find solutions to border insecurity. Would it in fact work?

The much-anticipated debut of the new fence was set for the summer of 2007. Then it was set back, and no new dates were given for quite when it would go live and start to play a role in securing the Tucson sector of the border. Were the difficulties simply the birth pangs of a promising new system—the next generation in border policing, imagined as part of the surveillance society—or was the system stillborn?

Finally, without any fanfare, and with none of the access anticipated by reporters who were keen to get a first look at how the high-tech barrier worked, it was quietly accepted by DHS in early 2008.

Clues to some of the glitches with the fence, and a broader hint at some of the problems inherent in its approach to contracting and technology, would become apparent in the release of a report by the watchdog Government Accountability Office, or GAO, just days later.

One of the problems was with the radar, which was supposed to be able to sweep the area within the purview of the towers, giving a real-time snapshot of anyone driving or walking up over the border, day or night, regardless of the weather.

But the GAO report later found that, far from providing actionable, real-time information on movements in the valley, the radar system was taking too long to relay and display that information in command centers.

Operators also discovered that the radars were giving false alerts, as they were being "activated by rain and other environmental factors," likely created by things such as the branches of trees stirred by the wind, technical sources unconnected to Boeing would later tell me.

There were other problems, too, with chunky laptops retrofitted into Border Patrol vehicles, which required agents to jab at the screen with styluses to retrieve information from the COP. But the problems were also larger. The ambitious technology, meant to provide field agents improved situational awareness, had been developed without sufficiently consulting the agents themselves about what they needed.

Much emphasis had been placed on relaying images to the agents on the line. One border policeman I spoke to told me that actually seeing what is going on out in the field isn't necessarily going to be that helpful to an agent at the moment of going out and making an arrest. "If I see a picture of a group of people moving through the desert, it is just a group of people moving through the desert. It doesn't improve my situational awareness," he told me.

In areas like the mountains around Arivaca where the Project 28 system was tried out, it is not possible to reach many of the most-trafficked areas in a vehicle. Agents often have to leave their trucks or SUVs to cut sign and walk up on a group of intruders, for as much as a mile or more. "Once you leave the vehicle," the officer pointed out, "that awareness is gone anyway, so the system is no help to you."

Then there was another practical issue. Many of the agents working out among the steep mountains, plunging canyons, and deep washes that comprise the eastern end of the Project 28 strip don't even patrol in SUVs. Instead, to reach the mountainous areas they either work their way in on horseback, as we have seen, or on four-wheel-drive quad bikes. On neither is it feasible to have a laptop computer system, however robust it might be. At least one agent I spoke to who works in the area on horseback said he wouldn't take a laptop out with him even if he were asked to, simply for fear of dropping it.

Also, most traffic moves over the border at night. The backlight from the screen would bathe the agents in light and erase any advantage accrued by stealth.

The fundamental problem appeared to be that, in its urgency to secure the border, the government had awarded a contract swiftly and demanded quick results. The virtual fence had been thrown up rapidly, without sufficient consultation with end users, the agents themselves, creating something that was overly complex and not necessarily useful to them as it was originally conceived.

Flawed as it was, the system nevertheless helped agents apprehend thousands of illegal immigrants and seize several tons of pot during trials in 2008. Elements including the ground radar, video cameras, and enhanced communications system were clearly helpful, and would likely prove useful in securing the empty spaces of the border in the future. The encouraging news is that similar systems have been developed by other contractors and have already proved highly effective in securing a perimeter—including one in use near the Arizona-Mexico border.

One firm, ICx Radar Systems, has designed and developed ground radar networks so sensitive they can detect someone walking at a range of six miles, and can detect someone crawling, even at near zero speeds, at a range of 150 yards.

Unlike the radars used in P-28, they have been designed from the ground up using a different technology; they don't have problems with false alerts caused by phenomena like rain or moving branches, and they have a solid track record of satisfying their clients.

Among those clients is the U.S. Air Force, which uses the firm's systems to secure the perimeters of more than 160 air bases around the world, as well as the Israel Defense Force, which has deployed ground radar to secure settlements in the disputed West Bank territories. They have also been used successfully since 2004 by the Marine Corps to secure an aerial bombing range in the desert near Yuma in far western Arizona, which was overrun by illegal immigrants straying into harm's way.

The radar system scans in a 360-degree sweep, and alerts a video camera system, which trains a camera automatically on the object detected and sends an audio nudge to operators, allowing them to immediately determine whether the alert is caused by a human intruder or by something such as a troop of javelina hogs.

The radar then tracks the object, automatically passing the video feed over from one camera to another, allowing the dispatchers to tell agents sent to intercept the intruder exactly what to expect. It works without all the cumbersome demands of having to bundle complex electronic data and relay it to agents in the field.

While the Altar Valley is, in many respects, ground zero for the problems of illegal immigration and drug trafficking, created by knowing and practiced smugglers, border police and other analysts I have spoken to feel that it might not be the best proving ground for new technologies to combat them.

There are plenty of places in the deserts of south and western Arizona, as well as whole sweeps of the Rio Grande Valley in Texas, which are largely flat. They would make ideal proving grounds for a system that is taking its first baby steps, and that uses technologies like ground radars and video cameras, which rely on clear lines of sight to work.

In a number of public comments following P-28's acceptance, Secretary Chertoff appears to have taken on board the need for greater consultation with Border Patrol in developing appropriate technologies for their needs. He also appears to be ready to ditch some of the more redundant elements of the system, such as the streaming video for field agents.

Chertoff has also made clear that P-28 is just a small element of a larger picture, and that the Department of Homeland Security will be pushing forward with other technologies in the future.

The benefits of getting the virtual fence right are considerable. Building physical barriers is an expensive business. Estimates for the steel pedestrian fences going up in Arizona range from $2 million to $4 million for every mile built, a figure several times the estimated cost of deploying a radar network, according to ICx.

With a virtual fence, the Border Patrol stand to get a system that could, if done right, really help them to secure the porous international line in a cost-effective way, and would also keep them safer by showing them what was coming up from Mexico.

A virtual system would also have untold benefits in terms of creating better neighborly relations with Mexico, where talk of building physical barriers generally gets people's backs up. The approach might even defuse some of the tensions between Washington and landowners on the Mexico border in Texas and Arizona, who are resisting giving the government access to their land to survey for physical barriers.

Finally, the kind of virtual fence that has been proposed on the border would likely have environmental benefits. A radar net, unlike the tall steel fences presently carving out hundreds of miles of the desert under SBI, would allow animals to carry on crossing over the border, including some of the unique fauna that lives in the Sky Islands, an ecologically rich highland chain in Arizona and Mexico—such as the increasingly rare jaguar.

The system, say environmentalists, would be able to distinguish between the pesky human interlopers slipping illegally over the international border and the migratory animals for whom it is purely an arbitrary line.

The role that technology will play in the future of border security will also impact not just the empty spaces of the international line where the Border Patrol works, but also the lives of inspectors working at dozens of ports of entry across the southwest border who process 350 million people who cross north each year in cars, trucks, buses, and on foot through the pedestrian lanes.

The U.S. government's approach to securing the ports is also multifaceted, starting with an initiative to standardize travel documents, and also involving a lot of new technologies.

In early 2008, the government eliminated the practice of accepting oral declarations of citizenship at the border, where for the longest time day-trippers and visitors to Mexico and Canada were simply allowed to walk or drive up to the line and tell the inspectors that they were American citizens.

Instead, they have to provide standardized travel documents brought in under the Western Hemisphere Travel Initiative, which seeks to harmonize entry requirements and make travel more secure.

The ports are already advanced in terms of the equipment they need to sort out the contraband and illegal immigrants from the legitimate trade goods and border crossers streaming up from Mexico each year by their millions.

U.S. Customs and Border Protection inspectors have highly effective dogs screening the aprons in front of the ports of entry, and at inspection points on highways and roads inland.

For the millions of pedestrians who often stand in snaking lines that reach back out of the ports of entry, inspectors have watch lists of known criminals on the lam. For people arriving in cars, they have a few details provided by license plate scanners. They present a history of when the car last crossed, and indicate if it had been stolen or used in a crime, or if its owner is sought by police.

The inspectors also have smart biometric systems including IDENT and IAFIS, and ever newer types of X-ray machines, now including so-called backscatter technologies that help them get a far better look at the travelers they process, and at the contraband that they might be trying to bring with them.

There is, however, no broadly implemented system that gives the border inspectors a heads-up on who is heading up to the line, a situation that leaves them at a disadvantage compared to agents at air- and seaports, who have passenger manifests that tell them in advance who is bound for the United States.

This knowledge has allowed authorities, on occasion, to turn back passenger aircraft carrying individuals they consider may present an imminent risk to homeland security, perhaps by hijacking a flight in transit and slamming it into a building. Officials at the increasingly busy border crossings say they would also find that capacity useful.

"Right now we can take advance information on airport and sea passengers, and we know what we are going to do with that person before they even get off the plane or the ship. But in this environment, we don't know what's going to happen until the car gets to the booth," former San Ysidro port director James Hynes told me during a visit to the border in 2006. "I think that ten years down the road, we will hopefully be in a position to receive advance electronic information on travelers before they arrive at the port."

Aside from increasing security, such a system would also speed up the processing of traffic coming up from Mexico, which on busy days at the ports can be backed up for hours, snarling up the streets with traffic right into the center of Tijuana, and causing traffic jams in the heart of other cities such as Nuevo Laredo, a very important trade hub south of Texas.

Getting it right is important for facilitating legitimate trade, where border crossers need to be able to get to work, to meetings, and to school on time, and where Mexican *maquiladoras*, for instance, gain a com-

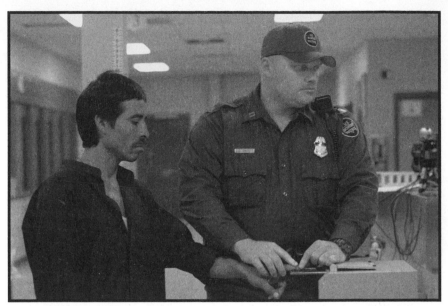

U.S. Border Patrol Supervisor Agent Don Watt uses the IAFIS system to scan the fingerprints of Curiel González from Mexico. The system matches the prints against criminal records and outstanding warrants held in a database, unmasking thousands of criminals including murderers, sex offenders, and armed robbers, often in just a few seconds. (Jeff Topping)

petitive advantage over China by cutting time to market for U.S. suppliers keen on inventory efficiencies.

The clues to how such a system might work lie with a program known as the Secure Electronic Network for Travelers Rapid Inspection, or SENTRI for short, a fast-track travel system that was first implemented at Otay Mesa in Southern California in the mid-1990s. At the time of writing, this program is in place at nine ports of entry along the border, from San Ysidro on the Pacific coast right across to Brownsville, Texas.

The program provides a dedicated lane for prescreened vehicles, drivers, and passengers taking part in a special program. To apply for the program, the drivers have to voluntarily submit to a background check against law enforcement, customs, and immigration databases, and have to give a complete set of prints, much like someone being booked by police.

The system is most often used by the thousands of people who live on one side of the border and commute to work, study, or shop each day on the other. It gives advance screening to legitimate travelers like the American managers of *maquiladoras* who prefer to commute daily to and from Mexico.

Once applicants have been vetted and approved, they are then given an RFID tag (radio frequency identification chip) that is embedded in a plastic decal stuck on the inside of their vehicle's windshield.

As the vehicle approaches the inspection booth, incoming radio waves power up the integrated circuit in the chip containing a file number. The file number triggers the participant's data to be retrieved and displayed on a screen in an inspector's both. Looking over the inspector's shoulder, you can see the information blink up on a split screen showing photographs of everyone who is authorized to be in the car alongside the driver, as well as details about the make and model of vehicle provided by license plate readers.

Drivers enrolled in the program typically roll up to and usually straight through the inspection lane in an average of around ten seconds, less than a third of the time taken to screen an average vehicle through the other lanes, often at the end of a bad-tempered wait of one, two, and sometimes three or more hours on busy days, spent weaving and cutting in and out of lanes trying to make up time on the way out of Mexico.

"At the moment we have just one dedicated SENTRI lane," Hynes told me back in 2006. "In the future we need seven or eight car lanes providing advance information. We'd like to know who they are, what they look like, how many times they've gone to Mexico. . . . With that, we can make an informed decision before the violator gets to us so we'll know how to respond."

Hynes cautioned that, with the high traffic volumes of above 40,000 cars a day running up to San Ysidro, any such expanded system would have to be able to provide information to inspectors instantly. "There can't be a seven- or eight-second delay. A seven- or eight-second delay with this traffic will back that line up to Mexico City," he said, pointing out of the window to the impressive snarl-up outside. "If we can do it, it would be a win-win situation for everyone."

In an interesting development, that kind of technology is also being developed and applied not just for vehicles, but for travel documents used by individuals heading up to the ports in cars, or walking up through the pedestrian halls.

New Passport Cards equipped with RFID chips were introduced by the U.S. State Department as part of an initiative to provide standardized and secure documents for Americans traveling to Canada, Mexico, Bermuda, and the Caribbean. The technology seeks to make the cards machine readable at a distance of up to twenty feet. In the summer of 2008, RFID technology was installed in vehicle lanes in El Paso and Nogales, to be followed by more than a dozen other ports on the U.S. and Canadian borders.

If the system is widely adopted and made to work, it might one day be possible for inspectors to look back along a line of traffic, or down a queue in the pedestrian hall, and know who is waiting in line, when they last crossed, and what prior history they might have. The system would not require the cards to be swiped. It would, however, have to have the capacity to cross-match the data dancing on the inspectors' monitors with biometric readers such as fingerprint scanners, to ensure that the travel document was being used by the bearer and not some near physical match—a common ploy on the border.

All these technologies are out there and being used at present in one form or another, either tracking vehicles on the border or for keeping tabs on inventory in the commercial world, so it is not too much of a stretch to imagine them being deployed at the ports of entry soon, although they face several hurdles in terms of concerns over encroachment of civil liberties and worries about the possibility of identity theft.

The fear is that the government will be able to track card bearers' movements not just at the port, but perhaps, one day, as they go about their daily lives. The U.S. government says all information about the bearer is stored in their computers and not in the RFID chip. Neverthe-less, there is also some lingering concern that it might be possible for identity thieves to access and steal that important information.*

As I consider the future of the line, I think that technology will play an increasingly large role both at the ports of entry and in the spaces in between. I sometimes try and imagine it.

I glimpse a grimy, high-tech border world at the ports of entry, a kind of Tex-Mex version of *Blade Runner,* where the good guys and the bad guys get more heavily burdened with technologies, while everybody else shuffles forward in ever longer lines, feeling more and more like FedEx packages.

In the spaces in between, I can see a greater use of ground radars, aerial drones, ground sensors, and manpower, as the U.S. government seeks to get a better hold on the line into the future.

When I try and imagine it, I am reminded of Nancy's fears, back in Arivaca, of Big Brother–style surveillance. It seems that in order to se-cure the border against illegal entry by smugglers, or economic mi-grants, a degree of freedom is perhaps going to have to be sacrificed by honest citizens, who will find their movements tracked by electronic devices and their images captured on cameras by Border Police and Homeland Security officials.

---

*Eileen Sullivan, "Passport Cards Raise Privacy Fears," Associated Press, January 1, 2008.

Afterword

Writing this book, I left aside the broader questions of what drives illegal immigration and the drug trade. For many border watchers, the only effective way of stopping economic migrants from trekking over the border is to staunch the demand for cheap, illegal labor by going after the U.S. employers who hire them. Others argue that the only way of effectively cutting off the flow of drugs of all sorts would be by legalizing them, and taking away the market in one fell swoop. They are compelling points of view.

Nevertheless, I have focused here on law enforcement, more specifically the duel between smugglers and police for control of the line. As I finish up this book, I feel that readers who will have followed me this far will want some kind of closure. The question I feel I have to answer is, what will happen on the border? Will the government get control of the international line by pursuing an enforcement-based strategy, and if so, what will that line look like in the future?

Crystal-ball gazing is an incredibly hubristic activity, and I feel loath to make predictions. I can, though, tell you what I will be looking out for in the months and years ahead on this storied line that has been my bread and butter and my passion for the last five years.

I continue to see the faces and hear the voices of the many people I have met during my journeys up and down this incredible border: smugglers, migrants, police, coyotes, and guards. All of them are fighting for dominance of this terrain and what it stands for—money, riches, the chance of a new life or the chance of a fast buck, security against crime, narcotics, and terrorists. Of all the futures I can imagine for this border, I know that these struggles will continue to be played out here, on the line.

I think the government is clearly getting a better hold on the line than ever before. The number of arrests in the past couple of years has fallen the length of the line. While the numbers are open to interpretation, I think it is clear that border police are proving more effective at catching illegal immigrants, and, in absolute terms, fewer are attempting that epic journey from Mexico than in previous years.

That same success has also had something of a perverse effect. As it gets increasingly difficult for illegal immigrants to make that journey alone, demand for professional services has gone up, and with it, prices. It has proved something of a market maker for ruthless and profit-hungry coyotes and drug traffickers, for whom smuggling has never been more profitable. The stakes have effectively been raised.

In the face of more effective policing, there is every indication that smugglers are becoming more violent and aggressive. Attacks on Border Patrol agents with rocks and fists are both up, and there have even been a number of reports of shootings. That tendency can only be expected to continue to get worse in the months and years ahead as the line becomes more fiercely contested by both the gamekeepers and the poachers.

The success in securing the more easily crossed areas of the border—the towns and cities and the flat lands of the line—is also likely to shift patterns of smuggling and illegal traffic. Illegal border crossers are already moving out to the more remote areas of the border, the mountains and the furthest reaches of the desert. Injuries, fatalities, and rescues are all likely to rise, as the areas will be the battleground in the future.

The police that I have focused on in this book—the agents on horses, the teams flying lights-out at night in Black Hawk helicopters, the SWAT teams and the Native American trackers, the specialists who hunt for tunnels and for corrupt inspectors—may very well play a greater role in the future, working largely out of sight, and far from the public eye.